Modern China and International Economic Law

This book series offers an essential forum for Chinese economic law scholars, as well as international scholars interested in China's practice in the context of international economic law. It is thus the aim of this book series to publish essential monographs/ compilations in the field of international economic law that focus on China, or on uniquely Chinese characteristics. This book series above all focuses on research that closely relates current practices with past history, and future policies with current circumstances, pursuing a philosophy of understanding legal practices by combining the past and present. Accordingly, top scholars in China and beyond its borders will be invited to contribute to this project from their respective areas of focus, which can cover broad topics related to international law in the current context of China's peaceful rise, such as China's economic policy with various countries, its participation in the WTO legal system and bilateral investment treaty practices, etc.; as well as more specific topics such as China's domestic legislation regarding foreign business, its unique "one country, two systems" policy and its implications on external economic interactions between different "systems" within China.

Bin Gu

Chinese Multilateralism in the Asian Infrastructure Investment Bank (AIIB)

中国国际经济法学会
Chinese Society of International Economic Law, CSIEL

Springer

Bin Gu
School of Law
Beijing Foreign Studies University
Beijing, China

ISSN 2364-8317 ISSN 2364-8325 (electronic)
Modern China and International Economic Law
ISBN 978-981-97-1218-2 ISBN 978-981-97-1219-9 (eBook)
https://doi.org/10.1007/978-981-97-1219-9

This Springer imprint is published by the registered company Springer Nature Singapore Pte Ltd.
The registered company address is: 152 Beach Road, #21-01/04 Gateway East, Singapore 189721, Singapore

Paper in this product is recyclable.

Preface

The Asian Infrastructure Investment Bank (AIIB) has grown into the eighth year of operation since its establishment in 2015. Cherishing an institutional culture of "lean, clean and green", the China-initiated multilateral development bank (MDB) has become the second largest after the World Bank by membership, reaching 109 members. The young Bank has been able to nimbly respond to the tumultuous world, getting "stronger, wiser and tougher", quoting its inaugural President Jin Liqun.

This book is a sequel to my first monograph, *The Law and Governance of the Asian Infrastructure Investment Bank*, published by Wolters Kluwer in 2018. It builds upon the previous one, and in each chapter digs into a different topic. The topics are chosen either because they are aspirational for the MDB family in large, or because they matter the dynamic reforms of global economic governance in general. This writing reflects the latest development of the Bank and has benefited from my numerous stimulating interviews and meetings with its highly skilled and cordial officers and staff, as always.

During the past few years, the interaction between the AIIB and peer international financial institutions (IFIs) has demonstrated a healthy trend of two-way emulation. This is vividly illustrated in Chap. 1 on a comparative study of their respective shareholding formulas, which are used to determine member countries' voting power in the institutions. Their shareholding formulas have been under continuous development and reform, as the world economic landscape evolves.

When it comes to the configuration of internal governance of the AIIB, the oversight mechanism was established in 2019 to ensure "proper checks and balances" between the Bank's non-resident Board and management. Chapter 2 examines this issue and suggests leaning towards the Oriental wisdom of advisory engagement, rather than the Western style of adversary checks, along the spectrum of oversight that best suits the Asian gene of the Bank and its purposes.

The AIIB's standards have been high and feasible. The third version of *Environmental and Social Framework* in 2021 enables the AIIB to firmly stand at the forefront of international best practices, along with other like-minded institutions in development finance. Additionally, the AIIB standards embody Asian wisdom—"voluntarism, flexibility and incremental progress", as revealed in Chap. 3.

Regarding institutional cooperation, the AIIB does not shy away from other Chinese initiatives, such as the Belt and Road Initiative (BRI), and the Multilateral Cooperation Center for Development Finance (MCDF), which both spearhead high quality in infrastructure investment. Chapter 4 investigates the MCDF in particular, which was established in 2020 and hosted by the AIIB. The writing pays special attention to the institutional nexus between the MCDF and the AIIB.

The issue of state-owned enterprises (SOEs) has far-reaching and significant implications against the background of China's rise and the reform of global economic governance. The question is essentially whether SOEs should be treated as public or private entities under international law. The final chapter, i.e., Chap. 5, explores this issue comprehensively, by comparing the laws of the AIIB, the World Bank, the World Trade Organization (WTO), and other institutions.

The above chapters were originally published as academic articles in leading international law journals, including *Journal of International Economic Law (JIEL), Review of European, Comparative & International Environmental Law (RECIEL), Asia Pacific Law Review*, and *Hong Kong Law Journal*, and is now restructured and streamlined in a coherent manner, with necessary revisions and updates. I feel thrilled to share with the reader my latest understanding about the AIIB, as well as China's approach toward global economic governance, as duly reflected in the story of the AIIB.

Annexed to the book are 16 newspaper columns that I have written since five years ago. Some of them are devoted to the AIIB, but others are beyond it. I tend to collect those op-eds in this monograph, as I did in my previous AIIB book, because their theme is consistently focused on *Chinese* multilateralism, an alternative to *American* multilateralism as an endeavor to respond to the global problems challenging us all today.

Finally, like the Bank itself, this book is a work in process, and it inevitably contains errors, omissions, and ambiguities, which will require correction, clarification, and further development in future editions. Questions and comments are warmly welcomed, by email to gubin@bfsu.edu.cn or gubin123@gmail.com.

Beijing, China Bin Gu

Contents

Chapter 1
Members' Shareholding: A GDP-Based Formula

Summary Shareholding formulas determine member countries' voice in capital-based international organizations. They are crucial for international finance and draw much attention in negotiations. In principle, these formulas reflect member countries' relative economic positions, but in practice, they serve as a starting point in negotiations, alongside other economic and political factors. This chapter investigates the unique shareholding formula of the Asian Infrastructure Investment Bank (AIIB) and compares it with those of the Bretton Woods institutions, that is, the International Monetary Fund (IMF), the International Bank for Reconstruction and Development (IBRD), and the International Finance Corporation (IFC). It shows that both the AIIB and the Bretton Woods institutions have learnt from each other's shareholding formulas. Built upon the Bretton Woods practice, the AIIB's GDP-based shareholding formula could stimulate the IMF to establish a new quota formula under the 16th general review of quotas, the IBRD to implement the results calculated from its 2016 Dynamic Formula, and the IFC to develop its own formula by the date of the next shareholding review in 2025.

1.1 Introduction

A country is related to an international financial institution (IFI) through its membership. The membership, in turn, results from the country's financial contribution to the institution. The size of the country's financial contribution, called capital shares,[1]

This chapter originally appeared in *Journal of International Economic Law* (2022)25(4), entitled "Shareholding Formulas in International Financial Institutions: Learning from the Asian Infrastructure Investment Bank", coauthor Dr. Tong Liu.

[1] Member countries' financial contributions to IFIs include monetary forms other than capital shares. For example, while IMF quotas (i.e., capital shares, special drawing right (SDR) 477 billion in total) are the main source of IMF financing, its borrowing arrangements (i.e., SDR 361 billion for multilateral borrowing and SDR 135 billion for bilateral borrowing) temporarily supplement quota resources. AIIB members may similarly contribute to a special or trust fund of the institution, besides their capital–share contribution.

B. Gu, *Chinese Multilateralism in the Asian Infrastructure Investment Bank (AIIB)*,
Modern China and International Economic Law,
https://doi.org/10.1007/978-981-97-1219-9_1

largely decides its voice in the IFI. In turn, the IFI's total capital stock, which sums up all members' financial contributions, determines the institution's power and influence in global governance.

Thus, the mechanism affecting capital distribution among IFI members—the shareholding formula—has long been a critical subject in international finance. Such a mechanism determines the amount of capital that a member country must subscribe to or has the right to subscribe.[2] The guiding principle for capital distribution in each IFI is that it should be proportionate to a member's relative position in terms of economic weight, because IFIs depend on the (continuous) financial contribution and support of members. A widely accepted parameter in measuring a country's weight in a modern economy is gross domestic product (GDP), which plays a dominant role in the mechanism of capital distribution in IFIs.

However, variables other than GDP may be considered in a shareholding formula. The choice of the other variables depends on the IFI's mission. For example, given the World Bank's mission of poverty reduction, its shareholding formula assigns weight to member countries' contributions to its soft-loan window, that is, the International Development Association (IDA).[3] A second example is the distribution of the International Monetary Fund's (IMF) capital shares (quotas), where variables such as economic openness, susceptibility to exogenous shock, and international reserves

---

[2] There are at least three versions in the Articles of Agreement (AOA, or the Charter) of the IFIs regarding a member's right (or obligation) to subscribe to a particular number of shares. Version 1: In some IFIs, capital shares are designated to a particular member as a ceiling, of which the member may subscribe at the maximum, but with no floor requirement. The arrangement is exemplified in the AIIB AOA Article 5.1: 'Each member shall subscribe to shares of the capital stock of the Bank.... **The initial number of shares available to be subscribed** by countries which become members in accordance with Article 58 shall be that set forth in Schedule A' (emphasis added). Echoed in practice, for example, Brazil, as an AIIB founding member, has subscribed 50 shares only out of the 31,810 capital shares designated to it in Schedule A. *See* further below in Section II. Version 2: Some institutions indeed have a floor or minimum requirement of capital subscription for each member. For example, International Bank for Reconstruction and Development (IBRD) AOA Article 2.3(a) stipulates that '**The minimum number of shares to be subscribed** by the original members shall be those set forth in Schedule A' (emphasis added). In Article 5.1 of AOA of the European Bank for Reconstruction and Development (EBRD), in addition to the provisions of the same effect as in the AIIB, it stipulates that 'No member shall have an initial subscription of less than one hundred (100) shares'. Version 3: In other institutions, the number of shares to be subscribed by a member, as specified in a schedule, is an exact requirement. For example, African Development Bank AOA Article 6.1 stipulates: '**The initial number of shares to be subscribed** by a State which acquires membership in accordance with paragraph 1 of article 64 of this Agreement shall be that set forth in this respect in annex A to this Agreement, which shall form an integral part thereof' (emphasis added). Asian Development Bank (ADB) follows suit.

[3] In this Chapter, the World Bank refers to both the IBRD and the IDA. This Chapter does not discuss the IDA's voting rights framework, where each member receives the votes to be allocated under IDA replenishments, which consist of subscription votes and membership votes. For example, IDA20, the latest replenishment, agrees upon 'A flat uniform vote price of $17,670 for all Non-Recipients, where Non-Recipients will receive additional subscription votes based on their replenishment contributions', while the combined voting power of Recipients will be boosted to 20.50% in recognition of the importance of poor countries' voice. IDA, 'IDA20 Final Replenishment Report: Building Back Better from the Crisis: Toward a Green, Resilient and Inclusive Future' (February 17, 2022) at 199 (Annex 17 'IDA Voting Rights Framework', paras 26–28).

are considered, given the IMF's role in maintaining member states' equilibrium of the balance of payments (see Fig. 1.1).

Meanwhile, IFIs are not merely economic but also political institutions, typically being a cooperative among sovereign states.[4] First, the IFI upholds democratic representation in its governance and operations, where every member's voice and participation should be guaranteed, which implies that the capital contribution is a major but not the only factor in deciding a member's voting power in an institution. In addition to capital shares derived from the shareholding formula, a minimum voting power for each member (known as basic votes), however small a member's capital contribution, is required in most IFIs.[5] Besides, other political factors are frequently considered when allocating capital shares, largely at the discretion of the initiating powers of the institution.[6] However, such considerations and relevant weights conferred can be opaque. After all, those factors are not reflected in any formula or mechanism.

This study selectively reviews the mechanisms of capital allocation in four IFIs, namely AIIB, IMF, IBRD, and IFC. Their selection is based on the following factors: IBRD, IMF, and IFC are Bretton Woods institutions, and they have long driven the global financial architecture. Under the World Bank Group (WBG), the World Bank, consisting of IBRD and IDA, is responsible for public (or sovereign-backed) financing through both hard-loan (for IBRD) and soft-loan (for IDA) windows, while the IFC is responsible for private-sector financing. The three financial institutions work together in the cause of development.

The AIIB is derived from the Bretton Woods system in terms of both corporate governance and modus operandi,[7] and it is now the second largest multilateral development bank (MDB) after the World Bank by membership.[8] With the DNA of Asian founders,[9] the AIIB increasingly presents itself as a global institution, featuring the so-called four globals: global membership, global investment, global procurement,

---

[4] The membership of some IFIs (such as the AIIB, the ADB, etc.) is also open to non-sovereign entities.

[5] Basic votes in the IBRD (plus IFC), IMF, AIIB, and ADB are currently set at 5.55%, 5.502%, 12%, and 20% of total votes respectively. It should be noted that the EBRD is a major exception with no basic votes. EBRD AOA, Article 29.1.

[6] For an account of the political nature dominated by the US in the IMF's quota distribution in 1944 and subsequent quota shifts, see Ayse Kaya, *Power and Global Economic Institutions* (Cambridge: Cambridge University Press, 2015), at 51–80.

[7] In terms of corporate governance, the AIIB resembles the World Bank and the IMF in establishing a three-layered governance structure, i.e., the Board of Governors, the Board of Directors, and management led by the President. The AIIB also sets up high environment, social and procurement requirements, comparable to those of the Bretton Woods institutions.

[8] European Parliamentary Research Service, 'Asian Infrastructure Investment Bank: How Lean, Clean and Green is the AIIB?' February 2021, at 3.

[9] A discussion of Asian values as embedded in the AIIB is available at David M. Ong, 'The Asian Infrastructure Investment Bank: Bringing "Asian Values" to Global Economic Governance?', 20 (3) Journal of International Economic Law (2017), 535–60.

IFIs	Current shareholding formulas	Key features of current formulas	This Chapter's proposals for reform
AIIB	The GDP-based formula	GDP measured with 60% at market rates and 40% at PPP rates, consistent with the formulas of IMF and IBRD. 75% of total capital stock reserved for regional members, and 25% for nonregional members.	Measure GDP with a weight of 40% at market rates and 60% at PPP rates.
IMF	The 2008 quota formula	$(0.5 * GDP + 0.3 * Openness + 0.15 * Variability + 0.05 * Reserves)^{0.95}$ 0.95 is the compression factor	Measure GDP with a weight of 40% at market rates and 60% at PPP rates. Increase the weight of GDP to 80%, the remaining 20% to indicate other IMF-specific mandates. Replace the compression factor with a higher percentage of basic votes (12%).
IBRD	The 2016 Dynamic Formula	$(0.8 * GDP + 0.2 * IDA)^{0.95}$ Where IDA = share of IDA replenishments, 80% last 3 replenishments, 20% historical.	Measure GDP with a weight of 40% at market rates and 60% at PPP rates. Replace the compression factor with a higher percentage of basic votes (12%). Implement calculated shareholdings from the Dynamic Formula as soon as possible.
IFC	N/A	Use IBRD shareholding as a baseline	A separate GDP-based formula should be developed.

Fig. 1.1 Shareholding formulas across the Four IFIs

and global recruitment.[10] In terms of functionality, the AIIB combines the roles of the IBRD and IFC. It provides both public- and private-sector financing, but lacks a soft-loan window similar to the IDA. In this regard, the AIIB has not only built itself based on Bretton Woods, given its commitment to embracing the new century as a new MDB,[11] but as this Chapter shows, its innovative elements with respect to the shareholding formula also explain the continuous reform and improvement of the Bretton Woods institutions.

This chapter does not consider the shareholding benchmarks of other peer regional MDBs, but presents a brief description of their initial capital allocation criteria.[12] For the Inter-American Development Bank, the US capital contribution served as the starting point, with the US as the majority shareholder; shareholdings of the other members closely followed their quotas in the IMF. For the African Development Bank, which consisted only of African members at the time of establishment, shareholding was based on the economic capacity of each member, with a formula consisting of three elements with different weighting: national gross product (65%), the amount of taxes collected (15%), and amount of exports (20%). For the Asian Development Bank, several formulas featuring economic capacity were used for regional members, and a minimum of US$ 5 million capital amount was contributed by non-regional members.[13]

1.2 The GDP-Based Formula in the AIIB

The AIIB adopts a GDP-based shareholding formula: GDP is the only parameter used to determine capital distribution among its members. The formula is stipulated in the Chief Negotiators' Report (the 'Report') on the AIIB Articles of Agreement (AOA). It is not an integral part of the AOA, a treaty, and may therefore be updated or revised much more easily than by amending the AOA itself. Notwithstanding, the Report functions as an authoritative explanatory instrument for the relevant parts

[10] In terms of global membership, the AIIB has 105 members across six continents except Antarctica. In terms of global investment, the AIIB has invested across Asia, Oceania, Europe, Africa, and Latin America. In terms of global procurement, the AIIB AOA explicitly authorizes the institution to do so. And in terms of global recruitment, AIIB staffs are from both members and non-member countries, including the US and Japan.

[11] *See* a succinct description of the AIIB's general feature—'heritage and innovation', Natalie Lichtenstein, *A Comparative Guide to the Asian Infrastructure Investment Bank* (Oxford: Oxford University Press, 2018), at 36–38.

[12] Andrés Rigo Sureda, 'The Law Applicable to the Activities of International Development Banks', in *Collected Courses of The Hague Academy of International Law* (Volume 308) (Brill Nijhoff, 2004), at 43.

[13] The split between regional and nonregional shares in the ADB is 60:40, as opposed to 75:25 in the AIIB, which is elaborated in Section II. Kai Yin Allison Haga, 'The Asian Infrastructure Investment Bank: A Qualified Success for Beijing's Economic Statecraft', 50 (3) Journal of Current Chinese Affairs (2021), at 399.

of the AOA.[14] Thus, the positioning of the shareholding formula in the AIIB, as attached to the AOA, offers it a higher legal status than those of the Bretton Woods institutions, which are resolutions of the Board of Governors.

However, the Report does not mention how to measure the GDP. According to a press release by the Chinese Ministry of Finance in 2015, GDP was measured both at market exchange rates with a 60% weight and at purchasing power parity (PPP) rates with a 40% weight.[15] Such measurement is consistent with the shareholding formulas of both the IBRD and IMF. That the method of measuring the GDP failed to appear in the Report (thus leaving the impression of being informal) probably reflects the awareness of those who drafted the AIIB Charter that the discussion of increasing the weight of PPP GDP had long existed in other IFIs, as discussed in Section III, and the AIIB's tendency to modify its measuring method readily in future reviews.

The GDP-based formula does not apply equally across all AIIB members, in contrast to the practice of the IBRD and IMF as global institutions. Rather, with the AIIB membership divided into both regional and non-regional groups, 75% of the authorized capital stock (i.e., US$100 billion) should be retained within the regional group, as indicated in the Chief Negotiators' Report.[16] Thus, regional members (i.e., the Asian and Oceania members, alongside Russia[17]) share the lion's share of US$75 billion, while non-regional members (such as G-7 countries other than the US and Japan (non-members of the AIIB), alongside African and Latin American members) share the remaining, smaller pie of US$25 billion. By the way, although the GDP-based formula is 'indicative only for non-regional members' (quoting the Chief Negotiators' Report), it was applied in capital allocation for these members.

If the US and Japan decide to participate in the AIIB someday, they would be treated as admitted members rather than founding members and receive treatment different from the founding members in capital distribution. Rather than reflecting their relative share of the global economy with the aid of the GDP-based formula, and thereby, overhauling each existing member's shareholding, the US and Japan would be entitled only to the unallocated authorized capital stock, which is small.[18] Another source of capital subscription for new members would be the shares previously

---

[14] The Chief Negotiators' Report identifies itself as 'part of the AIIB's basic documents, for future reference in interpreting the AIIB Articles'.

[15] Chinese Ministry of Finance, 'Press Release about the AIIB AOA' (Vice Minister Shi Yaobin answered reporters' questions on issues related to the AIIB Agreement), 29 June 2015 http://www.mof.gov.cn/zhengwuxinxi/caizhengxinwen/201506/t20150629_1262934.htm (visited 12 September 2021).

[16] Chief Negotiators' Report on the AIIB AOA, Article 5.3.

[17] Russia is not a country of Asia and Oceania based on the United Nations (UN) classification, which the AIIB officially adheres to in defining its regional membership. But the country is somehow classified as regional in Article 3.1 (a) of AIIB AOA and Schedule A thereof, thus being able to rank the third largest shareholder, and winning a vice presidency of Russian nationality in the AIIB.

[18] A small number of shares are left unallocated in both regional and nonregional groups after the initial capital allocation, as indicated in Schedule A of AIIB AOA. Those unallocated shares (16,150 shares for regional and 2336 shares for nonregional) are prepared for new members to join the Bank after its establishment, pursuant to the Chief Negotiators' Report.

allocated to the prospective founding members (PFMs), which failed to subscribe fully or in time.[19]

Brazil is one such founding member that subscribed to its capital shares neither fully nor in time. A PFM at the time of formation of the AIIB in 2015, Brazil was allocated 31,810 shares.[20] The country, however, only became a full member on November 24, 2020, almost four years later than anticipated,[21] and with just 50 shares subscribed (i.e., US$5 million), in part due to national fiscal difficulties.[22] The freed-up portion of 31,760 shares were added back to the unallocated capital stock of the AIIB, which are available for new members to subscribe.

Canada joined the AIIB after its establishment. It is allocated 9954 shares, much more than the total unallocated 2336 shares available for new non-regional members, as stipulated in Schedule A of AIIB AOA. As there has been no increase in the authorized capital stock of the AIIB, the gap must have been filled by the availability of such freed-up capital shares that were originally allocated to PFMs but eventually unsubscribed by them, as in the case of Brazil.

Shareholding determines a member's voting power in the AIIB. Specifically, capital subscription of each US$100 thousand equals one share, and each share equals one vote ('share votes'). A second important source of a member's voice is basic votes, which are automatic and equally distributed among the membership. The third component that counts for a member's voting power is PFM votes, which are exclusive to the 57 PFMs, amounting to 600 votes for each on fulfilling membership.[23] All votes across these three groups are equal in weight. Of the total votes in the AIIB, basic votes are designated at 12% under the AOA explicitly,[24] to ensure representation of smaller and poorer member countries; PFM votes are about 3%,[25] and share votes about 85%.

---

[19] The membership of Kuwait and South Africa, two prospective founding members, has been delayed for years since December 31, 2016—the original deadline of deposit of ratification instruments. The shares originally allocated to the two countries in AIIB AOA Schedule A could be subscribed by new members.

[20] See AIIB AOA, Schedule A.

[21] Ibid, Articles 58.1 stipulates: 'Instruments of ratification, acceptance or approval shall be deposited with the Depository not later than December 31, 2016, or if necessary, until such later date as may be decided by the Board of Governors by a Special Majority vote as provided in Article 28'.

[22] It is interesting to note that Korea is another founding member that did not subscribe fully; it subscribed 37,387 shares out of 37,388 allocated shares, i.e., only one share less than originally allocated in AIIB Schedule A. However, most AIIB founding members subscribed fully to the capital stock as allocated to them. AIIB, 'Members and Prospective Members of the Bank', 24 August 2021 https://www.aiib.org/en/about-aiib/governance/members-of-bank/index.html (visited 13 September 2021).

[23] A PFM becomes a member of the Bank only after 'its instrument of ratification, acceptance or approval is deposited'. AIIB AOA Article 58.1.

[24] The percentage of basic votes (12%) is stipulated in Ibid, Article 28.1.

[25] The percentage of PFM votes (3%) is concluded upon the condition that all PFMs fully subscribed their shares as allocated in AIIB Schedule A, which turned out to be not so. Lichtenstein, above n 11, at 152.

The AIIB Charter requires capital reviews at least every five years.[26] The purpose of capital review is twofold: to determine whether the authorized capital stock is sufficient, or should be increased, and whether the distribution of shareholding should be adjusted to reflect the evolution of members' relative economic positions. Under the AIIB Charter, as in the Charters of other IFIs, any increase in the authorized capital should be distributed in proportion to the existing shareholdings of members ('preemptive right').[27] Such an arrangement known as General Capital Increase, however, would fail to change members' relative shareholding positions, defeating the purpose of an equitable balance of voting power in capital review. The AIIB Charter, accordingly, accords members the right to relinquish their preemptive rights,[28] with the shares so relinquished to be subscribed by those underrepresented, aided by the GDP-based formula. This is known as Selective Capital Increase (SCI) in other IFIs,[29] which has the benefit of facilitating the result of shareholding (and voting power) adjustments across members.

Indeed, a successful shareholding realignment is premised on the overrepresented members' willingness to relinquish their preemptive rights.[30] In the Bretton Woods institutions, however, overrepresented member countries either expressly refuse to relinquish their preemptive rights or veto any increase in the authorized capital stock, despite its criticality amid global crises when the institutions' balance sheets are strained,[31] making the implementation of shareholding realignments a Herculean task, as revealed in the IBRD's 2020 shareholding review in Section IV.

A subject of much debate is China's veto power in the AIIB. Aided by the GDP-based formula applied within both regional and non-regional groups, respectively, China as a regional member is allocated about 31% of the total capital stock, making it the largest shareholder. China's shareholding is larger than those of the next five biggest shareholders combined (i.e., India, Russia, Germany, Republic of Korea, and Australia in order of largest shareholder after China to smallest shareholder).[32] With its shareholding translated into over 26% of total votes, China has veto power in decision-making that requires a super majority vote of 75% in favor.[33]

---

[26] AIIB AOA Article 5.4.

[27] Ibid, Article 5.4.

[28] Ibid stipulates 'No member shall be obligated to subscribe to any part of an increase of capital stock'.

[29] The practice of SCI is not rare in the Bretton Woods institutions, such as the 2018 SCI in the World Bank.

[30] As the Development Committee states, '...members' subscriptions should reflect their relative position in the world economy, subject to the right of each member to maintain its existing pro rata share in the capital on the occasion of any increase in the authorized capital (pre-emptive right)'. Development Committee (Joint Ministerial Committee of the Boards of Governors of the Bank and the Fund), 'Enhancing voice and participation of developing and transition countries in decision-making at the World Bank and IMF' (DC 2003–0002, 27 March 2003), at 11–12.

[31] Jonathan Wheatley, 'Multilateral development banks' balance sheets strained by global crises', *Financial Times*, 2 May 2022.

[32] See AIIB, above n 22.

[33] A super majority vote in the AIIB Board of Governors is defined as 'an affirmative vote of two-thirds of the total number of Governors, representing not less than three-fourths of the total

China claimed that it had no intention of seeking veto power during the establishment of AIIB.[34] It declared that it was ready to contribute 50% of the Bank's authorized capital only to make things happen.[35] Subsequently, as more countries applied to join the Bank, it became unnecessary for China to commit that amount of capital.[36] China stated that it was open to further diluting its share votes as more members expected to join the Bank in the future.[37]

However, China will remain the largest shareholder before the next capital stock increases. Even when there is a need for capital stock increase, the Board of Governors must decide through a super majority vote in favor, where China holds a veto power.[38] That super-majority-vote requirement ensures China's decisive role in such an event, in addition to its preemptive right.

As veto power exists in many IFIs, the potential control by veto leads to governance concerns: should any member ever have a veto over any IFI decision? Some misunderstandings deserve clarification to address this question. First, asymmetric capital contribution justifies asymmetric representation. Weighted voting, rather than equal voting for each member, has been widely accepted since the Bretton Woods Conference in 1944.[39] Veto power could be understood as a reward to the initiating powers who have exercised leadership while having to bear significant financial and diplomatic costs for the IFIs' establishment and maintenance. Second, veto power in the IFIs is derived from specific percentages of votes required for a few key decisions, as intended to draw majority support. By contrast, veto power in the UN Security

---

voting power of the members.' AIIB AOA Article 28. Super majority decisions include capital increases, modifying the regional shareholding percentage, assistance to non-members, increase in the lending limit, allocation of net income to other purposes, changes in the Board of Directors or its non-resident basis, election of the President and amendment of the AIIB Charter. Lichtenstein, above n 11, at 30.

[34] 'Chinese Deputy Minister of Finance says China has no intention to seek or drop a veto in the AIIB' (China's Vice Minister of Finance": The proposition that China seeks or gives up its one-vote veto power on the AIIB is untenable), 25 March 2015.

http://www.xinhuanet.com/politics/2015-03/25/c_1114763452.htm (visited 27 June 2022).

[35] 'Chinese Financial Minister says China does not seek a 50% capital subscription in the AIIB' (Lou Jiwei: The establishment of the AIIB is a win-win move, and China's investment does not necessarily have to reach 50%), 3 July 2014 http://www.gov.cn/xinwen/2014-07/03/content_2711747.htm (visited 27 June 2022).

[36] Ibid.

[37] Ibid.

[38] AIIB AOA Article 4.3.

[39] Harry Dexter White, one of the main architects of the Bretton Woods institutions, referred to the linkage between voting and financial contributions explicitly, 'If each member of the board were to be given an equal vote, then a small country that invested one million dollars would have as much power in making decisions as a country that has subscribed a hundred or a thousand times that amount'. Both advanced and non-advanced economies concurred with White in the Bretton Woods Conference. See Kaya, above n 6, at 55.

Council is derived from specific references to the five permanent members, as explicitly named by law.[40] The IFI version of veto power seems 'the lesser of two evils'. Finally, holding veto power does not necessarily mean using it, as what China does in the AIIB,[41] although the veto does not need to be used to influence governance, given the effect of its shadow. It concludes that the design of veto power in the IFIs is a rational choice, despite seemingly at a cost of equality and good governance.

1.3 The Quota Formula in the IMF

In the IMF, shareholding is referred to as a quota. A quota is denominated in special drawing right (SDR), while capital in the AIIB is denominated in the US dollar. Similar to capital shares in the AIIB, quotas in the IMF play multiple roles, namely they determine a member's financial contribution to the organization, decide its voting power, and decide new shares to be distributed to it in the case of a quota increase ('preemptive right').[42] However, the quota additionally decides how much a member state is allowed to draw (i.e., borrow) from the IMF. This unique function of the quota is due to the IMF's designated purpose of assisting members with maintaining equilibrium in their balance of payments, as opposed to the development purposes of an MDB.

A quota formula is traditionally designed to reflect IMF members' relative importance in the world economy, subject to negotiations of both economic and political considerations.The original formula used at the Bretton Woods Conference in 1944 contained four variables, namely, national income, gold and foreign exchange reserves, the five-year average of annual exports and imports, and a variability measure based on maximum fluctuations in exports over a five-year period.[43] This formula functioned as a point of departure in negotiations both at Bretton Woods and in ensuing IMF meetings.[44] Decades later, in the 1960s, the IMF introduced a set of five formulas, producing 'somewhat higher calculated quotas for members

---

[40] UN Charter Article 23.1 lists China, France, Russia, the United Kingdom and the US as permanent members of the Security Council, and Article 27.3 stipulates their veto power on non-procedural issues.

[41] Bin Gu, 'China, the US and what it means to be a hegemon', *The Straits Times*, 16 July 2022.

[42] For greater certainty, quota increase and distribution is distinct from SDR allocation, which can be done simply with a stroke of the pen. The IMF finished its largest ever SDR allocation in 2021, equivalent to 650 billion US dollars, in a bid to boost global liquidity among member states, in particular to cope with the impact of the COVID-19 crisis for most vulnerable countries. IMF members' existing quotas play a decisive role in SDR allocation, as they do in quota distribution. IMF, '2021 General SDR Allocation' https://www.imf.org/en/Topics/special-drawing-right/2021-SDR-Allocation (visited 3 June 2022).

[43] IMF, 'Quota Formula Review—Initial Considerations', 10 February 2012, at 6.

[44] Andreas F. Lowenfeld, *International Economic Law*, 2nd ed. (New York: Oxford University Press, 2008), at 610, quoting Horsefield.

with relatively small and more open economies'.[45] In 1983, the five formulas were further revised, with effects that 'the influence of variability of current receipts was reduced, GDP replaced national income, and reserves, which had been dropped earlier, were reintroduced'.[46] The current formula, known as the 2008 quota formula, is the outcome of the long-term effort to simplify the formulas.[47]

The 2008 quota formula has four variables: GDP (50%), openness (30%), variability (15%), and reserves (5%), all expressed in shares of global totals. Among them, in general, GDP captures members' relative positions in the world economy, measured in a blend of market exchange rates and PPP rates, weighing 60% and 40%, respectively; openness reflects members' degree of integration (mainly through trade) in the world market; variability illustrates members' exposure to exogenous shocks, and accordingly their potential need to draw from the IMF; and reserves represent members' ability to contribute to the organization. This formula includes a compression factor that reduces the dispersion in calculated quota shares across members, with the intended effect of redistributing quotas to the small and poor countries, and serving the purpose of democratic representation in the Fund.

The 2008 quota formula represents a major improvement upon its predecessors, if measured against the four guiding principles during the negotiations leading up to it, which are specifically that the formula should (1) be simple and transparent, so that the basis for differences in relative quota shares is readily understandable; (2) be consistent with the multiple roles of quotas, appropriately reflecting global economic and financial trends and capturing members' relative positions in the world economy; (3) result in calculated quota shares that are broadly acceptable to the membership; and (4) be feasible to implement based on timely, high quality, and widely available data.[48]

The 2008 quota formula has been guiding quota adjustments of the IMF ever since, which occurs every five years to reflect the changing world economic landscape.[49] Particularly, the 14th general review of quotas resulted in the historic IMF reform—the 2010 Quota and Governance Reform, which is known for 'a shift of more than 6 percent of quota shares to dynamic emerging market and developing countries and also from overrepresented to underrepresented countries, while protecting the quota shares and voting power of the poorest members'.[50] This historic IMF reform

[45] See IMF, n 43, at 6.

[46] Ibid, at 6.

[47] A group of external experts—the Quota Formula Review Group, after reviewing the five quota formulas, submitted a report to the IMF Executive Board in 2000, recommending the adoption of a single formula with two variables—market GDP and variability. IMF, 'External Review of the Quota Formulas' (EBAP/00/52, 5/1/00), 1 May 2000 https://www.imf.org/external/np/tre/quota/2000/eng/qfrg/annex/dload/EBAP52_Sup1.pdf (visited 24 August 2021).

[48] See IMF, above n 43, at 4.

[49] 'The Board of Governors shall at intervals of not more than five years conduct a general review, and if it deems it appropriate propose an adjustment, of the quotas of the members'. IMF AOA, Art. III Sect. 2(a).

[50] IMF, 'Press Release: Historic Quota and Governance Reforms Became Effective', 27 January 2016, https://www.imf.org/en/News/Articles/2015/09/14/01/49/pr1625a (visited 25 August 2021).

entered into force only after four years of delay by the US.[51] The fear of the US about its ratification is that '2010 will be a mere "down payment" on much bigger quota increases and reallocations to come',[52] which the US considers as the greatest threat to its veto power, its top priority.[53]

For all its historic improvement and positive results, the IMF's current quota formula remains problematic.[54] First, the weight assigned to GDP at 50%, combined with a blend of 60% at market exchange rates and 40% at PPP rates in measuring GDP, is inadequate and should be increased.[55] Second, regarding openness, indicators of members' integration in the global capital market lack adequate development, and thus do not feature prominently in the quota formula partially due to data limitations, as opposed to trade-based indicators used since the Bretton Woods Conference in 1944.[56] Third, some factors are highly correlated, such as the relationship between GDP and openness (e.g., consider a country with a high ratio of exports to GDP), which may result in double counting. Fourth, there is little empirical evidence of a relationship between variability, which seeks to capture members' potential need for IMF resources, and the actual demand for such resources.[57] Fifth, regarding reserves, the formula fails to distinguish members' ability to contribute to the IMF from their actual contributions, the latter of which should be assigned more weight. Six, the

[51] The reform, initially set to take effect by October 2012, took effect in 2016. 'Press Release: IMF Managing Director Christine Lagarde Welcomes U.S. Congressional Approval of the 2010 Quota and Governance Reforms', 18 December 2015, https://www.imf.org/en/News/Articles/2015/09/14/01/49/pr15573 (visited 30 March 2022).

[52] Robert H. Wade and Jakob Vestergaard, 'Why is the IMF at an Impasse, and What Can Be Done about it?', 6 (3) Global Policy (2015), at 294.

[53] Similarly, the US opposed the European Commission's proposal in 2015 for a single representation of the euro area in the IMF, which could form a constituency with more than 20% of the total votes and threaten the US's veto. Emanuel Castellarin, ' « La réforme institutionnelle du FMI: du 4ème au 7ème amendement. Conséquence du changement des rapports de forces dans le monde ou de l'enseignement des crises ?»,' in Michael Waibel (ed), *Les implications juridiques des crises financières mondiales* (Leyde, Brill/Nijhoff, 2020), at 153.

[54] Ernando S. De Leon, 'the IMF Quota Formula Review', Bangko Sentral Review (the Philippines) 2011, at 43–47, referring to the IMF staff paper 'Quota Formula Review—Initial Considerations' and other sources.

[55] IMF, 'Report of the Executive Board to the Board of Governors on the Outcome of the Quota Formula Review', 30 January 2013, at 2–3, http://www.imf.org/external/np/pp/eng/2013/013013.pdf (visited 15 August 2022). The G24 Secretariat, Ted Truman (arguing for the Cooper formula) and many other external reports argue for the substitution of PPP GDP for market-based GDP. The rationale is that PPP GDP more correctly measures the level of economic activity in emerging markets and developing countries where market prices of nontradeables tend to be significantly below those prices in advanced economies. See IMF, n 43, at 8.

[56] Openness is officially defined by the IMF as the annual average of the sum of current payments and current receipts (goods, services, income, and transfers) for a five-year period.

[57] See IMF, above n 55, at 3.

compression factor 'would reduce transparency and could dampen the formula's ability to capture dynamism over time'.[58]

Meanwhile, negotiation on a new quota formula to address the deficiencies of the current formula are ongoing. The negotiations initially set a deadline of January 2013.[59] It then became a crux in the subsequent 15th general quota review, which promised to conclude by January 2014. It was prolonged until an official declaration of failure in 2020.[60] The quota formula reforms remain top on the agenda of the ongoing 16th general quota review, scheduled to conclude by December 2023.[61] As committed, '[a]ny adjustment in quota shares would be expected to result in increases in the quota shares of dynamic economies (i.e., emerging market and developing countries) in line with their relative positions in the world economy'.[62] The demerits in the existing formula were discussed in the run up to its own establishment in 2008, and they continue to inform the ongoing negotiation. It is unfortunate that 'deadlines have come and gone, with next to no agreement'.[63]

The negotiation on a new quota formula should focus on the following principles. First, after more than a decade of deadlock, and during which the world economic landscape has experienced a fundamental overhaul, quota adjustments are needed even more urgently than in the case of the 2010 Quota and Governance Reform. The IMF cannot afford another failure inflicting damage to its credibility, effectiveness, and legitimacy. Second, a new quota formula is a prerequisite of the required quota adjustments. For the sake of transparency and predictability, the role of the formula is crucial for guiding quota adjustments, although historical experience shows that factors other than a quota formula were considered. Third, the four principles based on which the 2008 quota formula was developed, as discussed earlier, remain relevant today.[64] To implement those combined principles, the variable of GDP, and PPP

---

[58] See Leon, above n 54, at 45. Notwithstanding those defects, the compression factor (alongside PPP GDP) is agreed to be retained in the formula for 20 years, then to be revisited. See IMF, n 43, at 12.

[59] IMF, 'IMF Quota and Governance Reform—Elements of an Agreement', 31 October 2010, at 1.

[60] IMF, 'Fifteenth and Sixteenth General Reviews of Quotas—Report of the Executive Board to the Board of Governors' (attaching a Draft Board of Governors Resolution concluding the fifteenth general review of quotas with no increase in quota), 13 January 2020 https://www.imf.org/en/Publications/Policy-Papers/Issues/2020/02/13/Fifteenth-and-Sixteenth-General-Reviews-of-Quotas-Report-of-the-Executive-Board-to-the-Board-49049?sc_mode=1 (visited 15 August 2022).

[61] The Riyadh G20 leaders' communique stated, 'We remain committed to revisiting the adequacy of quotas and will continue the process of IMF governance reform under the 16th general review of quotas, including a new quota formula as a guide, by 15 December 2023.' G20 Leaders Declaration, Riyadh, 21–22 November 2020, para 14.

[62] IMF Board of Governors Resolution on 7 February 2020, https://www.imf.org/en/About/Factsheets/Sheets/2016/07/14/12/21/IMF-Quotas (visited 19 June 2022).

[63] This disappointing quote is from Jakob Vestergaard and Robert H. Wade, 'Still in the Woods: Gridlock in the IMF and the World Bank Puts Multilateralism at Risk', 6 (1) Global Policy (2015), at 4. Kaya's comment sheds light on the reason for the IMF stalemate, '[w]hile the formulae embody economic logic, such technical logic cannot be understood in a sterile manner that excludes politics.' See Kaya, above n 6, at 80.

[64] G20 Leaders Declaration, Los Cabos, 18–19 June 2012, para 33.

GDP in calculating GDP, may deserve a higher weight than that in the 2008 formula. Moreover, replacing the compression factor with an increased percentage of basic votes (e.g., from the current 5.5–12%[65]) of the total votes in the IMF would further transparency.

1.4 The Dynamic Formula in the IBRD

At the Bretton Woods Conference in 1944, the sequence of discussing the IMF first, followed by the IBRD, resulted in the IBRD mirroring the IMF, particularly on corporate governance.[66] Until 2010, the method for allocating capital shares to member states in the IBRD had depended on the outcome of IMF quota reviews for much of IBRD's history.

The historical link between the IBRD capital allocation and the IMF quota shares, while serving efficiency and convenience, is not appropriate, mainly because these two organizations have different mandates. Specifically, the IBRD focuses on supporting developing countries' long-term economic development, while the IMF works on the macroeconomic stability of member countries and the international monetary and financial system as a whole. Working toward the equilibrium of member states' balance of payments, the variables in the IMF quota formula capture both members' capacity to contribute to IMF resources and their potential needs to draw from the IMF. In comparison, IBRD members' capital shares have the former quality but lack the latter, that is, they do not determine the lending volume to the members. Particularly, the variables of openness, variability, and reserves in the 2008 quota formula, except GDP, are 'poor proxies' of the relationship between the IBRD and its members.[67]

Thus, in 2010, the IBRD decided to break this historical association with IMF quotas and established a unique formula to guide its own shareholding adjustments under the two-phased Voice Reform.[68] In 2010, a new shareholding formula was used in capital adjustments, which was later developed as the 2016 Dynamic Formula. The practice in 2010 marked the first time for the IBRD to depart from IMF quotas.

---

65 The percentage of basic votes out of the total votes in the IMF is less than half of their level at 11.3% in 1944, evidencing deepened inequality among members. See Castellarin, above 53, at 143.

66 As evidenced, Article V of the IBRD Charter is nearly an exact copy of Article XII of the IMF Charter, both articles being entitled as 'Organization and Management'.

67 World Bank, 'Repowering the World Bank for the 21st Century' (Report of the High-Level Commission on Modernization of World Bank Group Governance, known as the Zedillo Commission Report, 2009), at 25.

68 Voice Reform Phase 1, as agreed in 2008, increased the voting power of developing and transition countries (DTC) in the IBRD from 42.6 to 44.1% by increasing basic votes to 5.55% of total votes. Voice Reform Phase 2, as agreed in 2010, increased DTC voice further to over 47.19% by using a new shareholding formula, the basis for the later 2016 Dynamic Formula. Development Committee, 'World Bank Group Voice Reform: Enhancing Voice and Participation of Developing and Transition Countries in 2010 and Beyond' (DC2010-0006/1, 25 April 2010), at 2, 15–16.

Besides, the Voice Reform introduced regular shareholding reviews at five-year intervals, the first of which occurred in 2015.[69] The IBRD, unlike the IMF and AIIB, does not stipulate regular shareholding reviews in its Charter. Such efforts all fit into a greater campaign to enhance the voice and participation of developing and transition countries in the Bretton Woods institutions, conducted concurrently and in parallel with the IMF.[70]

In 2016, the IBRD Board of Governors formally endorsed its first shareholding formula, following and building on the first shareholding review report in 2015.[71] The so-called Dynamic Formula aims to achieve an equitable balance of voting power, while avoiding dilution of the voice of the poor and smallest countries.[72] It follows a few technically sound guidelines similar to the IMF's 2008 quota formula, such that the formula should be simple and transparent; broadly acceptable to the membership; and based on readily available, timely, and high-quality data.[73]

The Dynamic Formula has two variables: GDP and IDA contributions, weighing 80% and 20%, respectively. GDP, indicating members' economic weights, is measured as a combination of 60% market rates and 40% PPP rates, corresponding to the IMF and AIIB formulas. The IDA variable, indicating members' contributions to the World Bank's mission of poverty reduction, is measured as a combination of 80% three recent IDA replenishments and 20% historical replenishments to encourage new contributions while recognizing the generosity of past contributions.[74] A compression factor of 0.95 is introduced in the Dynamic Formula, similar to that of the IMF formula, serving to protect the poor and the smallest countries.

The IBRD's Dynamic Formula functions as a guide for each periodical shareholding review and as a starting point for capital realignments, similar to the IMF quota formula. As any capital realignment is a compromise, the Dynamic Formula is not intended 'as the final outcome for such realignment'.[75] For example, statistics show that the progress achieved at the 2018 Selective Capital Increase (SCI) has been reversed, with increased misalignment of 30 beneficiary countries from the SCI by the time of the 2020 shareholding review. Among them, China is misaligned by more than 6 percentage point, the largest ever.[76]

The IBRD decided not to adjust the shareholding in the 2020 shareholding review but to delay the consideration until the next review in 2025. One of the stated reasons was 'the timing of the Review in relation to the agreement on the capital package

---

69 Ibid, at 16.

70 Ibid, at 1, quoting 'Monterrey Consensus on Financing for Development', International Conference on Financing for Development, Monterrey, Mexico, 18–22 March 2002 (para 63).

71 Development Committee, 'Dynamic Formula—Report to the Governors Annual Meetings 2016' (DC2016-0010, 20 September 2016), at 1.

72 Ibid, at 2.

73 Ibid, at 2.

74 Ibid, at 4.

75 Ibid, at 3.

76 Development Committee, '2020 Shareholding Review: Concluding Report to Governors at the Annual Meetings' (DC2021-0008, 28 September 2021), para 10.

in 2018',[77] even though at the conclusion of which the IBRD had committed that it cannot replace the 2020 shareholding review. The 2020 review, instead, 'will provide an opportunity to review underrepresentation relative to updated calculated shareholding from the IBRD Dynamic Formula'.[78] Thus, the result of the 2020 review is ironic, and disappointing for those underrepresented member countries.[79]

With the rapid increase in China's GDP, delaying a new round of shareholding adjustment will increase the misalignment. The US's tactic of delaying the reform of the IBRD to suppress China's rising influence over it could backfire.[80] While the US dragged its heels in implementing the Bretton Woods reforms, a disappointed China started to 'walk on two legs', initiating the Belt and Road Initiative and the AIIB.[81] The longer the delay, the higher the disparities, the harder agreement on adjustment and the more the Bretton Woods organizations risk marginalization.[82]

1.5 Shareholding Distribution in the IFC

While the IBRD has the Dynamic Formula to guide its future shareholding reviews, should the IFC deserve a separate shareholding formula of its own, as a sister institution under the WBG, given that the IFC shareholding has a historical link to the IBRD shareholding? The WBG has been considering three main options for adopting a benchmark for future shareholding reviews in the IFC: (1) use IBRD shareholding as a baseline, as before; (2) use the 2016 Dynamic Formula as a baseline, although it was negotiated specifically for the IBRD; or (3) negotiate a separate shareholding formula for the IFC to better reflect its distinct private-sector mandate.[83]

---

[77] Ibid, paras 4 and 13. The World Bank's 2018 Capital Package, comprising the 2018 SCI and other reforms,made a US$13 billion increase in paid-in capital to IBRD and IFC, and increased China's voting power from 4.45% to 5.71%, among other achievements. Congressional Research Service, '2018 World Bank Capital Increased Proposal', 14 December 2018.

[78] Development Committee, 'World Bank/IMF Spring Meetings 2018: Development Committee Communiqué,' 21 April 2018, para 7 https://www.devcommittee.org/sites/dc/files/download/Communiques/2018-06/Communique%28E%29immediaterelease4-21.pdf (visited 16 February 2022).

[79] Kaya's comment on IMF quota shifts sheds light on the reason for the IBRD stalemate, 'the largest shareholders tend to prefer modest increases, compared to … some developing countries, which see the quota increase as the basis for … greater voice within the institution'. See Kaya, above n 6, at 66.

[80] Curiously, if calculated according to the Dynamic Formula, the US shareholding would *increase* by 1.48%, rather than decrease. See Development Committee, above n 76, at 13.

[81] Bin Gu, 'Chinese Multilateralism in the AIIB', 20 (1) Journal of International Economic Law (2017), at 143.

[82] Such warning is neither rare nor new. Jakob Vestergaard and Robert H. Wade used to warn acutely against 'further marginalization' of Bretton Woods institutions if the US kept delaying the shareholding reforms in those institutions. See Vestergaard and Wade, above n 63, at 10.

[83] Development Committee, '2020 Shareholding Review: Report to Governors at the Annual Meetings' (DC2020-0009, 16 October 2020), paras 18–21.

Next, we address these three options. First, should the IFC continue to use IBRD shareholding as a baseline? History tells us that it is a Herculean task to anchor IFC shareholding to IBRD shareholding over time because 'the shareholding distribution has diverged to some extent as the frequency and subscription of capital increases have differed, [and] members have joined at different times',[84] and thus, no parallelism between the two institutions has been maintained. The credibility of this option has further lost ground because the IBRD has managed to delink itself from IMF quotas in 2010. Given that the IBRD justified its decision on the ground of distinct mandates, the IFC with a distinct mandate from the IBRD can follow the same path.

The second option is that the IFC uses the Dynamic Formula as a baseline, if it deserves a separate benchmark. As the first option, this one sounds simple and automatic, and even echoes the spirit of 'one WBG'. However, it is technically inappropriate if one considers the two factors in the 2016 Dynamic Formula: only GDP is relevant to the character of the IFC, but the other factor of IDA contributions is out of the scope of the IFC's mandate. Capital distribution in an IFI is primarily decided by the members' economic size, while also being relevant to the organization's purpose, function, and mandates.

At this point the third option seems the only choice, that is, a separate shareholding formula for the IFC different from the Dynamic Formula. But there are concerns regarding this option. First and foremost, the option would violate a 'one WBG approach',[85] since the IBRD already has a shareholding formula. The concern is not genuine because the same people are the representatives on the Boards of Directors of the IBRD, IDA, and IFC, demonstrating the very 'one WBG approach'. The logical conclusion is a 'one Bretton Woods approach', which the IBRD rejected when it broke away from IMF shareholding in 2010. Another concern is that a separate shareholding formula for the IFC requires 'further technical work and negotiation' and continuing the status quo would represent 'a simple and practical approach in line with recent precedent that would provide a solid basis for future reviews'.[86] This argument is no less hypocritical and fictitious.

At the core of the current stalemate is the lack of collective political will over the reform of IFC shareholding. However, this does not mean that keeping the status quo is appropriate. Rather, it risks the IFC's long-term sustainability as shown by the history of IBRD shareholding reforms. Without a rules-based formula, future shareholding reviews in the IFC would be highly political, resulting in longer 'life

---

[84] See Development Committee, above n 76, para 15.

[85] The opponents argue that 'separate formulas in IBRD and IFC would imply divergence rather than convergence of the shareholding structures of the two institutions, which is not consistent with a one WBG approach, nor with approaches taken in the past'. See Development Committee, above 83, para 21.

[86] Ibid, para 21.

or death' negotiations, even down to compromises 'at a further than third decimal point'.[87]

A separate shareholding formula for the IFC is not only necessary but also viable. Mainly it should be a GDP-based formula, similar to the one used by the AIIB. This is because, in terms of mandates, the IFC is more alike to the AIIB than to the IBRD. Both IFC and AIIB prioritize private-sector investment,[88] and are free of a concessional loan function similar to IDA. Different from the AIIB, where its GDP-based formula applies separately within regional and non-regional groups, the formula should apply uniformly across member countries in the IFC. A GDP-based formula for the IFC also conforms to the rationale of the 2016 Dynamic Formula because it is tantamount to amplifying the weight of GDP in the Dynamic Formula to 100%, while dropping the other irrelevant factor of IDA contributions. The proposal would 'strengthen the WBG shareholding architecture by putting the shareholding frameworks for IFC and IBRD on an equal footing, in the spirit of one World Bank Group',[89] the ideal shareholding benchmark for the IFC.

The IFC shareholding review should adhere to the Lima Shareholding Principles, which were principally developed to guide the design of the IBRD shareholding benchmark but applicable to the prospective IFC shareholding benchmark discussion, as endorsed by the Governors of the World Bank at the 2015 annual meetings.[90] Particularly, the shareholding reviews should be conducted regularly, at least every five years, and the voice of poor and small countries should not be diluted in the governing body of the organization. Basic votes, as allocated to all members in the same amount, should be increased from the current 5.55% to over 10% of the total voting stock.[91]

[87] Vestergaard describes the shareholding negotiations in the World Bank as 'it took month after month of "24/7" negotiations, and blistered nerves all round, to even get changes of this [microscopic] magnitude, as Executive Directors and World Bank staff searched for compromises "at the third decimal point"'. See Vestergaard and Wade, above n 63, at 6.

[88] The AIIB has a lofty financing target of 50% for private sector projects by 2030. AIIB, 'Corporate Strategy: Financing Infrastructure for Tomorrow' (September 2020), at 27.

[89] See Development Committee, above n 76, para 20(iv).

[90] The Lima Shareholding Principles are (1) regular shareholding reviews every five years based on a dynamic formula, (2) to achieve an equitable balance of voting power, (3) that all voices are important, (4) small and poor countries' voting power not to be diluted, and (5) that shareholding brings both rights and responsibilities. See Development Committee, above n 76, paras 3 and 5.

[91] This level of 5.55% is stipulated in the IFC AOA, Article IV Sect. 3(a)(i). By comparison, the number of basic votes was set at 250 votes per member in the Bretton Woods institutions in 1944, amounting to an original level of over 10% of the total voting stock. Over time, however, the share of basic votes was eroded with the increase of capital subscription and share-votes allocation. Jakob Vestergaard and Robert H. Wade, 'Protecting Power: How Western States Retain the Dominant Voice in the World Bank's Governance', 46 World Development (2013), at 154.

1.6 Two-Way Emulation Between the AIIB, IMF, and IBRD

As a new multilateral organization derived from the Bretton Woods system, the success of the AIIB has built on its faithful inheritance of (and sincere cooperation with) the IMF and IBRD in terms of corporate governance and modus operandi. In turn, the AIIB's innovative elements have helped to improve of the Bretton Woods institutions. Such mutual emulation is also at work apparent with respect to shareholding formulas.

1.6.1 Two-Way Emulation Between the AIIB and the IMF

Although the IMF is mandated with a function distinct from the AIIB as an MDB, from a historical perspective, the two institutions have common factors, and they may have interacted with and even inspired each other. At the outset, the initiation of the AIIB in 2013 was a backlash against the continued US hegemony and blocking of reforms in Bretton Woods institutions.[92] Conversely, the establishment of AIIB in December 2015 led the US congress to approve the 2010 Quota and Governance Reform of the IMF immediately,[93] after four years of delay, as discussed in Section III. In 2021, the IMF made a historic program of allocating 650 billion US dollar-equivalent SDRs to members as a boost of global liquidity for post-COVID-19 economic recovery.[94] To benefit developing and least developed countries, as intended by the program, other countries with a strong external reserve position should channel their portion of allocated SDRs to the MDBs, which would effectively enhance the MDBs' lending capacity to the most needy countries. The AIIB is a candidate to be part of this mission.[95]

The AIIB chief negotiators chose a GDP-based shareholding formula, presumably having drawn upon the arduous reform of the IMF's 2008 quota formula, which was initiated after the completion of the 14th general review of quotas in 2010. Some

---

[92] The elaboration of the AIIB's role in correcting the 'unsustainable elements the existing world order' is available at Bin Gu, *The Law and Governance of the Asian Infrastructure Investment Bank* (The Netherlands: Wolters Kluwer, 2019), at 8–10.

[93] Vestergaard and Wade find that the US administration, which had agreed earlier on the IMF reform, conspired in a de facto manner with the US Congress in the delay of ratifying it. See Wade and Vestergaard, above n 52, at 292.

[94] IMF, 'IMF Governors Approve a Historic US$650 Billion SDR Allocation of Special Drawing Rights', 2 August 2021 https://www.imf.org/en/News/Articles/2021/07/30/pr21235-imf-governors-approve-a-historic-us-650-billion-sdr-allocation-of-special-drawing-rights (visited 27 February 2022).

[95] Only prescribed SDR holders may be eligible to receive SDRs as channeled to them. So far there are eight development institutions in the official list of prescribed SDR holders in the IMF, including the World Bank, the African Development Bank, and the Asian Development Bank. The AIIB is not currently among them. So, the AIIB needs to obtain the position of a subscribed holder to join the program. IMF, 'Guidance Note for Fund Staff on the Treatment and Use of SDR Allocations' (August 2021), at 38.

technical deficiencies and weaknesses embedded in the IMF's quota formula had been raised and discussed even in the run up to it and have been retained on the agenda of the ensuing negotiations until today. Among the most controversial issues are whether the GDP variable should have a heavier weight than 50% and whether the PPP GDP deserves a higher percentage than 40% as a measurement of GDP, as discussed in Section III. The architects of the AIIB Charter must have been aware of the IMF's discussion when they were designing their own shareholding formula, as the weight of GDP was increased eventually to 100%, while the 60/40 ratio for market GDP and PPP GDP, respectively, was retained for the sake of consistency.

The AIIB's GDP-based shareholding formula, blessed with the ideal feature of being 'simple and transparent', could inform the ongoing reform of the IMF quota formula. In a prospective new quota formula, the variable of GDP deserves a higher percentage, say 80%, and market GDP and PPP GDP may be blended in a reversed manner, that is, at a 40/60 ratio. If the proposal is adopted, it will affect the AIIB itself, which would probably change the combination of market GDP and PPP GDP correspondingly in the next capital review.[96] The AIIB could be more flexible than other IFIs in doing so, because its measurement of GDP is not even stipulated in a formal, legal document, as discussed in Section II. Such two-way emulation between the AIIB and the IMF should be healthy and sustainable, as it fits the overall purpose of a shareholding formula that reflects members' relative position in the world economy.

1.6.2 Two-Way Emulation Between the AIIB and the IBRD

The IBRD, unlike the IMF, may have directly impacted the AIIB's decision to adopt the GDP-based shareholding formula. As early as in the Voice Reform of 2010, the World Bank had designated a weight of 80% to the variable of GDP in capital adjustments and had members' IDA contributions to reflect the other mission of the World Bank—to fight poverty. The World Bank's practice, although lacking a formal formula to support it, possibly influenced the architects of the AIIB Charter during their subsequent negotiations on shareholding distribution.[97] As the AIIB has no such poverty-fighting function as that of the World Bank, there was no need for its chief negotiators to consider members' soft-loan contributions, if any, when designing the shareholding formula; the only remaining parameter was GDP. The choice of a GDP-based formula may have been encouraged by the World Bank's

[96] The Board of Governors carried out the first AIIB capital review in 2020, which resolved that the capital stock would remain unchanged subject to the next review, currently scheduled for 2025. AIIB Annual Report of 2020, at 18.

[97] Lichtenstein, the AIIB's inaugural General Counsel who was engaged in drafting the AOA, recalled that the AIIB Chief Negotiators were '[p]erhaps mindful of these [more than a decade of] World Bank Group discussions [leading up to the 2016 Dynamic Formula]', when recording their own standard of capital allocation. Lichtenstein, above n 11, at 114–15.

Voice Reform,[98] which served as a justification of emulation for the AIIB as a new bank eager to establish itself and to be recognized in the international community.

Conversely, the establishment of the AIIB shareholding formula up to 2015 probably contributed to the agreement on the 2016 Dynamic Formula of the IBRD.[99] Such proposition of two-way emulation is unsurprising as both Banks have closely interacted. In fact, there are many similarities between the organization of the AIIB and the suggestions of the Zedillo Commission Report on the World Bank modernization in 2009, including but not limited to suggestions on the shareholding formula, as discussed in Section IV.

The continuous success of the AIIB, including its shareholding formula, is likely to influence the IBRD's shareholding review. In particular, China should have a shareholding of over 12% in the IBRD, much higher than the current 6%, following the 2016 Dynamic Formula.[100] Although the Dynamic Formula is 'not for precise allocation of quotas',[101] a capital formula has traditionally served as a guide, a basis, or a point of departure for the discussion on capital distribution, and the gap between 12 and 6% is simply too stark to be ignored. The gap suggests that the implementation of the results of the Dynamic Formula is not satisfactory, and its designated function of reflecting countries' relative economic importance has not been fulfilled. Such failure continues to fail those underrepresented, as seen during the World Bank's 2020 shareholding review, and it undermines the institution's relevance and legitimacy to address global crises.

1.7 Conclusion and Outlook

Shareholding formulas have been an effective tool for capital adjustment among member countries in capital-based international organizations. As early as at the Bretton Woods Conference over seven decades ago, such formulas served in negotiations as a starting point, but not as an inflexible mechanism for the precise allocation of quotas. Since then, this role of shareholding formulas has expanded, but with variations across IFIs. Nowadays, shareholding formulas also highlight disparities between countries' calculated shareholding and actual shareholding. For example, if calculated according to the Dynamic Formula, China is even more misaligned and underrepresented in the IBRD, compared with at the time of agreement on the capital package in 2018.

With the aim of reflecting member countries' relative importance in the evolution of the global economic landscape, which has long been the leading principle of

[98] A group of emerging economies have long advocated increasing the weight of GDP in the shareholding formulas in the Bretton Woods institution.

[99] The AIIB Chief Negotiators' Report on the Charter, where the GDP-based capital allocation formula appears, was adopted on May 22, 2015, prior to the World Bank's 2016 Dynamic Formula.

[100] See Development Committee, above 83, at 11.

[101] The quote is borrowed from Lowenfeld, above n 44, at 610.

any shareholding realignment, a GDP-based shareholding formula and the relevant results calculated are gaining ground. As the Development Committee affirmed in 2003, '[t]he fundamental principle underlying the allocation of shares of the IBRD's capital stock to its members is that members' subscriptions should reflect their relative position in the world economy'.[102] The IMF executive directors reported similarly to the Board of Governors on the outcome of the quota formula review in 2013, 'GDP should remain the most important variable, with the largest weight in the formula and scope to further increase its weight. GDP is generally seen as the most comprehensive measure of economic size'.[103] Such a statement has been reiterated repeatedly by both Bretton Woods institutions.

A GDP-based shareholding formula needs to play a central role in allocating capital shares in future, if the relevance and legitimacy of the IFIs are to be preserved and the voice and participation of emerging economies and developing countries in them are to be increased. Statistics show that a dollar of GDP in Belgium is worth five times as many votes as a dollar of GDP in China in the IMF.[104] To correct such inequitable distribution of shareholding (and voting power), GDP deserves a much more prominent place in a new quota formula of the IMF, say a weight of 80%, and the other 20% to indicate other IMF-specific mandates, comparable to the structure of the Dynamic Formula in the IBRD. Moreover, the IFC deserves its own GDP-based shareholding formula to be inspired by the AIIB.

Meanwhile, governance and decision-making of IFIs must be democratic and allow for the representation of all members. This means that capital contributions alone cannot be the only source of voice and participation in it. Rather, the result of a capital formula is typically complemented by basic votes, which constitute a minimum voting power for those small and poor countries in the organization. Thus, a fixed percentage of basic votes as in the AIIB, rather than a fixed number of basic votes in other regional MDBs, proves to be a better choice, lest the share of basic votes be eroded with the increase of capital subscription and share-votes allocation over time.[105] Meanwhile, a compression factor is added to the formula in both the IMF and the IBRD to protect small and poor countries; nevertheless, the downside is that it dilutes the principle of 'simplicity and transparency', a hallmark of shareholding formulas. Therefore, the twin institutions may consider replacing the compression

[102] Development Committee, 'Enhancing voice and participation of developing and transition countries in decision-making at the World Bank and IMF' (DC 2003–0002, 27 March 2003) at 11–12.

[103] See IMF, above n 55, at 2–3.

[104] The statistics is based on a scenario of 2014, whereby the 2010 Quota and Governance go into effect. Today with the rapid increase of China's GDP, the disparity can only be more than five times. See Vestergaard and Wade, above n 63, at 4.

[105] For example, African Development Bank (AfDB) stipulates 625 basic votes for each member, and Inter-American Development Bank (IDB) stipulates 135 basic votes for each member. As share votes increase with capital increases, however, basic votes now represent a smaller percentage of total votes (less than one percent, as opposed to 50% for AfDB and 5% for IDB at the time of establishment respectively). Lichtenstein, above n 11, at 152.

factor with a higher fixed percentage of basic votes, say over 10% of the total votes, that is, their initial level in 1944, or 12% as in the AIIB case.

Overall, the relationship between the AIIB and the Bretton Woods institutions exhibits healthy, two-way emulation. This means that the AIIB builds on those traditional institutions, making use of both their positive and negative experiences. Conversely, the vigor and positive outcome of the AIIB produces a stimulus effect and helps to break gridlock in the ongoing reform of those old institutions.[106] For the sake of their respective 'credibility, effectiveness, and legitimacy', the IMF in particular needs a new quota formula to guide the 16th quota review after over a decade of fruitless negotiations. Meanwhile, the IBRD should speed up the implementation of the result of the Dynamic Formula to ease its strained balance sheet, and the IFC should seek to have its own shareholding formula by the next shareholding review in 2025.

[106] Haga observes other impacts made by the AIIB on the reform of peer institutions, which are not discussed in this Chapter. They include the World Bank's and the ADB's reform on lending policy (including their pivot to infrastructure projects), and the IMF approval of the inclusion of Chinese Renminbi in the SDR basket in 2015. See Haga, above n 13, at 414.

Chapter 2
Corporate Governance: The Non-resident Board

Summary The relationship between the Board and management has been a key issue of corporate governance for Bretton Woods institutions, and there is no exception to the AIIB. A new multilateral development bank (MDB) derived from Bretton Woods, the AIIB is now the second largest after the World Bank by membership. The institution of a non-resident Board of Directors in the AIIB deviates from the practice of most leading MDBs, and it was designed to avoid two dilemmas that have long bewildered traditional MDBs: the dual position of the Board members, and the co-managerial issue between the Board and management. The arrangement of the non-resident Board requires that project approval authority be delegated from the Board to the President, and in parallel to such delegation, a robust oversight mechanism should be established with a view to holding the empowered President and management accountable. Efforts to craft an oversight mechanism were made initially in the Accountability Framework and were completed in the Oversight Mechanism. As it strives for "appropriate separation of powers to ensure proper checks and balances" between the Board and management, the oversight mechanism should not hinder the pragmatic management of the AIIB from serving the changing needs of its members.

2.1 Introduction

The Asian Infrastructure Investment Bank (AIIB) has finished the first six years of foundation-building and is now entering a new phase of growth. The past six years witnessed the laying-out of corporate governance for the AIIB, which boasts a dual characteristic of heritage and innovation, vis-à-vis the traditional multilateral development bank (MDB) family. Specifically, it inherits the three layers of governance structure featuring the MDBs, i.e., the Board of Governors, the Board

This chapter originally appeared in *Asia Pacific Law Review* (2022)30(2), entitled "International organization and corporate governance: the case of the AIIB", coauthor Ms. Chengjin Xu.

B. Gu, *Chinese Multilateralism in the Asian Infrastructure Investment Bank (AIIB)*, Modern China and International Economic Law,
https://doi.org/10.1007/978-981-97-1219-9_2

of Directors,[1] and management led by the President. Meanwhile, the AIIB's Board of Directors is non-resident in nature, contrasting the Executive Board of peer institutions. This novel design led to somewhat tricky, nuanced, and complex evolutions of the relationship between the Board and management during the past few years.

In particular, AIIB Board of Directors issued the Accountability Framework and the Oversight Mechanism consecutively during the past three years or so, in a bid to addressing the Board and management relationship. In these important internal law documents, project approval authority is delegated to the President in principle, with numerous exceptions reserved to the Board still. The arrangement of power delegation lends justification to holding the President and management accountable in operations in a more vigorous manner, compared with other MDBs free from similar power delegation. The Complaints-resolution, Evaluation and Integrity Unit (CEIU) is created to do the job of accountability, and in addition, the Directors' Forum is instituted to supervise the President's conduct.

This chapter is committed to exploring the dynamics of corporate governance reform for the AIIB, in the context of the MDB family and their history. It argues that the reform work is reminiscent of the debut of Bretton Woods institutions over seven decades ago and represents the development trend of MDB governance. What the AIIB has achieved in governance and accountability may be an aspiration, and even a beacon, for the World Bank and others, which have endeavored in a similar direction of reform but with few achievements. Section 2 overviews the MDBs' traditional governance structure, and identifies the problems therein. Section 2 investigates the AIIB's non-resident Board and project approval authority. Section 4 examines the oversight mechanism responsible for holding the President accountable. Section 5 concludes.

2.2 The MDBs' Traditional Governance Structure and the Problems Therein

The founding fathers of the Bretton Woods institutions designed the three-layered organizational structure for the International Bank for Reconstruction and Development (IBRD), later known as the World Bank, as copied from the design of the International Monetary Fund (IMF).[2] The structure was obviously modeled upon the

[1] This book uses "the Board" as the shortened name for the Board of Directors, not for the Board of Governors, as the practice of the MDBs goes, except as indicated otherwise.

[2] At the Breton Woods Conference in 1944, the relevant provisions of the IMF charter were discussed first and very little time was left to discuss the provisions of the IBRD charter. The negotiators decided to borrow directly the result of the IMF negotiation, including governance structure. Ibrahim Shihata, *World Bank Legal Papers* (Martinus Nijhoff Publishers, 2000) at 641. As a key US delegate reflected later, "We spent very little time on organization [of the IBRD] in the Bank Committee. As a consequence, no serious attempt was made to structure the organization in a different fashion, possibly more appropriate to its purpose." World Bank, "Repowering the World Bank for the twenty-first Century" (Report of the High-Level Commission on Modernization of World Bank

practice in the private sector: The Board of Governors mirrors a shareholder meeting, which generally meets once a year, and the Board of Directors and management even share the name of their counterparts in a private corporate. All other major MDBs, as followers, essentially copied the structure of the World Bank in the ensuing decades.

A rough sketch of the composition and power of the governance in these MDBs is thus: The Board of Governors comprises representatives of every Bank member, most of which are sovereign nations, but non-sovereigns are also involved in some MDBs.[3] Each member has a seat in the Board of Governors and holds varied voting power, depending mainly upon the capital share they each subscribe.[4] While the Board of Governors is vested with almost all powers in the Bank,[5] most of these powers are not reserved to it, rather being delegated to other layers of governance.[6] Decision-making in the Board of Governors, with delegations of each member at present, becomes unavoidably ceremonial, and it is particularly so as membership increases over time.

The Board of Directors is a much smaller, condensed decision-making body. For example, 25 Board members represent 189-member countries in the World Bank, while 12 Directors represent 105 members of the AIIB.[7] Each Director constitutes a constituency. While some Directors represent one member each, others represent over twenty-member countries each, revealing power disparity in membership. The Board's powers, as delegated by the Board of Governors, are enormous and they may vary with nuanced differences across Banks. These powers typically involve policy and strategy making, project approval, and management oversight.

Management led by the President is the third layer of organizational structure for an MDB. This layer represents the independent legal personality of an MDB as an international organization in the Bank structure, as distinct from any individual Bank member. In other words, Bank management and their staff serve the interest

---

Group Governance, known as the Zedillo Commission Report, 2009), at 18, quoting Edward S. Mason and Robert E. Asher.

[3] For example, World Bank membership can only be sovereign, while the Asian Development Bank (ADB) is more inclusive, having China's Taiwan and Hong Kong as its members. AIIB membership is open to members of both the World Bank and the Asian Development Bank. AIIB Articles of Agreement (AOA), Article 3.1.

[4] In the design of voting power allocation in an MDB, the bulk of voting power is allocated to Bank members based on their capital shares subscribed each; a small part of it (5.5% for World Bank, 12% for AIIB and 20% for ADB) is allocated equally among members.

[5] In the World Bank, however, the power of amending the Bank charter is subject additionally to the approval of national authorities, which reflects the US's persistent distrust of an international organization, as well its efforts to maximize political power in it. IBRD Articles of Agreement, Article VIII (a).

[6] The few powers reserved to the Board of Governors are considered to be the most important for the Bank, among which are the amendment of the Bank charter, the approval of new membership, the size of authorized capital, and the size of the Board.

[7] It is noted that in the AIIB, as a growing MDB, there are 13 prospective members out of the membership of 105; technically, the prospective members are not represented in the Board of Directors until full membership. The list of the prospective members is available at https://www.aiib.org/en/about-aiib/governance/members-of-bank/index.html

of the Bank, or the whole membership, but not of any particular member only. The President, leading this international civil servant team, is responsible for the ordinary or current business of the Bank, under the general direction and oversight of the Board of Directors.

Two dilemmas emerge or exist in corporate governance for a traditional MDB: the dual position of the Board members, and the co-managerial issue between the Board and management. The dilemmas both arise from the executive nature of the Board of Directors in traditional MDBs, and it is exactly where the AIIB departs as a new bank of the new century, achieving "a major advance on the arrangements in the World Bank and ADB".[8]

1. The dual position of the Directors

In a traditional MDB, a resident Director is inherently executive, and is closely involved in bank daily business. He represents the member or members appointing/electing him on the one hand (so-called political counterweight), and functions as an officer of the MDB meanwhile. This dual position creates a potential conflict of interest, due to the often-unavoidable disparity in claims of interest between a certain member and the Bank (i.e., the whole membership). A survey of current and former executive Directors in the IMF—whose governance structure mirrors that of the World Bank—shows that 68% of those surveyed believe that their dual roles conflict "occasionally" (54%) or "frequently" (14%).[9] In practice, an executive Director is highly motivated to defend, or seek, national interests before the Board, because of the prospect that his political career is determined by his home country authority. All the while, he tends less to prioritize the Bank's interest, even though he normally receives salary from the Bank. What is worse, neither the Director nor the Board will be punished when they fail to fulfill their fiduciary duties to the Bank.

2. The co-managerial issue between the Board and management

An MDB's raison d'être is to finance projects. In practice both the executive Board and management are responsible for Bank operations, due to the unclear demarcation of the roles of the two bodies. The Bank charter describes the Board's role as responsible for the Bank's "general operations",[10] and the President's role as responsible for its "ordinary/current business", while both terms are not defined, nor distinguished. In the practice of traditional MDBs, the President and his team prepare a project and propose it to the Board, which in turn decides to approve it or not. This leads to several problems.

---

[8] Mike Callaghan and Paul Hubbard, "The Asian Infrastructure Investment Bank: Multilateralism on the Silk Road" (2016) 9 *China Economic Journal*, Issue 2, 116-139, at 132.

[9] Zedillo Commission Report, at 32, quoting an IMF Independent Evaluation Office survey.

[10] It is noted that the charters of the World Bank and the AIIB are nuancedly different in relevant parts, where the former states that the Board is "responsible for the ***conduct*** of the general operations of the Bank" (IBRD AOA Article V, Section 4(a)), while the latter states that the Board is "responsible for the ***direction*** of the general operations of the Bank" (AIIB AOA Article 26). The wording difference tells that the AIIB Board should avoid intervening in daily operations, consistent with its non-resident nature.

First, the Board cannot hold the management accountable. While the management has de facto power over whether to finance a project, the decision formally lies with the Board. In other situations, particularly those pertaining to major projects, the Board often discusses and produces concrete opinions, which management has to follow. This makes it even hard to hold management accountable if anything goes wrong with the project, and the Board has little incentive to do so as well.[11] Everybody's responsibility is nobody's responsibility.

Second, the executive Director intervenes in project preparation and implementation. Although the processes of project preparation and implementation hinge upon the President, the executive Director has a natural obligation to promote the business interest of his own nationality, and therefore, has a motive to intervene. For example, he may do his best in assisting the firms of his nationality to win a project bidding, while other firms may be disadvantaged in competition.[12]

Third, the Board is stuck in day-to-day operations and has no time for policy-making and management oversight. The operational businesses consumed so much of the Board's meeting time, that only 6% of total boardroom time was spent on monitoring and evaluation, according to the Zedillo Commission Report.[13] Aligned with such finding, another external review committee suggested that "Executive Directors should not be involved in managing day-to-day operations, but should be setting strategic directions and overseeing management performance".[14]

2.3 AIIB's Non-resident Board and Project Approval Authority

The AIIB is well positioned to avoid the problems brought forth by an executive Board in traditional MDBs: the dual position of the Directors and the co-managerial dilemma between the Board and management, as discussed above. The founders of the AIIB indeed designed a non-resident Board of Directors during the negotiating

[11] Zedillo Commission Report, at 31.

[12] Take American executive Directors in most leading MDBs for example. They help American firms in two respects specifically: first, on business information, executive Directors are able to provide US business with accurate and timely procurement information—the "early warning" so desired by US business. Second, on procurement contracts, executive directors make sure that US business be treated fairly during MDB procurement practices; otherwise, they may pursue the reversal of the awards of contracts, or the cancellation of bank loans. United States Congress, *Multilateral Development Bank Procurement* (Classic Reprint Series) (London: Forgotten Books&c Ltd., 2015) Hearing Before the Subcommittee on International Development, Finance, Trade and Monetary Policy of the Committee on Banking, Finance and Urban Affairs, House of Representatives, 103rd Congress, First Session, November 18, 1993, at 16, 40-41, 51 and 71.

[13] Zedillo Commission Report at 34.

[14] Zedillo Commission Report at 33-34, quoting the External Review Committee on Bank-Fund Collaboration ("Malan Report").

period from 2013 through 2015. It means that the Board does not reside in the headquarters of Beijing, void of the executive nature typically seen in a traditional MDB. This becomes AIIB's hallmark signature, further prompting other complementary innovations in AIIB governance in the ensuing years. One of those requisite changes is the delegation of project approval authority from the Board to management, since the authority needs plenty of time, money, personnel, and skills, which a non-resident Board cannot afford.

1. A non-resident Board

A non-resident Board for an MDB is not a new idea. From a historical viewpoint, that idea was first put forth by Lord Keynes, when he was the head of the UK delegation at the Bretton Woods Conference in 1944. Keynes' proposal of a non-resident Board for Bretton Woods institutions was persistently resisted by his counterpart Harry White of the US, and eventually White's proposal of an executive Board prevailed.[15] The choice facilitated the US to exert its political influence in the IMF and the IBRD, and weakened the organizations' independence.

The issue of Board residency was raised again in the negotiation on the charters of the African Development Bank (1963), the Asian Development Bank (1965) and the European Bank for Reconstruction and Development (EBRD) (1990), before the resident Board option was agreed. During the negotiation on the EBRD charter, for example, the US prevailed over the European countries, arguing that the Board should "have a powerful voice in day-to-day functions, as to assure that the vague compromises in negotiations would be implemented".[16]

Meanwhile, the dual position of the Directors and the co-managerial dilemma, as corollaries to the executive Board, became issues of rising tensions and caused public concerns amid the ensuing decades. In 2009 the Zedillo Commission Report, a high-profile external review report sponsored by the World Bank, recommended that the World Bank should formally rescind the resident Board and substitute it with a non-resident one, among other reformative suggestions. However, that report effected no change on Board residency in the World Bank.

A few other development banks adopt a non-resident Board. For example, the European Investment Bank (EIB)'s non-resident Board meets at least six times a year.[17] An atypical MDB,[18] the EIB nevertheless contributed substantially to the

[15] Regarding the history of negotiation on Board residency, see Benn Steil, *The Battle of Bretton Woods* (Princeton University Press, 2013), at 301-2. Ibrahim Shihata, *World Bank Legal Papers* (Martinus Nijhoff Publishers, 2000) at 641.

[16] Natalie Lichtenstein, *A Comparative Guide to the Asian Infrastructure Investment Bank* (Oxford: Oxford University Press, 2018) at 137.

[17] Rules of Procedure of the European Investment Bank Article 11.1.

[18] The EIB is the European Union's policy-driven bank, established in 1958 under the Treaty of Rome. It is the world's largest international public lending institution with a subscribed capital base of EUR 249 billion in 2020. Although it is not an MDB in a strict sense, it is often considered as a member of the MDB family. https://www.eib.org/en/about/key-figures/data.htm (visited August 9, 2021).

drafting of the AIIB charter, with its non-resident Board arrangement being an immediate inspiration for the AIIB. Besides the EIB, there are a few smaller, less influential regional development banks with a non-resident Board, including the Andean Development Corporation, the Caribbean Development Bank, Nordic Investment Bank, the International Fund for Agricultural Development, and the New Development Bank. A non-resident Boardis also the norm in private companies.[19]

A non-resident Board enables the MDB to function as an autonomous international organization, free from daily operating interventions by Board members. It produces the following merits: First, it saves a large financial and human cost for the Bank,[20] and frees up considerable time for the Board to do jobs of policy and strategy formulation and management oversight. Second, the impact of the dual role of the Directors and conflict of interest therefrom is to be reduced to the largest extent possible, if not eliminated. The Directors are paid by their home country authority and function duly in a membership representational role in the Board. Third, the division of labor is expected to be clearly delineated between the Board and management, eliminating the co-managerial problem by delegating project approval authority to the President, as discussed below.

2. Project approval authority

With a non-resident Board built in the AIIB organization, the Bank founders naturally expected to delegate to management the authority to approve a project, thus delineating appropriately the labor and responsibility between the Board and management.[21] The co-managerial confusion incurred by an executive Board should not occur in a new development bank of the new century. Accordingly, the AIIB Board had an explicit plan to consider such power delegation to the President by late 2016,[22] the first year of Bank operations. The plan was eventually substantiated in the Accountability Framework, as adopted by the Board of Directors and effective as of January 2019.

The Accountability Framework distinguishes itself in setting rules for project approval authority, while describing the Board's dual role of policy making and

---

[19] Natalie Lichtenstein, *A Comparative Guide to the Asian Infrastructure Investment Bank* (Oxford: Oxford University Press, 2018) at 136-7.

[20] For example, the World Bank's Board members cost 70 million US dollars a year, with hundreds of Bank staff serving them exclusively. Natalie Lichtenstein, *A Comparative Guide to the Asian Infrastructure Investment Bank* (Oxford: Oxford University Press, 2018) at 136-7, quoting Dollar.

[21] AIIB Articles of Agreement stipulates that the Board shall "take decisions concerning operations of the Bank", and "by a majority representing not less than three-fourths of the total voting power of the members, decide on the delegation of such authority to the President". AIIB Articles of Agreement Article 26(iii).

[22] AIIB Operational Policy on Financing, a major internal legal document, stipulates that "The Board is expected to consider (in late 2016) a delegation of authority to the President to approve certain Financings and subsequent changes related to them." AIIB Operational Policy on Financing (January 2016) para 3.5.1, footnote 17.

management oversight incidentally.[23] On project approval authority, the Framework stipulates the delegation of such authority to the President as the norm, while the reservation of it to the Board as the exception. Given its theme, an appropriate name of the Accountability Framework should be "The Project Approval Authority Framework"; the theme of accountability in the existing name is instead fulfilled in a later major policy—the Oversight Mechanism, which will be discussed in the next section.

The Accountability Framework sets specifically three exceptional categories, whereby project approval authority should be reserved to the Board.[24] Respectively, Category I "Precedent Setting" refers to the first project in a member (sovereign or non-sovereign backed), or in a sector, or to utilize a new financial instrument, or to be co-financed for the first time with a particular partner using the partner's standards. Category II "Significant Strategic and Policy Issues" refers to a non-regional project,[25] or a project with no pre-set Bank sector strategy,[26] or a project to derogate from Bank standards,[27] or a project in a territory in dispute or with cross-border characteristics. And Category III "Risk Tolerances" refers to a project exceeding a certain threshold of AIIB funding amounts.[28] It is well discerned from these limiting conditions that the delegation process will be progressive and gradual, as committed by the Accountability Framework.[29] It can be even bumpy, complicated, and conflicting internally.[30] In 2019, the first year the Accountability Framework went into operation, the President approved three projects, and in 2020 he approved three more.[31]

---

[23] As expected, three main parts are explicitly laid out in sequence in the Paper on the Accountability Framework: (1) The Role of the Board of Directors— Policy and Strategy; (2) Delegation Principles and Project Approval Process; and (3) Holding the President to Account.

[24] AIIB Paper on the Accountability Framework (effective January 1, 2019), para. 19.

[25] A non-regional project is defined as a project in the regions outside Asia and Oceania, according to the AIIB Chief Negotiators' Explanatory Notes (an interpretative instrument to AIIB Articles of Agreement), but Russia is deemed as regional.

[26] The AIIB has established strategies in major sectors such as energy, transport, water, urban development, and digital infrastructure.

[27] This may refer to two situations: using the borrower country systems, or using a co-financier's standards. AIIB Procurement Policy (January 2016), para. 5.4. AIIB Environmental and Social Framework (May 2021), pp.13 and 30.

[28] For example, the threshold amount of the AIIB's economic capital (ECap) utilized by the Bank's financing in a project is $25 million. It is an easy threshold for an infrastructure project, rendering the President with a hollow power of project approval accordingly.

[29] AIIB Paper on the Accountability Framework (effective January 1, 2019), para. 21.

[30] It is noted that in the situation of co-financing with another bank, a conflict may well arise, because under Category I the project approval authority is delegated to the President after the first time of co-financing, while under Category II that authority may still be reserved to the Board.

[31] The President-approved projects in 2019 were (1) India: Rajasthan 250 MW Solar Project—Hero Future Energies, (2) Pakistan: Karachi Bus Rapid Transit Red Line Project and (3) Bangladesh: Power System Upgrade and Expansion. In 2020 the President-approved projects were (1) Bangladesh: Dhaka and West Zone Transmission Grid Expansion Project, (2) Bangladesh: Rural Water, Sanitation and Hygiene for Human Capital Development Project and (3) India: Ayana Anantapumaru NTPC Solar Project. *See* AIIB Annual Report and Financials 2019, at 15-16; AIIB Annual Report and Financials 2020, at 20.

Given the purpose of the Accountability Framework—a clear demarcation of responsibility between the Board and management, it is difficult to justify why the Board reserves such a bulk of project approval power. Under Category III, for example, a presumption appears that the Board should be in a better position than the President to analyze and decide upon the merits of a project proposal, whereby large financial resources are to be committed.[32] This presumption is hardly true even for an MDB with a resident Board, which involves in Bank business and is assisted by large pools of professional staff; let alone for the AIIB of a non-resident Board.

With so much power for project approval still reserved to the Board, the value of crafting a non-resident Board for the AIIB is dwindled. The division of labor and responsibility between the Board and management remains unclear, and the co-managerial problem remains in the AIIB, inconsistent with the stated purpose in the Accountability Framework. The Board may still have to spend a considerable time on projects, which those MDBs with executive Directors have long considered to change. Even in much of its history, the Board of the IBRD rescinded project-approval powers gradually to some degree in various forms, including the streamlined arrangement,[33] under which a series of projects with similar characteristics need not to be approved one by one by the Board. Instead, only the first of such series, alongside other major projects in terms of costs and impacts, should go through the Board discussion and approval procedure.

Therefore, AIIB operations should fall within the mandate of the President and his operating team, and they are supposed to make business decisions with technical capacities and professionality. Meanwhile, the non-resident Directors, in their membership representational roles, are inherently political, and should be kept from intervening in daily businesses in principle. Admittedly, there are cases of particular sensitivity— for example a project in a territory of dispute,[34] and the Board may step in, but such project proposal tends to be excluded from management consideration even in the first place. Most exceptions to power delegation in the Accountability Framework, however, fail to be of sensitive nature.

Alas, the Board of Directors is reluctant to let go the power of project approval. Besides those reserved powers to the Board as discussed above, the President has to

---

[32] AIIB Paper on the Accountability Framework (effective January 1, 2019), para. 20.

[33] Regarding the streamlined arrangement, as featured in the evolution of project approval authority between the Board and management in the World Bank, see Ibrahim Shihata, *World Bank Legal Papers* (Martinus Nijhoff Publishers 2000) at 643-6. As for a comprehensive review of project approval arrangements in other MDBs equivalent to that of the World Bank, *see* African Development Bank, 'Comparative Study of Board Processes, Procedures and Practices in International Financial Institutions' (February 2018), at 17–18.

[34] As an enlightening reference, when the World Bank had to consider whether to continue funding a project (after the project was approved) that became a controversial matter of interest to several member countries, such as the Narmada project in India and the Yacyreta dam project in Argentina, Board involvement may be inevitable, and management as decision-maker would normally be expected to follow the clear sense of the Board. Ibrahim Shihata, *World Bank Legal Papers* (Martinus Nijhoff Publishers 2000) at 722.

report to the Board every quarter with a summary of all projects approved.[35] If one Director raises concerns, a project may have to be brought to the Board's table.[36] At this point one may well wonder why the Board prefers to gripping upon the project, if its oversight of management is robust at all. Now, let us turn to the AIIB's oversight mechanism and see how it works.

2.4 Hold the President Accountable

The arrangement of a non-resident Board requires the delegation of project approval authority to the President. As the AIIB itself acknowledges, "It is in line with best modern governance practice, fit for a new MDB with a nonresident Board like AIIB."[37] In parallel to such delegation, a robust oversight mechanism should be in place with a view to holding the empowered President and management accountable for non-compliance with the Board-approved policies, rules and procedures. Efforts to craft such an oversight mechanism were initially made in the Accountability Framework in 2018, and were completed in the Oversight Mechanism in 2019.

To build an oversight mechanism is an explicit legal mandate for the AIIB. Article 26.3 of the charter provides for the delegation of operational power. Article 26.4, the immediately following paragraph, envisions the establishment of an oversight mechanism to oversee management in operations, in the context of such delegation.[38] The Chief Negotiators' Explanatory Notes, offering authoritative interpretation to the charter, elaborate further in relevant part that "the oversight mechanism to be established ...would be designed in line with the principles of transparency, openness, independence and accountability, and would address such areas as audit, evaluation, fraud and corruption, project complaints and staff grievances...". The AIIB Environmental and Social Framework, a major legal document based upon the charter, affirms project-affected people's right to resort to the oversight mechanism for relief.[39] The

[35] AIIB Paper on the Accountability Framework (effective January 1, 2019), para. 31 stipulates thus: "[the President] provides the BoD with regular updates on AIIB's program, including total investment volume (nominal and in economic capital terms), as well as important breakdowns by regions, countries, sectors and investment grade."

[36] AIIB Paper on the Accountability Framework (effective January 1, 2019), para. 23 stipulates thus: "A Director may ask that a project be considered and decided upon by the BoD at any time from the first time a project is included in the pipeline until a date which is fourteen (14) calendar days after Management provides the BoD with a final Project Summary Document (PSD)."

[37] AIIB Annual Report and Financials 2019, at 16.

[38] Article 26.4 of AIIB Articles of Agreement provides that the Board of Directors shall "supervise the management and operation of the Bank on a regular basis, and establish an oversight mechanism for that purpose, in line with principles of transparency, openness, independence and accountability".

[39] AIIB Environmental and Social Framework, in its old version of February 2016, first envisioned an oversight mechanism to be established for project-affected people to seek relief, and in the latest, revised version of May 2021, it reaffirmed the mechanism that had been established priorly. AIIB Environmental and Social Framework (May 2021), para. 72.

Accountability Framework sketches the oversight mechanism formally for the first time, drawing three lines of internal defense,[40] and a fourth independent line—the Complaints-resolution, Evaluation and Integrity Unit (CEIU). All those arrangements serve to hold the President and management accountable, as they are delegated with project approval power, as discussed above.

The Oversight Mechanism marks the latest of such efforts, building upon the work of the Accountability Framework, while enhancing it tremendously from an external independence perspective. According to this legal document, the oversight mechanism comprises three major institutions: the CEIU, the Administrative Tribunal,[41] and external audit.[42] And the Directors' Forum, a new form of Board members' meeting, is established to facilitate the Board's work of oversight. The Directors' Forum is chaired by a Director, namely the Dean, rather than by the President, who is designated as chair of the Board pursuant to the Bank charter. As the Forum is dedicated to an oversight function, the President is disallowed to attend it. The creation of the Directors' Forum in the Oversight Mechanism, alongside the CEIU as created in 2016, sets the AIIB apart from other MDBs, and they deserve detailed investigation and analysis.

1. CEIU

The CEIU has been in operation since 2016, well before the issuance of the Terms of Reference for the CEIU, a separate legal document as attached to the Oversight Mechanism. As its name reveals, the CEIU has three distinct functions: *C* is the initial for Complaints-resolution (originally Compliance), pointing to project-related complaints; *E* is the initial for Evaluation (originally Effectiveness), referring to project evaluation; and *I* is for Integrity, referring to anti-fraud and corruption in project bidding and implementation. Other MDBs have those similar functions, but

---

[40] The first line of defense (LOD) refers to the Bank's operational management, whereby project reviews pass through the Screening Committee, the Executive Committee and the Investment Committee; the second line refers to compliance and risk management; and the third refers to the Bank's internal audit function. Bank officers responsible for the three lines of defense all report to the President, and thus are under management control, except that along the second and third lines, both the Chief Risk Officer (CRO) and the Chief Internal Audit Officer additionally participate in the Board's Audit and Risk Committee, thus producing a sense of independence from the President.

[41] The Administrative Tribunal, an independent, staff grievances mechanism in the MDBs, functions as the last resort for a Bank staff who has been grieved by, or dissatisfied with, an internal administrative decision. AIIB is required to establish an administrative tribunal per Article 13.4 of the Staff Regulation, and in the Staff Rules, such administrative tribunal is described as "an independent Reviewer appointed by the President from a panel maintained by the General Counsel". The independent reviewer is appointed in a dispute-specific manner, and his recommendation is subject to the President's final decision (so called "Administrative Review Decision"). AIIB Staff Rules (January 2022), Rule 8.01/6 and 8.01/10. https://www.aiib.org/en/about-aiib/basic-documents/_download/staff-regulations/AIIB-Staff-Rules_January-2022.pdf

[42] External auditors provide an independent "assessment on part of the first, second and/or third LOD", assuring the Board on the Bank's effective internal controls over financial reporting. AIIB Paper on the Oversight Mechanism (July 10, 2019) para.25. AIIB's external auditor is PricewaterhouseCoopers.

carry them out in different units—only the AIIB synergizes them under one roof, which is a major innovation in governance. The Managing Director of the CEIU (i.e., the MD-CEIU) reports directly to the Board, enabling its independence from the President.

The first function of the CEIU is project-related complaints resolution. This function is embodied in the Project-Affected People's Mechanism (PPM), which is established pursuant to the Bank charter and the relevant Explanatory Notes as quoted above, and the Environmental and Social Policy (ESP) in specific.[43] PPM provides "an opportunity for an independent review of submissions from Project-affected people who believe they have been or are likely to be adversely affected by AIIB's failure to implement the ESP".[44] This mechanism has a traditional function of "compliance-review", which is common among major MDBs. It also has two other mandates: "project processing queries" which seek quick resolution over simple matters, and "dispute resolution" which in essence facilitates a settlement between the Bank, the complainant and/or the borrower. By comparison, the "compliance-review" function seems more formal and legalistic than the other two functions, which may well serve the purposes of economy and efficiency. The fact that the name of the CEIU was changed from the original C for Compliance is due to considerations of these expanded mandates. In contrast, a similar function under the World Bank, as carried out by the Inspection Panel, focuses on compliance review only. In instituting the compliance review function, the CEIU establishes a project-tailored task force chaired by the MD-CEIU, and its members are external specialists or Bank staff.[45] In contrast, the World Bank Inspection Panel is a standing body, comprising three independent members serving a non-renewable five-year term each.[46] Therefore, the compliance review function of the AIIB seems to have a similar feature of flexibility, as its two other mandates do.

The second function of the CEIU is project evaluation. This function aims to assess whether AIIB-funded projects have implemented AIIB policies and strategies, and whether they have produced expected results.[47] The function is comprehended in the Learning and Evaluation Policy, as approved by the Board on May 19, 2021. Under the policy, learning and evaluation serves the Bank's culture of continuous improvement, and it is a Bank-wide responsibility, with shared but distinct roles of the Board, the CEIU and management.[48] A model relationship in evaluation is thus:

---

[43] AIIB Environmental and Social Policy provides that "People who believe they have been or are likely to be adversely affected by a failure of the Bank to implement the ESP may also submit complaints to the Bank's oversight mechanism in accordance with the policies and procedures to be established by the Bank for such mechanism." AIIB Environmental and Social Policy (February 2016), p.24.

[44] AIIB Paper on the Project-Affected People's Mechanism (December 7, 2018), section 2.1.

[45] AIIB Rules of Procedure of the Project-Affected People's Mechanism (December 21, 2018), pp.19 and 27.

[46] The World Bank Inspection Panel Resolution (September 8, 2020) paras.3 and 4.

[47] Terms of Reference for the Complaints-resolution, Evaluation and Integrity Unit (July 10, 2019), Section C.

[48] AIIB Learning and Evaluation Policy (approved May 19, 2021), at 2.

"independence is accompanied by collegiality and constructive two-way engagement between CEIU and Management".[49] In principle, evaluation adheres to international best practice, in particular as outlined by the Development Assistance Committee of the OECD.[50] In practice it should follow a balanced and evidence-based approach, identifying the results achieved under a project, whether intended or not, positive or negative, to understand the reasons behind, as well as what may be learned for future projects.[51] The application scope of this policy is comprehensive, covering both types of projects approved by the Board and the President,[52] as well as both phases of projects under implementation and after completion.[53] Since AIIB-funded projects are mostly at an early stage of development at this moment and "several years will pass before evaluation can occur at project completion, or even midterm",[54] the CEIU is essentially learning and accumulating experience along this line of function.

The third function of CEIU is anti-fraud and corruption. The Prohibited Practice Policy (PPP), pursuant to Article 13.9 of the Bank charter,[55] stipulates the mechanism and procedures for tackling business fraud and corruption behaviors, committed by firms and individuals in the procurement and implementation activities relevant to a project funded by the AIIB. The firms or individuals having committed a prohibited practice as stipulated in the PPP,[56] would be debarred from bidding AIIB-funded projects for a certain period or forever. They may further be cross-debarred by other MDBs, enhancing the chilling effect and compelling corporate compliance in international project procurement markets. As a new and active participant in global anti-fraud and corruption campaign, the AIIB has cross-debarred over 1000 firms

---

[49] AIIB Learning and Evaluation Policy (approved May 19, 2021), at 5.

[50] AIIB Learning and Evaluation Policy (approved May 19, 2021), at 5.

[51] AIIB Learning and Evaluation Policy (approved May 19, 2021), at 5 and 7.

[52] To evaluate projects whose approval power has been delegated to the President is emphasized in particular, and such evaluation will be used to decide whether the delegated authority should be called in or not. AIIB Paper on the Accountability Framework (effective January 1, 2019), para. 27. *Also* AIIB Paper on the Oversight Mechanism (July 10, 2019), para.31.

[53] AIIB Learning and Evaluation Policy (approved May 19, 2021), at 7-8.

[54] AIIB Annual Report and Financials 2017, p.42. A similar sense of earliness is expressed in AIIB Paper on the Oversight Mechanism (July 10, 2019) para.35, stating that "in the coming five years, only a limited number of projects will have been completed and be available for meaningful evaluation."

[55] Article 13.9 of the Bank charter provides, "The Bank shall take the necessary measures to ensure that the proceeds of any financing provide, guaranteed or participated in by the Bank are used only for the purposes for which the financing was granted and with due attention to considerations of economy and efficiency." This legal clause, referred to as the "fiduciary duty" clause, lays out the legal and policy basis for the AIIB's project-level anti-corruption efforts.

[56] In the PPP, there are seven types of prohibited practices: corrupt practice, fraudulent practice, coercive practice, collusive practice, obstructive practice, misuse of resources and theft. Other MDB's sanctions regimes stipulate similar types of prohibited practices. See Gu Bin, *The Law and Governance of the Asian Infrastructure Investment Bank* (The Netherlands: Wolters Kluwer, 2019), at 147-8.

and individuals originally debarred by five other MDBs,[57] by referencing the Agreement for Mutual Enforcement of Debarment Decisions (AMEDD) which the AIIB unilaterally commits to adhere to. The PPP provides for a two-tiered quasi-judicial system,[58] where the adjudicator announces sanctions decisions while the accused entities or individuals are allowed to defend themselves. The World Bank, by the way, has adjudicated hundreds of cases under the system of its own, prompting an emerging area of international law.

In sum, the success of the CEIU dwells upon its relationship with the President, which should strike a healthy balance between independence and engagement.[59] It is better to precaution the President beforehand, rather than punishing his team after an issue occurs. In other words, with a spectrum having adversary checks and advisory engagement at both ends, the MD-CEIU should be inclined towards the end of advisory engagement, rather than leaning closer to adversary checks. Such approach is most conducive to the fulfillment of the Bank purpose—infrastructure and other productive development—as stipulated in its charter, because it is helpful to get things done.

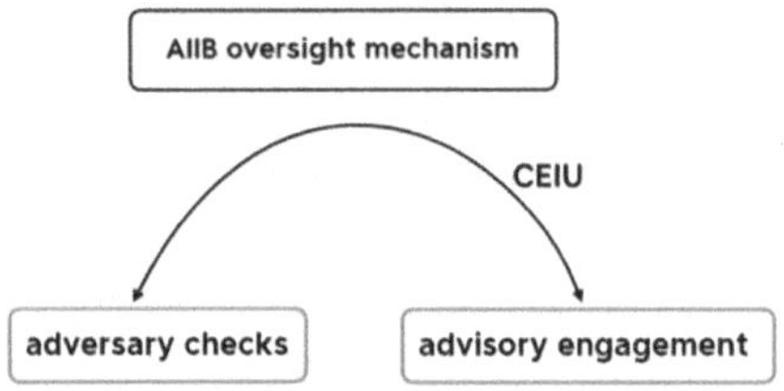

Meanwhile, the MD-CEIU should be wary of his own independent role, for example when attending senior management team meetings as an observer.[60] He shall not be "captured" by management in an unhealthy proximity between evaluator and evaluee.[61] To this end, the MD-CEIU shall not be considered as part of senior

[57] The five MDBs are Asian Development Bank, African Development Bank, European Bank for Reconstruction and Development, Inter-American Development Bank, and World Bank Group. In 2020 the AIIB had the first group of firms and individuals debarred by itself, all happening to be Chinese in nationality. https://www.aiib.org/en/about-aiib/who-we-are/debarment-list/index.html (visited August 12, 2021).

[58] The AIIB's appellate mechanism, namely the Sanctions Panel, was established after three members were appointed in 2020, marking the debut of the operation of the system. https://www.aiib.org/en/news-events/news/2020/Three-Members-Appointed-to-AIIBs-Inaugural-Sanctions-Panel.html (visited August 12, 2021)

[59] AIIB Corporate Strategy: Financing Infrastructure for Tomorrow (September 2020), at 9.

[60] It is a practice in AIIB that the President invites the MD-CEIU to attend the Management Meeting and Executive Committee, in order to enable CEIU to be well informed of important decision-making, and to play a constructive role in expeditiously raising concerns with Management for resolution. AIIB Paper on the Accountability Framework (effective January 1, 2019), para. 37.

[61] This comment is borrowed from the Zedillo Commission Report para. 113, which points out the problems existing in the oversight role of the Independent Evaluation Group, a central safety net unit in the World Bank.

management, and the seniority of the position may be uplifted to a vice-president level.[62]

2. The Directors' Forum

As part of the oversight mechanism, the Directors' Forum may function in several scenarios. First, it serves the need of the MD-CEIU to have a forum to meet with the members of the Board without the President present in an informal setting. The need to do so is essentially to avoid the intervention of the President in a Board meeting, where he chairs and has an immense power of agenda-setting. Second, the Directors' Forum may also be a platform for the members of the Board to meet among themselves, or with "a consultant who facilitates the performance review of the President."[63] A venue for sharing information and exchanging ideas, nevertheless, the Forum is neither a formal meeting of the Board, nor a decision-making body.

The position of the Dean is created to chair the Directors' Forum, and he must be the longest serving Director of a different nationality to that of the President.[64] The Dean may also chair the Board meeting in the following two situations: the review of the performance of the President, and consideration of his alleged misconduct.[65] The former may include the President's exercise of delegated project approval authority,[66] while the latter means the President's "knowing or reckless violation" of AIIB rules, regulations and procedures.[67] In those two situations, the Board meeting appears no difference to the Directors' Forum, since the President is absent from both. But be reminded that the Board is a decision-making body in those situations, while the Forum is not in nature.

---

[62] It is noted that the head of CEIU has gained increased importance in corporate hierarchy already, as revealed in the change of the title; it was initially entitled Director General, as in AIIB Policy on Prohibited Practices (Dec. 8, 2016), section 9.2, and now is renamed Managing Director.

[63] AIIB Paper on the Oversight Mechanism (July 10, 2019), para.39.1–3.

[64] AIIB Paper on the Oversight Mechanism (July 10, 2019), para.41.

[65] "The President, or, in the absence of the President, the Vice President so designated by the President, shall act as Chair of the Board. In the event of their absence from any meeting, or part thereof, the Dean will act as Chair. The President, Vice Presidents and Directors shall not act as Chair of a meeting in the event of a conflict of interest related to an item on the agenda at that meeting." AIIB Rules of Procedure of the Board of Directors (amended July 10, 2019), section 3(a).

[66] The exercise of delegated authority is part of the President's annual performance review, according to AIIB Regulation on the Accountability Framework, section 5.3. However, detailed requirements for such review are unclear, as the Terms of Reference for the Board of Director's Annual Review of the Performance of the President is not publicly available. That said document, where the President's annual performance review is to be stipulated, was identified and approved in the Decision on the Accountability Framework by the Board on April 11, 2018.

[67] The misconduct of Bank personnel, including the President, is defined as the knowing or reckless violation of Bank policies, rules, directives, or the Code of Conduct, and the conviction of a serious crime in a national court system. AIIB Code of Conduct for Bank Personnel (adopted January 16, 2016), paras. 36–37.

(1) The Directors' Forum in comparison

Like the AIIB, the Board members in other MDBs hold similar, informal meetings where they may discuss issues concerning them, and such occasions are not recognized as the Board meeting. For example, in the history of the World Bank, there were occasions bearing various names for the Directors to meet informally,[68] the best known among which was the Committee of the Whole. As one of the Board's many committees, the Committee of the Whole was to make recommendations to the Board, or merely to exchange views on matters of interest to the Board. What the Committee of the Whole is famous for in history is the preparation of the draft conventions for establishing two new international organizations under the World Bank Group—the ICSID and the MIGA, among other things.[69] Two sharp differences exist between the Committee of the Whole and the Directors' Forum in the AIIB. First, the AIIB Directors' Forum is tasked to facilitate the supervision over the President, while the Committee of the Whole (and other informal Board meetings in the World Bank) has nothing to do with this. Second, accordingly, the AIIB President is disallowed to attend the Directors' Forum, while the World Bank President often participates and even chairs the Committee of the Whole.

The Board may hold "Executive Session" in the World Bank, different from the usual meeting. In such session, particularly sensitive information is provided to the Board, or discussed by the Board, and "attendance by staff is limited, and no staff summary of the proceedings is provided", according to the World Bank former General Counsel Shihata.[70] However, such sensitive information includes neither the review of presidential performance nor of his alleged misconduct, different from the AIIB.[71] There was, for a long time indeed, no formal process for the Board to evaluate presidential performance in the World Bank, which had been criticized.[72] Therefore, it is sensible for the AIIB to design the Directors' Forum for appropriate checks and balances against the President, complementing the CEIU in the context of a non-resident Board in particular. Meanwhile, one should bear in mind that the

---

[68] These occasions include the Committee of the Whole, a Board seminar, and a retreat.

[69] The Committee of the Whole also did the following things: (1) the recommendations of the "Pearson Commission" in 1968, which carried out a general review of "the impact of external assistance on the development of the poorer nations over the past two decades", as reflected in the Bank's experience; (2) the discussion of Policy Framework Papers (PFPs) before forwarding them to the IMF Executive Board; (3) the discussion of the draft agenda of the Development Committee; (4) the discussion of the draft of the President's Report to the Development Committee; (5) the preliminary discussion of the Bank's annual budget before the Board's discussion and approval; (6) the discussion of a Bank-Fund collaboration memorandum before its finalization in 1989; etc.. Regarding an elaboration on the history and function of the Committee of the Whole, see Ibrahim Shihata, *World Bank Legal Papers* (Martinus Nijhoff Publishers 2000) at 672–4, 696, 718.

[70] Shihata gives an example of the so-called "particularly sensitive information", which is the staff's assessment of market conditions in connection with Bank borrowings. Ibrahim Shihata, *World Bank Legal Papers* (Martinus Nijhoff Publishers 2000) at 673.

[71] "All matters relating to alleged misconduct of the President will be considered by the Board in Executive Session, chaired by the Dean". AIIB Rules of Procedure of the Board of Directors (amended July 10, 2019), section 3(h).

[72] Zedillo Commission Report, at 34.

Directors' Forum is no decision-making body and should refrain from abusing its position and acting as a de facto Board.

(2) The Dean in comparison

Like the AIIB, other MDBs have similar occasions where the Board be chaired by a Director called the Dean. For example, the Board of the World Bank, when considering "the appointment of the President or the terms and conditions of his or her service contract or any matter thereto", selects a Director as chair or the Dean.[73] In such situations, the issues under discussion have conflict of interest potentials, and are thus inappropriate for the President to chair the Board. And the Dean selected in these situations is by practice the longest serving Director in the World Bank, similar to that of the AIIB. However, the Dean in the AIIB is novel in two respects. First, he has a designated term of service of two years, renewable once,[74] and he cannot be from the same member as the President. In contrast, the Dean in the World Bank seems to be temporarily selected to chair a particular Board meeting, and there is no requirement on his nationality. Second, the Dean in the AIIB seems to have a more focused mandate than the Dean in the World Bank, i.e., to check and balance the President under the oversight mechanism.[75] Therefore, by comparison, the institution of the AIIB may well bestow upon the Dean with enormous power to leverage against the President, either through the Directors' Forum or the formal meeting of the Board.

In sum, the Directors' Forum and the Dean are the most forceful components to hold the President accountable, under the AIIB Oversight Mechanism. They facilitate the MD-CEIU to report to the Board members without the President present, and make convenient for them to discipline the President. The success of such institutions depends upon their appropriate, balanced and healthy implementation, which may incentivize the President to play his leadership role and to sharpen staff's accountability to him, while not unduly stifling the morale and actions of his team. Further, the Directors' Forum must not be an *alter ego* Board, acting as a de facto decision maker. Given that the Directors' Forum comprises nobody but Board members, it is reasonable to anticipate that the discussion in the Forum would naturally lead to the decision of the Board at a later stage. The Forum has to strike a tricky and subtle

[73] World Bank Rules of Procedure for Meetings of the Executive Directors (amended July 22, 2019), section 2(f).

[74] AIIB Paper on the Oversight Mechanism (July 10, 2019), para.41.

[75] In contrast, the Dean of the World Bank Board has varied mandates, including: (1) the negotiation of the terms and conditions of the contract of the President along with the Co-Dean; (2) the Corporate Secretary consults with the Dean during the process of informal consultations to select members of the Board Ethics and Standing Committees; (3) to chair the meetings of the Steering Committee, which is the meeting of Executive Directors with Senior Management to set the Board's work program; (4) to organize meetings for Executive Directors among themselves or with Management, the UN or other high level experts to exchange views informally; and (5) to coordinate with the Dean of the IMF's Board on matters of mutual interest such as the Annual Meetings, the remuneration of the heads of the two institutions, and corporate governance issues. https://www.worldbank.org/en/about/leadership/directors/eds11 (visited August 17, 2021)

balance by avoiding effects of decision-making while playing its due role of facilitating the Board's work. Any inappropriate maneuver would not only risk violating the Forum's mandate, but also superseding the power of supervising management, which is exclusive to the Board.

2.5 Conclusion

The AIIB as an MDB embracing the twenty-first century, commits to draw upon the lessons learned in other MDBs of the past century, and keeps abreast of both innovation and inheritance in corporate governance. A non-resident Board makes possible a clear division of labor and responsibility between the Board and management. And to make it really happen, the delegation of power for project approval to management is a key step. Further, such delegation should be safeguarded by an oversight mechanism, enabling the Board to supervise management in project operations. The CEIU is established as a watchdog within the Bank, and the Directors' Forum is designed to facilitate the communication between the Board and the MD-CEIU. Such communication channel is headed by the Dean, which is a standing rather than temporary position, enabling the supervision work to be effective and meaningful.

In AIIB corporate governance, the most challenging task is the design of an oversight mechanism, which should reflect "an appropriate separation of powers to ensure proper checks and balances".[76] The key is to figure out where the degree of "appropriateness", or "properness", lies along a spectrum. If the power of oversight is weak or insufficient, a repetition of the World Bank leadership scandal in 2007 may well occur to the AIIB someday in future.[77] A President dictated by his own will or the will of a particular power might bring catastrophe to the reputation of the international organization, on top of his own. However, if the oversight power is of adversary nature or over-stretched, the President and his team may feel unduly bound to take some bold but necessary action, thus missing the opportunity to promote the cause of the Bank.

To help crack this hard nut of "appropriateness" in AIIB corporate governance, the right thing to do is to assess whether the oversight mechanism and the implementation thereof serve the dual purposes of the Bank—infrastructure connectivity and institutional collaboration, as designated in the Bank charter.[78] For examples, the

[76] AIIB Paper on the Oversight Mechanism (July 10, 2019), para.14.

[77] Paul Wolfowitz was forced to resign after serving two years of World Bank Presidency, due to a scandal involving his girlfriend, as well as his arbitrary and controversial policy approach towards borrowing states. Sarah Babb, *Behind the Development Banks* (Chicago: The University of Chicago Press, 2009), at 225–26. The Wolfowitz scandal is a case study of accountability gaps. The Zedillo Commission Report, "Executive summary", at xiv.

[78] AIIB AOA Article 1.1 states that "The purpose of the Bank shall be to: (i) foster sustainable economic development, create wealth and improve infrastructure connectivity in Asia by investing in infrastructure and other productive sectors; and (ii) promote regional cooperation and partnership

AIIB actively involves both in Belt and Road investments and in the MCDF secretariat service,[79] which are conducive to its purposes, and should not be discouraged by the oversight mechanism.[80] Another example is the AIIB's stringent restraint on non-regional investments, and it must be relaxed.[81] AIIB President should be delegated the power to co-finance with other MDBs beyond Asia, because it is good for institutional collaboration and regional connectivity under the Bank purposes. The maneuver of such power by the President should not be compromised by the oversight mechanism.

Finally, a philosophical question is whether a checks-and-balances culture suits the purpose of the AIIB. A purposive interpretation has been dominant in the history of the World Bank, contributing to the success of the organization. This is because, facing ever changing circumstances, the World Bank needs to rely upon a powerful executive branch to be able to make adaption and even innovation, by interpreting the Bank charter flexibly. As former General Counsel Shihata argued,[82]

> A purposive and broad interpretation of the Articles to enable the Bank to serve the changing needs of its members is in my view a legally sound approach which I have supported since joining the Bank in 1983 as its General Counsel, as long as this does not violate explicit prohibitions in these Articles or conflict with the Bank's stated purposes.[83]

Another former General Counsel Broches echoed,[84]

> ...the Bank's powers are not limited to those that are granted in express terms. The fact that an operation or transaction is not expressly authorized or contemplated by a specific provision of the Articles, does not mean that the Bank has no power to undertake it. Whether it has or does not have a particular power must be determined in the light of the Bank's purposes, by which all the Bank's decisions must be guided. For a finding that the Bank has such power, the power need not be shown to be necessarily or even reasonably implicit in any power given expressly by the Articles. It is enough that its exercise may further the

in addressing development challenges by working in close collaboration with other multilateral and bilateral development institutions."

[79] On the relationship between the AIIB, the Belt and Road and the Multilateral Cooperation Center for Development Finance (MCDF), see Gu Bin, "MCDF: A New Beacon of Multilateralism in Development Finance", *Journal of International Economic Law* (2020) 23 (3), 665–684, at 668–72. Simply put, almost all AIIB-funded projects may be characterized as Belt and Road projects, because they have mostly laid along the Belt and Road routes. And the MCDF Secretariat is hosted by the AIIB.

[80] As regards criticism of cooperation between the AIIB, the Belt and Road and the MCDF, see Korinna Horta and Wawa Wang, "The Beijing-led Asian Infrastructure Investment Bank: Global Leader in Infrastructure Finance, at What Cost?" (E-paper published by the Heinrich Böll Foundation October 2021), at 3, 8 and 14–15.

[81] On a detailed critique of the AIIB's non-regional investment policy, see Gu Bin, "AIIB should broaden horizons to gain global impact", *Global Times*, December 16, 2018.

[82] Ibrahim F.I. Shihata was World Bank General Counsel from 1983 to 1998.

[83] Ibrahim Shihata, *World Bank Legal Papers* (Martinus Nijhoff Publishers 2000) at 217.

[84] Aron Broches was World Bank General Counsel from 1959 to 1979. Both Broches and Shihata are towering figures in the World Bank legal history, who consistently applied a purposive interpretation of the bank charter in a forceful manner, and the two quotes here reflect their shared legal philosophy.

> achievement of the Bank's purposes, and that it is not prohibited by or inconsistent with the Bank's Articles of Agreement.[85]

An oversight mechanism fervent with separation of powers, or checks and balances, therefore, would risk hindering the pragmatic management of the AIIB from making such efforts. As Alvarez infers from a discussion of the United Nations, "separation of powers" does exist, as a matter of fact, in an international organization, but "checks and balances" seems to be more America-specific, and one should be cautious to introduce the concept into an international organization.[86] Even American history reveals that "checks and balances", as crafted by James Madison, was resisted by George Washington and Alexander Hamilton relentlessly in early American political practice.[87] It is advisable, therefore, to lean towards the oriental wisdom of advisory engagement, rather than the western style of adversary checks, along the spectrum of oversight that best suits the Asian gene of the Bank and its purposes.[88]

---

[85] Aron Broches, *Selected Essays, World Bank, ICSID, and other Subjects of Public and Private International Law* (Martinus Nijhoff Publishers 1995) at 28.

[86] As international organization (IO) defenders suggest, "many of the frustrating delays in achieving legal standards in IO settings reflect the numerous 'checks and balances' built into IO processes by states intent on keeping their IO agents in line." Jose E. Alvarez, *International Organizations as Law-makers* (New York: Oxford University Press 2005) at 66, 70, 73–74, 634.

[87] In their numerous major political battles, James Madison was a fervent supporter of a legislature-centered national system, while George Washington and Alexander Hamilton favored a powerful executive branch. Ron Chernow, *Washington: A Life* (The Penguin Press 2010) at 533–9, 575, 591, 648–9, 771.

[88] Such suggestion on the relationship between the Board and management is echoed elsewhere, for example, by an official report of the African Development Bank, where "social capital" (referring to trust) is emphasized among the Executive Directors and in particular between Executive Directors and management. In the report social capital is compared to the oil that lubricates the complex machine, and developing and nurturing such social capital is "a particular important role for the President and the Dean of the Board, assisted by the Secretary General and the General Counsel." African Development Bank, 'Comparative Study of Board Processes, Procedures and Practices in International Financial Institutions' (February 2018), at 34–35.

Chapter 3
Operational Standards: Environmental and Social Framework 2021

Summary The AIIB's new Environmental and Social Framework (ESF) features a relationship of heritage and innovation, compared with the ESF of the World Bank and other multilateral development banks (MDBs). The innovative elements are not only embodied in a few specific institutions shiny with traditional Asian wisdom of 'voluntarism, flexibility and incremental progress', but are also observed in the AIIB's frontier environmental, social and governance portfolio investments in global capital markets. Drawing upon the World Bank, the alternative use of client systems enables the AIIB to maintain high and feasible standards, without having to intervene in national politics. In the Project-affected People's Mechanism, three complaints resolution functions are streamlined under one roof, catering for the nature and degree of seriousness of the dispute involved and marking a major innovation in the design of an accountability mechanism among leading MDBs. The two requirements of exhaustion of project-level remedies and free, prior and informed consultation expect to function equivalently to the World Bank standards in effect, although they appear to reduce the protection of project-affected people.

3.1 Introduction

In May 2021, the Asian Infrastructure Investment Bank (AIIB) promulgated the new Environmental and Social Framework (ESF). It is a legal tool to regulate the behavior of AIIB staff, as well as of AIIB clients, in an AIIB-financed project, and the purpose is to safeguard project-affected people from possible negative impacts or risks in regard to environmental and social aspects. In effect as of 1 October 2021, this new ESF is a major legal instrument to help the AIIB to achieve the 'highest

This chapter originally appeared in *Review of European, Comparative & International Environmental Law*, 5 September 2022, entitled "A legal study of the AIIB's new Environmental and Social Framework".

B. Gu, *Chinese Multilateralism in the Asian Infrastructure Investment Bank (AIIB)*,
Modern China and International Economic Law,
https://doi.org/10.1007/978-981-97-1219-9_3

possible standards',[1] as embodied in its trademark corporate culture of 'lean, clean and green'.[2]

The original ESF of the AIIB came into force in February 2016, as one of the very first few legal documents identified as 'major policies'.[3] The ESF was immediately put into use, applying to the first batch of four projects that were prepared even before the AIIB went into operation in January 2016.[4] The ESF was revised in February 2019, after three years of use, as committed in the initial ESF.[5] However, the 2019 version did not make substantive changes *vis-à-vis* the original framework; rather, it featured more nominal updates than substantive revisions. For example, it substituted the language 'oversight mechanism' in the 2016 ESF—generally described as a grievance relief mechanism for local people—with a 'Project-affected People's Mechanism' (PPM), reflecting new developments.[6] Two years later, an overhaul of the ESF was eventually made, after two rounds of wide and comprehensive public consultations (albeit much of the work was carried out virtually, instead of

---

[1] The quote is from a statement by then AIIB President-designate Jin Liqun; it has been reiterated both in AIIB official documents and on the AIIB's official website. See AIIB, 'Statement by Jin Liqun at a Press Conference in Tbilisi' (26 August 2015) < https://www.aiib.org/en/news-events/news/2015/Statement-by-Jin-Liqun-at-a-Press-Conference-in-Tbilisi.html > .

[2] The three words are commonly defined as follows: 'lean', meaning with a small, efficient management team and highly skilled staff; 'clean', meaning an ethical organization with zero tolerance for corruption; and 'green', an institution that is built on respect for the environment. Nevertheless, the technical definitions vary across AIIB official documents.

[3] 'Major policies' is a legal term defined to explicitly include the ESF, and they require a higher three-quarters majority of total voting power within the Board of Directors for approval. By comparison, 'other policies' require a simple majority of the votes cast within the Board of Directors for approval. AIIB, 'Articles of Agreement' < https://www.aiib.org/en/about-aiib/basic-documents/articles-of-agreement/index.html > (AIIB AOA) art 26.2 and Explanatory Notes on Article 26 as attached to the Chief Negotiators' Report on AIIB AOA.

[4] Of the first batch of AIIB projects located in Bangladesh, Indonesia, Pakistan and Tajikistan, totalling US$509 million in loans, three projects were co-financed with peer institutions including the World Bank, the Asian Development Bank (ADB), and the European Bank for Reconstruction and Development (EBRD), and those projects applied the co-financers' ESFs, respectively, with each considered to be 'materially consistent' with AIIB's ESF; the only project using the AIIB's own ESF was the standalone one in Bangladesh. The AIIB 2016 ESF explicitly authorized the use of the co-financier's ESF, stating that '[t]he Bank may agree, on a case-by-case basis, to the application of the environmental and social policies and procedures of multilateral development banks and bilateral development organizations who are co-financing the Project, provided that the Bank is satisfied that they are consistent with the Bank's Articles of Agreement and materially consistent with the ESP and ESSs, and that appropriate monitoring procedures are in place'. AIIB, '2016 Environmental and Social Framework' (February 2016) (AIIB 2016 ESF) 'Environmental and Social Policy (ESP)', para 10.

[5] The 2016 ESF warranted that 'updates would be introduced to the framework, and further improvements to the ESP and ESSs would be recommended to the Board of Directors for approval' at the end of 'the first three years of the Bank's operation'. AIIB 2016 ESF (n 4) 'Introduction', para 4.

[6] The PPM was established in accordance with the Policy on the Project-affected People's Mechanism in 2018, during the interval between the 2016 and 2019 ESF of the AIIB. See AIIB, 'Policy on the Project-affected People's Mechanism' (7 December 2018) < https://www.aiib.org/en/policies-strategies/operational-policies/policy-on-the-project-affected-mechanism.html > (AIIB Policy on the PPM).

face-to-face consultations, due to the outbreak of COVID-19). This 2021 version offers stronger climate change provisions in alignment with the Paris Agreement and uses environmental, social and governance (ESG) approaches to capital market investments, among other innovative arrangements.

All the while, the AIIB demonstrates the Asian wisdom of 'voluntarism, flexibility and incremental progress' throughout the ESF. 'Voluntarism' originates in Chinese society as non-missionary,[7] which contrasts a hegemon's intention to impose its will and seek predominance over others. As reflected in the ESF, cooperation with the client is prioritized, and interference in national politics is forbidden. In terms of 'flexibility', an institution should be nimble and agile in serving its purpose, and the design and implementation of the institution should be geared to its object and purpose because being responsive and efficient is key.[8] Neither an overly bureaucratic institution nor a one-size-fits-all approach is advisable. 'Incremental progress' means that the standards in development should aim both high and for *feasibility*, catering for the particularities of a society, including its limited awareness and capacity, rather than wishing to build Rome in one day. No doubt that the three elements of wisdom are inherently intertwined.

The ESF is standard practice among MDBs,[9] as a community of international organizations committed to sustainable development financing.[10] Sustainable development encompasses more than economy, expanding to ESG aspects featuring high standards, as society progresses.[11] The World Bank adopted the first ESF of its kind in the late 1980s,[12] under the pressure of widespread protests by local people and civil societies due to environmental deteriorations and human rights violations inflicted in the course of its own projects. Other MDBs followed the initiative of the World Bank and enacted their own ESFs. Each of these ESFs has since experienced more than

---

[7] In a non-missionary culture, China has never sought to export its political system and values; rather, it has seen others come to it. As Confucius said, '远人不服，则修文德以来之' (translated literally as: If people from afar do not submit, influence them to do so by means of virtue and civil culture). For an elaboration of this aspect of the Chinese culture, see H Kissinger, *World Order* (Penguin Books 2015) 213–233.

[8] As Deng Xiaoping famously said: 'Be it a black cat or a white cat, it is a good cat as long as it can catch mice'.

[9] Some regional MDBs still use the traditional name of safeguards, such as the ADB and the African Development Bank (AfDB), while others adopt the term ESF, such as the AIIB, the New Development Bank (NDB) and the Inter-American Development Bank (IDB).

[10] The EBRD may be considered an exception in the sense that it was created in 1991 to promote privatization in the former Soviet Union countries.

[11] An overview of the evolution from economic growth to more inclusive aspects in the understanding of sustainable development can be found in P Dann, *The Law of Development Cooperation* (Cambridge University Press 2013) 101–125.

[12] The genesis of the World Bank's ESF was the Operational Manual Statement on Environmental Aspects of World Bank Work (OMS) in 1984, subsequently updated as Operational Directives (ODs) in 1987, as Operational Policies and Bank Procedures (OP/BP) in 1992, as safeguard policies in 1997, and ultimately, bearing the current name of ESF in 2016.

one round of revision in response to ever-changing circumstances and in a general direction of convergence or even towards a *droit commun.*[13]

This chapter is committed to a nuanced critique of the AIIB ESF's institutional merits and implications, as reflected in past and ongoing practices where relevant. The study is comparative, i.e., involving comparison with the ESFs of peer institutions, in particular that of the World Bank (IBRD/IDA).[14] Wherever necessary, comparison is also made to the International Finance Corporation's (IFC) Sustainability Framework, which includes the Performance Standards as a globally recognized environmental and social benchmark in the private sector.[15] Section 3.2 investigates the status of the ESF as internal law in the corpus of international institutional law. Through Sect. 3.3, 3.4, 3.5, 3.6, four institutional innovations in the AIIB's ESF are explored, respectively. Section 3.3 specifically dwells on the AIIB's ESG portfolio investments, and Sect. 3.4 examines the use of a country or corporate system (UCS). Functioning as 'escape clauses' alternating the ESF, both of these institutions are authorized explicitly by the ESF, considered as composite parts of it and required to be consistent with it either materially or spiritually. Section 3.5 deals with the complaints resolution system available for local communities. Section 3.6 focuses on the system of free, prior, and informed consultation (FPICon) for indigenous peoples. Section 3.7 concludes.

---

[13] The notion of *droit commun* is defined as a process through which various organizations develop and implement similar standards, rules or procedures. A *droit commun* allows for the emergence of a distinct legal corpus of the harmonized standards, rules and procedures that the institutions have in common. See L Boisson de Chazournes, 'Partnership, Emulation, and Coordination: Toward the Emergency of a *Droit Commun* in the Field of Development Finance' in H Cisse, DD Bradlow, B Kingsbury (eds), *The World Bank Legal Review*, Vol. 3 (World Bank 2012) 174. The AIIB ESF's explicit authorization of the use of a co-financer's ESF in an AIIB-financed project, as discussed above, may contribute to the prospect of a *droit commun*.

[14] The World Bank means the International Bank for Reconstruction and Development (IBRD) and the International Development Association (IDA). The World Bank ESF was drafted from 2012 through 2016, a period largely coinciding with the establishment of the AIIB. Presumably, the AIIB's ESF had been built upon that of the World Bank, with the assistance of a former World Bank senior expert, Stephen Lintner.

[15] Under the World Bank Group, IBRD/IDA serves the public sector, and IFC/MIGA serves the private sector, applying different safeguard systems. See IFC, 'Sustainability Framework' (1 January 2012) < https://www.ifc.org/wps/wcm/connect/topics_ext_content/ifc_external_corporate_site/sustainability-at-ifc/publications/publications_handbook_sustainabilityframework > . By contrast, other MDBs, such as the AIIB, ADB, AfDB, European Investment Bank (EIB) and IDB, which are eligible to invest in both public and private sectors, apply the same operational safeguards to both sectors, with their procedural requirements adjusted to the particular circumstances of private sector activities.

3.2 Legal Status of the ESF

The ESF is an internal law approved by the Board of Directors of the AIIB, and accompanying the ESF is an implementing directive issued by the President. There are many rules, regulations, and procedures of such an internal nature, and they are often theme- or sector-specific.

3.2.1 Categorization of AIIB Internal Laws: A Brief Description

The AIIB's legal corpus grew to be comprehensive and complicated after the first five-year start-up phase (January 2016 to January 2021). The corpus consists of the AIIB Articles of Agreement (AOA), commonly known as the Charter, and numerous internal laws, which are derived or developed from the Charter. These internal laws may be further roughly divided into three categories.[16] The first category is governance-related and thematic. For instance, on the Board's oversight power,[17] the Accountability Framework was initially made in 2018, followed by an Oversight Mechanism (OM) in 2019. On anti-corruption and fraud, the AIIB has a Policy on Prohibited Practice.[18] On environmental and social standards, the ESF has been put in place. And on avoidance and settlement of environmental and social disputes, the AIIB has the PPM. There are some other internal legal documents related to AIIB governance, covering issues such as transparency, sovereign-backed loans, project and corporate procurement and a few special funds including the Project Preparation Special Fund.

The second category includes sector strategies. As its name suggests, the AIIB focuses on investment in infrastructure,[19] which is an undefined, broad, and evolving concept. Infrastructure traditionally encompasses such areas as transport, energy, and urban developments; meanwhile, it may cover new types of infrastructure such

---

16 All the texts of these internal laws are readily available on the AIIB's official website: < https://www.aiib.org/en/index.html > .

17 The non-resident Board of Directors shall 'supervise the management and operation of the Bank on a regular basis, and establish an oversight mechanism for that purpose, in line with principles of transparency, openness, independence and accountability'. AIIB AOA (n 3) art 26(iv).

18 For a detailed discussion of this policy, see B Gu, *The Law and Governance of the Asian Infrastructure Investment Bank* (Wolters Kluwer 2019) 143–172.

19 To be accurate, the scope of AIIB investments breaks down into two elements under AIIB AOA (n 3) art 1(1): 'infrastructure' and 'other productive sectors'. 'Infrastructure' itself is a broad sector encompassing both physical and electronic elements. The concept of 'other productive sectors' can be even broader, echoing the term 'productive' first used in the International Bank for Reconstruction and Development (IBRD) Charter in 1944, whereby the word choice meant to exclude 'such non-productive lending as financing of war and budget deficits and refinancing of old debts'. N Lichtenstein, *A Comparative Guide to the Asian Infrastructure Investment Bank* (Oxford University Press 2018) 42–43, 50–51.

as digital infrastructure (5G), broadband, and satellites. The AIIB Board of Directors approves sector-specific strategies as guidance for Bank operations in relevant sectors,[20] and those strategies may be revised or updated in response to changing circumstances. For example, the AIIB has revised its energy strategy, with a major aim to stop financing new coal power, a concurrent step with other MDBs toward green financing.[21]

The third category covers other rules and regulations at the overall level of the Bank. The foremost is the Corporate Strategy of 2020, governing the long-term development of the Bank from 2021 through 2030. As the growth-phase strategic plan, this policy identifies four cross-cutting operational 'thematic priorities' for the AIIB: (i) green infrastructure, (ii) connectivity and regional cooperation, (iii) technology-enabled infrastructure, and (iv) private capital mobilization. In particular, it sets a climate financing target at 50% of actual financing approvals by 2025 and 50 % for private sector projects by 2030.[22] Another noted policy in this category is the Strategy on Financing Operations in Non-Regional Members, which limits the AIIB's non-regional investment to no more than 15% of total financing in order to maintain the Bank's Asian gene.[23] Also in this policy, project approval authority is delegated to the President, as required under the Charter,[24] with a few exceptions where the Board of Directors retains that power.

3.2.2 *Internal Laws as a New Source of International Law*

The above legal documents of the AIIB are "internal", not because they have no external effect upon the outside world; indeed, those documents all produce external legal effects. The internal nature, instead, is a description of their approval by the Board of Directors, the President, or other internal organs of the AIIB,[25] as opposed to the Articles of Agreement as an international treaty agreed by, and binding upon, all AIIB members. While the AIIB's Charter and its internal laws are often grouped

---

[20] These sector-specific strategies include the Transport Sector Strategy, Sustainable Cities Strategy, Water Strategy, Digital Infrastructure Sector Strategy, etc.

[21] AIIB,'ENergy Sector Strategy: Sustainable Energy for Tomorrow'(Nov. 22, 2022), paras. 53–58. A discussion of no-coal investments in international development is available at B Gu, 'China's Belt and Road Initiative Should Stop Financing New Coal Power' (Financial Times, 5 July 2021).

[22] AIIB, 'Corporate Strategy: Financing Infrastructure for Tomorrow' (September 2020) 27.

[23] The text of this strategy can be found at < https://www.aiib.org/en/policies-strategies/strategies/financing-operations.html > . For a detailed critique of the AIIB's non-regional investment policy, see B Gu, 'AIIB Should Broaden Horizons to Gain Global Impact' (Global Times, 16 December 2018).

[24] The Board shall 'take decisions concerning operations of the Bank', and 'by a majority representing not less than three-fourths of the total voting power of the members, decide on the delegation of such authority to the President'. AIIB AOA (n 3) art 26(iii).

[25] While the internal organs competent to enact internal laws are many, the Board of Directors is deemed as the "legislative" branch, if roughly compared to the national system.

together as the "AIIB law", internal laws per se deserve an appropriate explanation under international law. In the case of the ESF, for example, the following questions may arise: Is the ESF a source of international law as encompassed by Article 38 of the Statute of International Court of Justice (ICJ)?[26] If not, what is the status of the ESF then in the broader international legal order?

Article 38 of ICJ Statute has been known to exhaust the sources of international law,[27] but the Article itself does not state so. It has neither been updated since adoption to reflect the ensuing many decades of international legal developments,[28] among which the foremost has been the law of international organizations.[29] As a legal output of an international organization, the ESF is not a treaty agreed directly by states; neither is it a custom, without seeking to find consistent practice and *opinio juris* of states; nor does it represent "general principles of law", which is of fairly limited scope and intended to close the gap that might be uncovered in international law.[30] As a result, the ESF, alongside the bulk of international institutional law, except for the international organization's Charter, has difficulty in finding an appropriate place in the corpus of traditional international law.

Instead, these internal laws are a new source of modern international law, since international organizations possess legal personality and separate will, just as states do on the international plane.[31] The lawmaking of international organizations, while not creating immediate hard obligations upon states, has a legislative nature.[32] With the organizations' intent to create norms and the legitimacy in creating them, states habitually comply with them. In the case of the ESF, its framing is a power delegated by all AIIB members in the Articles of Agreement which stipulates that "[t]he Bank shall ensure that each of its operations complies with ... policies addressing environmental and social impacts".[33] Blessed with "greater consultation (in open

---

[26] The three sources of international law, as stipulated in Article 38 of ICJ Statute, are: international conventions, international custom, and general principles of law.

[27] Malcolm N. Shaw, *International Law* (Cambridge University Press 2008, 6th ed.), pp.70–71.

[28] It is noted that Article 38 of ICJ Statute was primarily drafted for the Permanent Court of International Justice during the inter-war period, well before international organizations became proliferated after World War II. James Crawford, *Brownlie's Principles of Public International Law* (Oxford University Press 2012, 8th ed.), pp.21–22.

[29] In this light Alvarez criticizes that 'we continue to pour an increasingly rich normative output [of international organizations] into old bottles labeled "treaty," "custom," or (much more rarely) "general principles"'. Jose E. Alvarez, *International Organizations as Law-makers* (Oxford University Press 2005) Preface p. x.

[30] Malcolm N. Shaw, *International Law* (Cambridge University Press, 2008, 6th ed.), pp.98–99.

[31] It is noted that the degree of legal personality and corporate will varies across international organizations, ranging from the contractual type (such as Shanghai Cooperation Organization, SCO), to the constitutional type (such as European Union, and, to a lesser extent, the AIIB).

[32] White comments that 'even though the term "legislation" is often confined to hard lawmaking, there is no reason why its meaning—as the process of enacting law—should not be extended to softer forms of lawmaking.' Nigel D. White, 'Lawmaking', in Jacob Katz Cogan, Ian Hurd, Ian Johnstone (eds), *The Oxford Handbook of International Organizations* (New York: Oxford University Press 2016), p. 566.

[33] AIIB AOA, Article 13.4.

meetings), greater transparency, and ultimately greater representation of the international community",[34] as described briefly in the Introduction, the enacting of the ESF realizes the greater common will of AIIB membership, which is formally represented through the Board of Directors within the AIIB.

The legal impact of the ESF may go far beyond the projects which the AIIB finances. With numerous projects and billions of dollars invested across the globe, the ESF extends to regulate the behaviors of each borrowing state and participating market entity. The AIIB, alongside other like-minded MDBs in the development financing community, effectively functions as a norm-setter and regulator in environmental and social safeguards.[35] They are at the forefront of promoting international law-making and implementation in relevant fields, claiming to be mutually reinforcing each other vis a vis the Paris Agreement, and UN laws on biodiversity, labor, and social rights. Indeed, the ESFs of those MDBs may incrementally form "international custom, as evidence of a general practice accepted as law".[36]

3.2.3 The Legal Effects of the ESF in an AIIB-Financed Project

The new ESF is clearly articulated in legal language and structure, and it comprises the following parts: an introduction, a vision statement, the Environmental and Social Policy (ESP) and an exclusion list (i.e., a taboo for the AIIB to invest in). The introduction and vision are often identified as soft law and non-binding. The other two parts—i.e., the ESP and the exclusion list—are both legally binding upon the AIIB and applicable to any AIIB-financed project. Accompanying the ESP are three Environmental and Social Standards (ESSs),[37] which are only binding upon the borrower, while the AIIB has an obligation to monitor their implementation.

The project agreement between the AIIB and the borrower is the conduit for the ESF to produce legal effects at the project level. There are three perspectives to understand the legal effects. First, at the phase of project preparation, the borrower must assess possible environmental and social risks or impacts, measured against the ESF, with respect to the proposed project, and provide corresponding mitigating

[34] This quote of White is believed to contribute to the legitimacy of a norm. Nigel D. White, 'Lawmaking', in Jacob Katz Cogan, Ian Hurd, Ian Johnstone (eds), *The Oxford Handbook of International Organizations* (New York: Oxford University Press 2016), p. 569.

[35] As Dann and Riegner comment, "the Safeguards had become a globally diffused normative model for socially and environmentally sound development", by way of "diffus[ing] horizontally into the laws and practices of other MDBs and private banks and vertically into domestic legal orders beyond individual projects", eventually transcending the World Bank "from lender to norm-setter". Philipp Dann and Michael Riegner, "The World Bank's Environmental and Social Safeguards and the evolution of global order", Leiden Journal of International Law (2019), 32, pp. 538, 545–7.

[36] It is a language borrowed from Article 38 of ICJ Statute.

[37] The three ESSs are entitled, respectively, 'Environmental and Social Assessment and Management', 'Land Acquisition and Involuntary Resettlement' and 'Indigenous Peoples'.

measures. The AIIB is to evaluate the adequacy of the borrower's preparatory work and decide on approval (or not) of the project proposal. Second, by incorporating the requirements of the ESF in the project agreement,[38] the borrower has an obligation to implement the ESSs, while the AIIB, as the lender, must monitor the implementation process. Third, during the procurement of the project, the borrower must write the requirements of the ESF into the tender documents, and later, into the project contracts, which are binding upon bidders and contractors, as relevant. Thus, the legal effects of the ESF apply all through the lifecycle of the project, including but not limited to the phases of project preparation, implementation, and procurement. In this connection, the ESF is binding (directly or indirectly) upon the AIIB, borrowers (including both governments and corporations) and contracting entities.

A highly contentious topic is the applicability of the doctrine of *lex specialis* in a conflict between the internal laws of an international organization and general international law. As stated in Article 64 of the draft Articles on the Responsibility of International Organizations (ARIO), '[t]hese articles do not apply where and to the extent that … are governed by special rules of international law. Such special rules of international law may be contained in the rules of the organization applicable to the relations between an international organization and its members'.[39] The internal laws of the AIIB, including the ESF, with external legal effects as noted above, may qualify as such 'special rules of international law' and may thus override general international law in a conflict of norms. This prospect risks the abuse of Article 64, however, by giving international organizations an easy escape route from their responsibilities. The contention incurred here, while outside the focus of this book, is worth exploring elsewhere.[40]

---

[38] While the text of a project agreement is not publicly available, a summary of each project is posted on the AIIB official website as a 'looking glass' into how the ESF governs. For example, regarding the Oman Broadband project, it states: 'According to AIIB's Environmental and Social Framework, the Project is classified as Category B. As required for a Category B project, an Environmental and Social Management Plan (ESMP) has been developed'; AIIB, 'Oman: Oman Broadband Infrastructure' < https://www.aiib.org/en/projects/details/2017/approved/Oman-Oman-Broadband-Infrastructure.html > . Regarding another project, the Beijing coal-to-gas project, it similarly states: 'Per the Bank's Environmental and Social Policy, the Project is assigned as Category B. As part of Project preparation, the environmental and social impacts were assessed and mitigation measures proposed in an Environmental and Social Management Plan (ESMP)'; AIIB, 'China: Beijing Air Quality Improvement and Coal Replacement' < https://www.aiib.org/en/projects/details/2017/approved/China-Beijing-Air-Quality-Improvement-and-Coal-Replacement.html > . The ESMP is a commitment made by the borrower and approved by the AIIB, and the text of an ESMP is available on the websites of both the borrower and the AIIB.

[39] Draft Articles on the Responsibility of International Organizations, in 'Report of the International Law Commission, Sixty-Third Session' UN Doc A/66/10 (2011) para 87ff.

[40] See L Gasbarri, *The Concept of an International Organization in International Law* (Oxford University Press 2021) 41–44.

3.3 ESG Approaches to Capital Markets Operations

3.3.1 The General Landscape of the AIIB's ESG Portfolio Investments

Pursuant to the AIIB Charter, the Bank's investment areas are 'infrastructure and other productive sectors',[41] which normally means specific infrastructure projects, including physical, digital, and social ones, but it may also invest in publicly traded securities in support of capital market engagement in infrastructure development.[42] In such cases, the Bank will engage an asset manager or an investment advisor, leveraging the latter's expertise to make individual investment decisions, rather than doing the job by itself. The engaged asset manager is expected to invest in infrastructure-related corporate bonds, thereby still serving the purpose of the AIIB. Furthermore, as its text is designed for 'a private, bilateral agreement' between the AIIB and the borrower, the ESF does not apply readily to portfolio investments featuring 'a public, hub-and-spoke relationship' between a bond issuer and numerous institutional investors (i.e., the position of the AIIB).[43] In this context, a special ESG framework is put in place, in lieu of the AIIB ESP, for the Bank to assess environmental and social risks involving such portfolio investments. For example, the Asia Climate Bond Portfolio explains in the project summary that the common ESP is 'designed to apply to more conventional investment projects where creation of physical assets is being financed and has not envisaged projects such as this one, where environmental and social compliance is more suitably assessed at the corporate rather than asset level'.[44]

The ESG framework is created under the auspices of the AIIB and applied in investment operations by an asset manager, who should report periodically to the AIIB about its implementation. While being operation-specific, the AIIB ESG frameworks are similar to each other across operations, in terms of structure, language, and content. Above all, they are explicitly authorized by the AIIB ESF and required to

[41] AIIB AOA (n 3) art 1(1).

[42] AIIB, 'Environmental and Social Framework (ESF)' (May 2021) < https://www.aiib.org/en/policies-strategies/framework-agreements/environmental-social-framework.html > (AIIB ESF 2021) Vision, paras 29–30. The authorization of such special investments is derived from AIIB AOA (n 3) art 16(9), which states: 'The Bank may exercise such other powers and establish such rules and regulations as may be necessary or appropriate in furtherance of its purpose and functions, consistent with the provisions of this Agreement.'

[43] Specifically, capital markets investment is 'governed by the terms of the publicly traded securities; the environmental and social assessment of any potential investment is made on the basis of publicly available information; reporting is made to all securities holders in the same manner; and environmental and social performance is more suitably assessed at the corporate rather than asset level by measuring publicly available ESG information against widely acknowledged benchmarks'. AIIB ESF 2021 (n 42) ESP, para 12.

[44] AIIB, 'Project Summary Information: Asia Climate Bond Portfolio' PD000312 (22 April 2021) < https://www.aiib.org/en/projects/details/2019/approved/Multicountry-Asia-Climate-Bond-Portfolio.html > .

be consistent with its 'spirit and vision'.[45] To the extent that it is a form of 'applying the ESF to capital market projects',[46] the ESG framework may be considered as a composite part of the ESF. Probably unaware of such high-standard dimensions of the ESG framework, as well as the inherent limit of the AIIB ESF as described in the previous paragraph, some critics wrongly blame the AIIB for lowering standards by choosing 'to forgo its own standards for this new dynamic frontier of investment'.[47]

The AIIB's ESG portfolio investments are an innovative form of public–private partnership (PPP), which has three key features. First, the AIIB partners with an asset manager in making bond investments, as well as in developing ESG standards. Second, the AIIB expects to crowd in more private capital in the ESG campaign in capital markets by unleashing its own portfolio.[48] Third, the AIIB fund expects to invest in corporate bonds and green bonds (i.e., non-sovereign), which should be infrastructure-related, promoting an ESG culture and awareness among private issuer entities.[49] Such ESG portfolio investments, though authorized 'in special circumstances' and accounting for a very small proportion of the AIIB's overall portfolio so far,[50] are expected to contribute to the lofty financing target of 50% for private sector projects by 2030, as provided for in the AIIB Corporate Strategy of 2020.[51]

The AIIB's ESG portfolio investments represent 'a new and dynamic frontier' for traditional MDBs, as acknowledged in the ESF.[52] It invests in bond markets, guided by the ESG credentials of corporate issuers, and in the form of public–private partnership. By contrast, neither the World Bank nor the IFC acknowledges ESG portfolio investments in their ESFs.[53] Partnering with an asset manager, the AIIB

---

[45] '[ESG portfolio] investments would require the use of an appropriate ESG framework against which environmental and social risks can be addressed.' AIIB ESF 2021 (n 42) vision, para 29; and ESP, para 13.

[46] AIIB, 'Environmental, Social and Governance Credentials' (April 2022) < https://www.aiib.org/en/treasury/_common/_download/AIIB-ESG-Credentials-Slides-20220401.pdf > 6.

[47] K Horta and W Wang, 'The Beijing-led Asian Infrastructure Investment Bank: Global Leader in Infrastructure Finance, at What Cost?' (Heinrich Böll Foundation October 2021) 13, 29.

[48] The AIIB's Asia Climate Bond Portfolio, for example, 'expects to mobilize another US$500 million from climate change-focused institutional investors'. AIIB (n 44).

[49] With respect to the AIIB's Asian ESG Enhanced Credit Managed Portfolio, for example, the investment focus is explicitly on quasi-sovereign bonds (e.g., those issued by State-owned enterprises), corporate bonds and green bonds; sovereign bonds, project bonds and derivatives are outside consideration. AIIB, 'Project Summary Information: Asian ESG Enhanced Credit Managed Portfolio' 000,152 (March 2019) < https://www.aiib.org/en/projects/details/2018/approved/Multicountry-AIIB-Asia-ESG-Enhanced-Credit-Managed-Portfolio.html > .

[50] '[T]he Bank intends, *in special circumstances*, to support investments in a portfolio of publicly traded securities'. AIIB ESF 2021 (n 42) Vision, para 29 (emphasis added).

[51] AIIB, 'Corporate Strategy: Financing Infrastructure for Tomorrow' (September 2020) 21.

[52] 'Mobilization by development finance institutions of financial resources for infrastructure development through investments in publicly traded securities (i.e. stocks and bonds) using environmental, social and governance (ESG) approaches is *a new and dynamic frontier*'; AIIB ESF 2021 (n 42) Vision, para 29 (emphasis added).

[53] An exceptional provision, which is general in nature, is that '[g]iven the importance of the private sector's role in the reduction of greenhouse gas (GHG) emissions, IFC will engage in innovative investments'. IFC (n 15) Policy on Environmental and Social Sustainability, para 10.

has the ambition to promote ESG market education across Asian capital markets, which are at an early development phase, compared with mature markets such as the United States and Western Europe.[54] In the process, the AIIB expects to be a norm setter in this emerging area. As indicated in its Sustainable Capital Markets Initiative (SCMI), a winner of the Environmental Finance's 2021 Impact Awards,[55] the 'AIIB and the investment advisor will work to develop relevant benchmarks/indices based on learnings from the two portfolios, … [and] to test and report on ESG integration techniques applied to infrastructure-linked corporate bonds'.[56] The AIIB-Amundi Climate Change Investment Framework is such a pilot knowledge product concerning climate bonds investments; in particular, it translates the key objectives of the Paris Agreement into fundamental metrics to assess an issuer's level of alignment with climate change mitigation and adaptation objectives.[57]

The AIIB's ESG portfolio investment in capital markets differs from its own ESG rating by a professional, third-party rating agency. The latter is a rating of the AIIB at the corporate level as evaluated by assessment of the track records of the AIIB's conventional projects, as well as portfolio investments, from the ESG perspective.[58] Additionally, the AIIB's ESG rating is solicited by institutional investors in capital markets, rather than by the AIIB itself, which boosts the credibility of the rating result.[59]

[54] Statistics indicate that, among the top 20 countries for annual green bonds issuance in 2020, the United States led national rankings (US$51.1 billion), with Germany second (US$40.2 billion), France third (US$32.1 billion), China fourth (US$17.2 billion) and the Netherlands fifth (US$ 17 billion). See the Climate Bonds Initiative, 'Record $269.5bn Green Issuance for 2020: Late Surge Sees Pandemic Year Pip 2019 Total by $3bn (24 January 2021) < https://www.climatebonds.net/2021/01/record-2695bn-green-issuance-2020-late-surge-sees-pandemic-year-pip-2019-total-3bn > .

[55] Environmental Finance, 'IMPACT Awards 2021' < https://www.environmental-finance.com/content/awards/impact-awards-2021/corporate-statements/making-an-impact-in-asian-infrastructure.html > .

[56] AIIB, 'Asia Climate Bond Portfolio ESG Framework' (Version 1, March 2020) < https://www.aiib.org/en/projects/details/2019/approved/_download/Multicountry/ESG-Framework-for-ACB-Portfolio-April-9-2020.pdf > 7–8.

[57] AIIB, 'AIIB-Amundi Climate Change Investment Framework' < https://www.aiib.org/en/policies-strategies/framework-agreements/climate-change-investment-framework/index.html > .

[58] At the time of writing, the AIIB is rated C + in terms of ESG performance. Among the 32 peer institutions rated by ISS ESG, an ESG rating agency, only three, as industry leaders, have ratings higher than C + ; they are the ADB (B), the Council of Europe Development Bank (CEB) (B-) and the EBRD (B-). See < https://www.aiib.org/en/treasury/esg/index.html > .

[59] An investor-paid, rather than issuer-paid, rating arrangement helps to avoid the notorious conflicts of interest that exist in the credit rating industry and contributed to the 2008 global financial crisis.

3.3.2 *Two Case Studies of the AIIB's ESG Portfolio Investments*

At the time of writing, the AIIB had created two innovative ESG portfolio projects. One is the Asian ESG Enhanced Credit Managed Portfolio ('Credit Portfolio') and the other is the Asia Climate Bond Portfolio ('ACB Portfolio'), approved by the Board of Directors in 2018 and 2019, respectively.[60] Each project is equipped with a specific ESG framework, modeled on the same template and similar to each other and applied by asset managers in both the pre- and post-investment phases. The asset managers of the Credit Portfolio and the ACB Portfolio are two European asset managers, Aberdeen Standard Investments and Amundi respectively, with an initial volume of US$500 million for each.

For both projects, the ESG investment process involves two lists of exclusions, consistent with the exclusion list in the AIIB ESF, i.e., product- and norms-based, whereby the covered issuers should not be considered. Under product-based exclusions specifically, weapons, alcohol, tobacco, gambling, and asbestos are covered, whereby the asset manager will not invest in issuers that derive more than 10% of their turnover from the manufacture or sale of such products.[61] Regarding the norms-based exclusions, by contrast, they are 'both difficult to obtain information [about] and to assess what qualifies for exclusion',[62] because they are defined in the ESG framework as violations of internationally recognized ESG standards, which are themselves evolving. In this light, an 'ESG Focus List and escalation process' has been developed, whereby the AIIB and the asset manager may identify and engage with issuer companies involved in ESG controversies, including both scenarios of deteriorating ESG performance and activities involving product- or norms-based exclusions during the post-investment phase.[63]

The ESG Focus List and escalation process comprises four steps for issuers in proportion to their degree of deterioration in ESG performance (see Fig. 3.1).[64] First is *observation*, meaning the flagging of companies involved in ESG controversy for more frequent monitoring and review; second is *notification*, meaning engagement with issuer companies to investigate and determine the materiality of ESG issues; third is *ESG Focus List designation*, meaning the designation of companies that have material ESG issues with which the AIIB is engaging; and fourth is *divestment*, meaning consideration for divestment after unsatisfactory engagements.

[60] The authority of portfolio investments is retained by the Board, rather than being delegated to the President as had been expected in the institutional context of a non-resident Board of the AIIB. AIIB ESF 2021 (n 42) ESP, para 14.

[61] AIIB, 'Asian ESG Enhanced Credit Managed Portfolio ESG Framework' (Version 1, July 2019) 3–4. <https://www.aiib.org/en/projects/approved/2018/_download/regional/ESG-enhanced-credit-managed-portfolio.pdf>.

[62] Ibid 4.

[63] Ibid 5.

[64] Figure 3.1 is from the 'ESG Focus List and Escalation Process', as included in ibid 6.

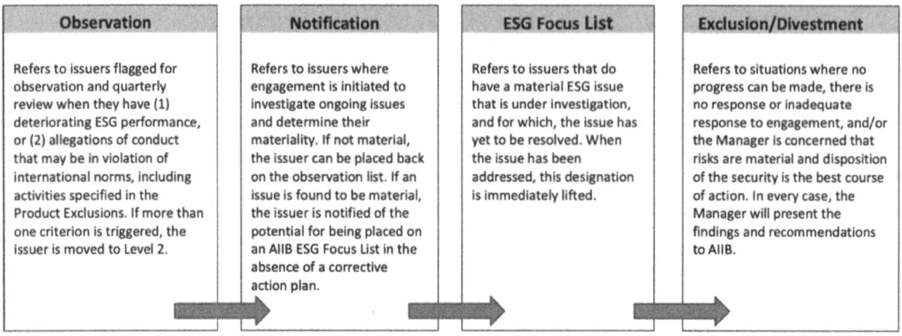

Fig. 3.1 Steps of the ESG Focus List and escalation process

	ESF Element	ESG Controversies
Environmental	Pollution Prevention Resource Efficiency Climate Change Biodiversity	• Local pollution • Overuse and wasting of resources • Global climate impacts • Impacts on critical habitats or protected areas
Social	Vulnerable Groups and Discrimination Indigenous Peoples Gender Involuntary Resettlement Cultural Resources Labor and Working Conditions	• Social discrimination • Impacts to Indigenous Peoples • Controversies related to involuntary resettlement • Impacts to cultural resources • Forced labor or child labor • Poor employment conditions • Occupational health and safety issues
Governance	Business Ethics Corporate Governance Transparency	• Corruption, bribery, extortion, money laundering • Fraud

Fig. 3.2 ESF elements for consideration during engagement with issuers

During engagement with issuers, the ESF elements to be considered (Fig. 3.2)[65] are pollution prevention, resource efficiency, climate change and biodiversity (in the environmental dimension); vulnerable groups and discrimination, Indigenous peoples, gender, involuntary resettlement, cultural resources and labour and working conditions (in the social dimension); and business ethics, corporate governance and transparency (in the governance dimension).

The above-mentioned steps, featuring incremental escalation, incentivize the bond issuers involved in ESG controversies to take corrective actions as agreed by the AIIB and to roll back in compliance with ESG standards. In this respect, the process indeed compensates for the accountability void left by the non-applicability of the PPM with respect to an ESG portfolio investment.[66] Regarding investment practices,

[65] Figure 3.2 is from the 'Guidelines for AIIB's ESG Focus List and Escalation Process', as annexed to ibid 9.

[66] 'The Policy on the PPM would not apply to the AIIB's operation of ESG portfolio investments'. AIIB ESF 2021 (n 42) para 14.

for example, the AIIB once engaged with a Russian steel company involved in environmental, health and safety controversies. The company then undertook corrective actions, including refraining from developing any coal production capacity, improving board oversight of ESG issues, and adopting the Investor Mining and Tailings Safety Initiative.[67]

There is a third project that may be categorized as atypical ESG portfolio investments. The AIIB, jointly with Clifford Capital, established a corporate platform in 2019, namely Bayfront Infrastructure Management, each subscribing 30% (US$54 million) and 70% (US$126 million) of the equity stock, respectively.[68] As a Singapore-based entity, Bayfront purchases infrastructure loans from banks (most of whom have adopted the Equator Principles), securitizes them and sells to institutional investors as rated and listed debt securities. Governing Bayfront's loan selection is neither the AIIB's ESF nor an ESG framework but rather Bayfront's own ESF, supplemented by a Sustainable Finance Framework for the sustainable tranche of the operation.[69] The first of its kind in Asia, the platform is expected to relieve 'financial institutions that currently originate and hold [infrastructure] loans to maturity but will increasingly be constrained from doing so with the advent of Basel III regulations',[70] serving the ultimate goal of 'infrastructure private capital mobilization', per the project name. In 2021, the AIIB made an anchor investment of US$60 million into a Bayfront-sponsored debt securities product, and it again agreed to defer to Bayfront's ESF.[71]

The AIIB sees the capital markets as holding the key to unlocking the trillions of dollars needed for infrastructure investment, and ESG approaches in debt capital markets lag behind those in equity. Learning from its own portfolio investments in ESG bond markets, the AIIB is expected to create new benchmarks for infrastructure investment over time, which 'could be an ESG index for Asia Emerging Markets or

---

[67] The story was told by Dong-Ik Lee, an AIIB Director General, in an interview with the online magazine Environmental Finance (n 55).

[68] AIIB, 'Project Summary Information: Infrastructure Private Capital Mobilization Platform' PD000274 (9 August 2019).

[69] This information is found in the project summary of a later project. See AIIB, 'Project Summary Information: Asia Infrastructure Securitization Program' P000492 (11 June 2021). The rationale for the derogation from the application of the AIIB ESP is that '[t]he ESP is designed for lending to conventional project finance investments and is not 'fit for purpose' for capital markets instruments'; see < https://www.aiib.org/en/projects/details/2021/_download/singapore/AIIB-PSI-Asia-Infra-Securitization-Project-vF.pdf > . Bayfront's ESF can be found at < https://www.bayfront.sg/environmental-social-framework > , and its Sustainable Finance Framework can be found at < https://www.bayfront.sg/sustainable-finance > .

[70] AIIB (n 68). Commercial banks and private capital are generally risk averse to infrastructure investment, which features longer maturities and uncertainty. Securitization thus relieves them of such disadvantages, as well as of the stringent capital adequacy requirements for investments involving longer maturities under Basel III.

[71] AIIB (n 69).

an index on infrastructure-related issuers',[72] that is, a guide for investors on ESG performance in Asia and infrastructure-related issuances, promoting infrastructure as an asset class. Such efforts should be welcomed, as they would be helpful to prevent greenwashing in the ESG bond market, whose relevant standards have been ill-defined so far.[73]

This type of frontier investment differs from a financial intermediary (FI) project, the financing structure of which involves the provision of funds to or through an FI for the project, with a much wider and more general investment scope.[74] Another difference is that the ESP still governs FI projects, where the FI nevertheless adopts an environmental and social management system. By contrast, the ESP in its entirety does not apply to an ESG portfolio investment. The third difference is that the accountability mechanism of the AIIB, i.e., the PPM, as discussed below in Sect. 3.5, is still applicable to an FI project, while it does not apply to an ESG portfolio investment, where, instead, the ESG Focus List and escalation process should apply. Incidentally, development financial institutions' investments through private equity funds, which are essentially of the FI type, should not be so greedy as to stretch into 'generalist' private equity funds; rather, they should focus on specialized funds to stay within the thematic orbit of development, as advocated in the recent report *BIO as a Sustainable Development Actor*.[75]

3.4 Use of Client Systems

The AIIB ESF demonstrates 'voluntarism, flexibility and incremental progress' by allowing subrogate use of client systems (UCS) to replace its own standards,[76] when the client systems are 'adequate to address the environmental and social risks and impacts of the Project' and 'materially consistent with the objectives of the ESP and relevant ESSs'.[77] Given that national law applies naturally within the territory of a borrower State, the UCS relieves the borrower of the burden of dual compliance with

[72] Courtney Lowrance, 'The Rise of Sustainable Capital Markets' (AIIB Blog, 12 July 2019) < https://www.aiib.org/en/news-events/media-center/blog/2019/The-Rise-of-Sustainable-Capital-Markets.html > .

[73] 'Greenwashing in Finance: Europe's Push to Police ESG Investing' (Financial Times, 10 March 2021); 'Sustainable Funds Must Work Harder to Vet Their Investments' (Financial Times, 4 August 2020).

[74] For example, in the case of AIIB, an FI project includes 'medium- to long-term corporate or project finance, lending to small and medium enterprises, trade finance, housing finance and micro-finance'. AIIB ESF 2021 (n 42) Vision, para 28. The IFC may invest in a similar FI project; see IFC Sustainability Framework (n 15) Policy on Environmental and Social Sustainability, para 32.

[75] G Jokubauskaite et al., 'The Belgian Investment Company for Developing Countries (BIO) as a Sustainable Development Actor' (April 2022) 43–53.

[76] The accurate name of the UCS in the AIIB ESF is 'use of country and corporate systems', which means that both private and public clients may be eligible for the UCS.

[77] AIIB ESF 2021 (n 42) ESP, para 54.1.

both the AIIB standards and domestic systems. It thus benefits the borrower with project flexibility and ownership.

The UCS originated in 2005, when the World Bank initiated the pilot use of country systems in a total of 15 projects in two consecutive phases,[78] mainly aimed at emerging economies with relatively strong legal systems and administrative capacities. However, interest in this 'escape clause' gradually dissipated because, as diplomatically stated, '[t]here is an inconsistency between client expectations of the purpose of UCS and that presumed by the Bank', among other reasons.[79] Mindful of the reputational risk involving the UCS, the World Bank maintained an obligation of supervision, rather than transferring safeguard responsibilities to clients, which effectively increased the time and cost of project preparation and supervision, rather than decreasing them as intended.[80] Worse, the experimental UCS was project-based and did not automatically extend to subsequent projects and other sectors. Consequently, the UCS has rarely been practiced ever since, if at all.[81]

The UCS of the AIIB first appeared in the 2016 ESF. Like others,[82] it has not yet been implemented in lending practices. The AIIB may share similar concerns as the World Bank in applying the UCS. That is, in the eyes of critics, the UCS represents a 'discourse–content–decoupling' strategy entailing decoupling the high-standard discourse advanced by the ESF from its actually moderate content in response to competing legitimacy demands from the borrower State on the one hand and human rights-oriented audiences on the other.[83] Given timing convergence, the AIIB's UCS drafting work presumably may have interacted with that of the World Bank in 2016. Three major points are worth elaborating after a comparative reading of both texts, which are similar to each other.

---

78 World Bank, 'Safeguards and Sustainability Policies in a Changing World: An Independent Evaluation of World Bank Group Experience' (World Bank 2010) 85.

79 Ibid.

80 This counterproductive result is inferred from the interview conducted by the Independent Evaluation Group with World Bank officers. World Bank (n 78) 86.

81 The Eskom Project in South Africa is among the very few recent World Bank projects involving the UCS, and it is one of the largest projects (US$3.75 billion) the World Bank has financed. The project was initiated as a UCS pilot in 2009 and closed in 2021. World Bank, 'Eskom Investment Support Project' < https://projects.worldbank.org/en/projects-operations/document-detail/P116410?type=projects > .

82 Similarly, other MDBs that are authorized with the UCS, including the ADB and IDB, have not implemented the authority in investment projects. World Bank, 'Comparative Review of Multilateral Development Bank Safeguard Systems' (May 2015) ix, 111.

83 MVC Ormaza and FC Ebert, 'The World Bank, Human Rights, and Organizational Legitimacy Strategies: The Case of the 2016 Environmental and Social Safeguards' (2019) 32 Leiden Journal of International Law 487.

First, the principles on UCS eligibility are similarly worded for both Banks, emphasizing the client system's 'material consistency' with ESF standards.[84] Where both the World Bank and the AIIB affirm that the client system comprises three elements, namely competent authorities, applicable laws, and implementation capacity,[85] there are no detailed methods for assessing their 'material consistency' with the ESF,[86] thus rendering enormous discretion or 'flexibility' to both Banks' investment teams. There are three specific aspects of concerns[87]: (i) it is unclear whether the borrowers' systems are anchored to the objectives of the ESF, to the requirements of the relevant ESSs, or both; (ii) the objectives of the ESF are considered to be too vague for a 'material consistency' test and need clarifications; and (iii) the definition of 'material consistency', as well as the methodology of determining it, is lacking. Suppose that the assessment is focused on the objectives of the ESF. It will wield too much discretion for the Bank team, and the Bank standards risk being rendered futile. If it is anchored to the specific requirements of the ESF, it will be challenging for the Bank team to conclude 'material consistency', at least at the level of legal texts. This is because 'no two leaves are alike', let alone vastly different local systems among borrower countries. To strike a fine balance, a good reference may be the Eskom Project, which examined South Africa's domestic legal system and concluded broad consistency with 'the objectives and applicable operational principles' as set out in the World Bank's safeguards.[88]

Second, the issue of human rights is particularly challenging for the assessment of 'material consistency'. The protection of human rights is an integral part of the ESF, as it is inherently embodied in such ESF standards as involuntary resettlements, the protection of Indigenous people, the prohibition of forced labour, etc. However,

---

[84] The World Bank seems satisfied with a relatively soft principle, i.e. the UCS 'is likely to address the risks and impacts of the project'. However, what difference the wording choices of 'be likely to' for the World Bank and 'adequate' for the AIIB would make in practice is yet unknown. See IBRD Environmental and Social Framework (ESF) < https://thedocs.worldbank.org/en/doc/837721522762050108-0290022018/original/ESFFramework.pdf > ESP, para 23. AIIB ESF 2021 (n 42) ESP, para 54.1.

[85] Dann has commented interestingly that the three criteria in the test of a client system all involve *legal and administrative* rather than economic performance. This shows that '[s]overeignty becomes contingent upon good governance', and the World Bank eventually becomes the arbiter of sovereignty. P Dann and M Riegner, 'The World Bank's Environmental and Social Safeguards and the Evolution of Global Order' (2019) 32 Leiden Journal of International Law 559.

[86] The World Bank used to draft a working methodology as guidance for its project team to make such an assessment, which remained very vague in text, nevertheless. World Bank, 'Information Note: Assessing the Borrower's Environmental and Social Framework' (4 August 2016). It should be noted that the information note's applicability is yet unknown, given its working draft status as presented on the World Bank website.

[87] Parties with such concerns include the US government and a few civil society organizations, as revealed during the consultation phase of the World Bank ESF. World Bank, 'Review and Update of the World Bank's Environmental and Social Safeguard Policies Phase 3 Feedback Summary (US)' (24–26 February 2016).

[88] World Bank, 'Inspection Panel Investigation Report (Report No. 64977-ZA) on South Africa: Eskom Investment Support Project' (IBRD Loan No. 78620-ZA) (21 November 2011) < https://www.inspectionpanel.org/panel-cases/eskom-investment-support-project > paras 170–194.

the definition of 'human rights' varies starkly between donor and borrower countries, as well as among other stakeholders. As expected, the topic of human rights was politically sensitive during the development of the ESF. The ESF in principle encourages borrower countries to respect human rights in projects the AIIB finances, but 'all in a manner consistent with its Articles of Agreement',[89] i.e., subject to non-intervention in the political affairs of borrower countries.[90] This is concurred with in the ESF of the World Bank.[91] The AIIB further affirms that the protection of human rights should take care of 'local conditions',[92] which essentially means deferring to national law. The term 'local conditions', nevertheless, fails to appear in the World Bank's ESF. While the principled approaches to human rights are generally shared by the MDBs, they risk watering down the protection of local people in the eyes of some critics.[93] Human rights are, after all, stipulated 'voluntarily and flexibly' in the non-binding vision statement of the ESF for both the World Bank and the AIIB,[94] rather than in the relatively strong ESP or ESSs.[95] That said, local people under the

---

[89] AIIB ESF 2021 (n 42) Vision, para 13.

[90] 'The Bank, its President, officers and staff shall not interfere in the political affairs of any member, nor shall they be influenced in their decisions by the political character of the member concerned. Only economic considerations shall be relevant to their decisions.' AIIB AOA (n 3) 31(2).

[91] The World Bank's ESF supports human rights 'in a manner consistent with its Articles of Agreement' (IBRD ESF (n 84) Vision, para 3), specifying that the World Bank should make funding decisions with no regard to political or non-economic influences or considerations and should refrain from interfering in the political affairs of members. See IBRD, 'Articles of Agreement' < https://www.worldbank.org/en/about/articles-of-agreement/ibrd-articles-of-agreement > art III, Sect. 3.5(b) and art IV, Sect. 10.

[92] AIIB ESF 2021 (n 42) Vision, para 13. This interpretation may be inferred from a general encompassing statement at the beginning of the same paragraph, which states that 'The Bank believes that social development and inclusion are critical for sound development. For the Bank, inclusion means empowering people to participate in and benefit from the development process in a manner consistent with *local conditions*'; ibid (emphasis added).

[93] Jokubauskaite has even commented that '[t]he choice of *not* addressing human rights in the [IBRD] ESF gives more discretion for the borrower to opt for mitigation and compensation measures, rather than trying to ensure more effective prevention of human rights violations'. G Jokubauskaite, 'The World Bank Environmental and Social Framework in a Wider Realm of Public International Law' (2019) 32 Leiden Journal of International Law 462 (emphasis in original).

[94] A critique of the positioning of human rights in the vision statement is available at European Parliamentary Research Service, 'Asian Infrastructure Investment Bank: How Lean, Clean and Green is the AIIB?' (February 2021) 8.

[95] Under the AIIB ESF 2021 (n 42), ESS 3 ('Indigenous Peoples') states its objective as 'to design and implement Projects in a way that fosters full respect for Indigenous Peoples' identity, dignity, [and] human rights'; under the IBRD ESF (n 84), ESS 7 ('Indigenous Peoples') states its objective as 'to ensure that the development process fosters full respect for the human rights'; and under the IFC Sustainability Framework (n 15), Policy on Environmental and Social Sustainability and Performance Standard 1 both recognise 'the responsibility of business to respect human rights', and Performance Standard 7 states its objective as 'to ensure that the development process fosters full respect for the human rights'. Nevertheless, all these are considered to be limited for human rights protection.

UCS may still resort to the PPM for human rights protection,[96] as relevant to specific ESF standards.

Third, the AIIB seems less ambitious than the World Bank in strengthening the borrowers' systems by means of the UCS. The World Bank has placed the strengthening of borrowers' systems at the core of the UCS, starting with the pilot UCS in 2005, and its ESF reinforces this endeavor, stipulating an 'overview assessment' at the borrower level, independent of the conventional project-level assessment.[97] The overview assessment is devoted to strengthening the borrowers' systems by 'identify[ing] aspects of the existing framework that can be strengthen[ed], and the capacity-building needed to support this',[98] and is expected to contribute to 'the ultimate victory of the Bank's good governance agenda'.[99]An overview assessment, by helping to strengthen the borrowers' systems, would then contribute to the prospect of scaling up their use in subsequent projects, which is in the interest of rising economies.[100] The logic here is that the UCS is contingent upon assessment of the borrowers' systems; the higher the standards of the latter, the more likely the UCS is to be used.

By contrast, the AIIB seems to take a moderate approach to strengthening the borrowers' systems. A comparative reading of the ESF texts of both Banks leads to this conclusion. First, the title of the World Bank's UCS is '[u]se and *strengthening* of borrower's environmental and social framework' (emphasis added), while it is '[u]se of country and corporate systems' for the AIIB. Second, the gap-filling measures identified during the project-level assessment of UCS are explicitly used to strengthen the borrowers' systems in the World Bank, but there is no equivalent provision in the ESF of the AIIB. And third, compared to the World Bank, the AIIB lacks a corresponding 'overview assessment' provision, and its assessment of the UCS is made on a project-by-project basis.[101] However, the AIIB may also decide the UCS 'for a specific sector or specific Client',[102] which, notwithstanding in an implicit form, may be understood as an incremental step toward an 'overview assessment'. The rationale behind the AIIB's approach is probably to avoid being read otherwise as an excessive intrusion in national politics, and, if so, it amounts to a balancing of 'voluntarism' and 'incremental progress'.

---

[96] 'Use of a Client's systems (including in situations described in Sect. 61, Adoption by the Client of a Development Partner's Environmental and Social Policy) does not preclude access of Project-affected people to the Project-level [Grievance Redress Mechanism, or GRM] or to the PPM.' AIIB ESF 2021 (n 42) ESP, para 59.3.

[97] IBRD ESF (n 84) ESP, para 29.

[98] Ibid.

[99] Dann and Riegner (n 85).

[100] This prospect echoes the call of major rising economies, such as Brazil, India and South Africa, during the consultations leading up to the World Bank's 2016 ESF. It also increases the attraction of the UCS to them. As Jokubauskaite has commented, these economies are probably the main 'winners' of the ESF reform. Jokubauskaite (n 93).

[101] AIIB ESF 2021 (n 42) ESP, para 54.

[102] Ibid ESP, para 55.

It is noted that the World Bank conditions the overview assessment upon the request of the borrower, plus the Bank's own feasibility study.[103] Drawing on this observation, the AIIB is advised to incorporate the system of overview assessment to scale up the use of the UCS in the next round of ESF revisions, a gesture of 'incremental progress' itself. Alternatively, the Multilateral Cooperation Center for Development Finance (MCDF), an international initiative hosted by the AIIB, may compensate for this void, as the MCDF is dedicated to a primary mandate of capacity building in both new partners (mainly banks) and beneficiary countries (mainly low-income countries) to help them to adopt and apply high standards in environmental and social aspects.[104]

3.5 Private Complaints and Dispute Settlement

What legal remedies are available for the local community adversely affected in environmental or social aspects by an AIIB-financed project? The AIIB establishes the PPM to address the issue.[105] Formally independent of the ESF, the PPM investigates project-related environmental and social complaints and identifies harms caused by Bank staff's non-compliance with the ESP. Bank management, in response, decides corrective actions to redress such grievances. Institutionally, the PPM is independent from Bank management and reports directly to the Board of Directors, who exercise oversight and supervisory power with respect to Bank management. Accountability mechanisms, as they are known among other MDBs, are an instrument by which private actors can hold an international organization directly accountable for the consequences of its failure to follow its own rules and procedures. It builds a legally significant non-contractual relationship between an international organization and private parties.[106]

The PPM encompasses three distinct functions: project processing queries, dispute resolution, and compliance review.[107] The function of 'project processing queries' refers to the quick resolution of private concerns over simple matters, for example,

---

[103] IBRD ESF (n 84) ESP, para 29.

[104] MCDF, 'Partnering to Advance High-quality Infrastructure and Connectivity' (2021) 13, 23–25.

[105] The AIIB Charter requires the Board of Directors to establish an oversight mechanism to supervise Bank operations (AIIB AOA (n 3) art 26(iv)). The 2016 ESF of the AIIB required the oversight mechanism to be established to receive private complaints over environmental and social harms caused by a Bank-financed project (AIIB ESF 2021 (n 42) ESP, para 64). In December 2018, the PPM was formally established by the Policy on the PPM, the Directive on the PPM and the Rules of Procedure of the PPM, all entering into effect on 31 March 2019.

[106] DD Bradlow, 'International Organizations and Private Complaints: The Case of the World Bank Inspection Panel' (1994) 34 Virginia Journal of International Law 554.

[107] The complex functions may well explain why the Complaints-resolution, Evaluation and Integrity Unit (CEIU), as the administrator of the PPM, changed the meaning of its initial letter C in its name from the original 'compliance' (confined to the third function) to the current 'complaints-resolution'.

over complaints involving project dust and noise.[108] The function of 'dispute resolution' is to resolve disputes between the client (a borrower government, typically) and private actors, facilitating a voluntary agreement through mediation or by other means.[109] This function may expand and encompass other stakeholders, such as contractors.[110] The third function, 'compliance review', points to complaints from private parties over the AIIB's failure to adhere to its own ESP, corresponding to the traditional accountability mechanism in the MDBs. The AIIB streamlines the three functions under one roof, establishing implementation methods for each and catering for the nature and degree of seriousness of the dispute involved. This marks a major innovation in the design of an accountability mechanism among leading MDBs.[111]

Private parties are free to choose which function they wish to pursue and to cease it at any time in order to resort to another that is deemed more appropriate.[112] This reflects 'voluntarism and flexibility' in resolving disputes. In 2020, the World Bank revised its accountability mechanism, adding the 'dispute resolution' function for the

---

[108] AIIB Policy on the PPM (n 6) para 2.1.1. The function of 'project processing queries', while being similar to the World Bank's Grievance Redress Service (GRS) in terms of attempting to resolve a private concern promptly, differs in two respects. First, the scope of complaints subject to the GRS is much wider and may well extend any complaint type subject to an Inspection Panel review. Second, the GRS is an internal accountability system, reporting to World Bank senior management, while the PPM, through the Managing Director of the CEIU, reports to the Board. See also World Bank, 'Grievance Redress Service' < https://www.worldbank.org/en/projects-operations/products-and-services/grievance-redress-service >.

[109] The result may take the form of 'a time-bound and monitorable dispute resolution agreement or memorandum of understanding' between the disputing parties, and the PPM is responsible for monitoring its implementation. AIIB, 'Rules of Procedure of the PPM' (21 December 2018) < https://www.aiib.org/en/policies-strategies/operational-policies/policy-on-the-project-affected-mechanism.html > (Rules of Procedure of the PPM) para 6.6.

[110] Ibid para 6.6.1. By comparison, under the World Bank's accountability mechanism, the newly added dispute resolution service, as applying between the borrower and a private complainant, does not explicitly deal with any extension to such other stakeholders, though it may do so in practice, upon agreement between the borrower and the complainant. The World Bank Accountability Mechanism (8 September 2020) < https://www.inspectionpanel.org/sites/www.inspectionpanel.org/files/documents/AccountabilityMechanismResolution.pdf > para 9.

[111] No other major MDBs merge the three functions, let alone distinguish the 'project processing queries' function from others. For example, the IFC's accountability mechanism, the Compliance Advisor Ombudsman, has the two functions of dispute resolution and compliance, while lacking an explicit mandate of dealing with project processing queries ('IFC/MIGA Independent Accountability Mechanism (CAO) Policy' (28 June 2021) paras 62–146). Similarly, the EBRD's accountability mechanism, the Independent Project Accountability Mechanism, distinctively has two functions of problem solving and compliance; the problem-solving function, by definition 'supports dialogue between Requesters and Clients to resolve the environmental, social and public disclosure issues underlying a Request, without attributing blame or fault.' EBRD, 'Project Accountability Policy' (April 2019) Section III, para 1.1.a.

[112] The limitation on private parties' freedom of choice is eligibility of submissions (*inter alia*, parallel pursuit of remedy is disallowed under the Policy on the PPM (n 6) para 5.2.5), plus time limits for filing submissions (Rules of Procedure of the PPM (n 109) paras 4–5). The eligibility requirements, common among the MDBs' independent accountability mechanisms (IAMs), are quite extensive, a point of criticism concerning the effectiveness of IAMs.

first time,[113] which is, nevertheless, embedded 'in the context of [an] Inspection Panel Request for Inspection',[114] in contrast to the AIIB, where dispute resolution is independent of compliance review. Meanwhile, under the World Bank's new Inspection Panel procedure in 2020, the past practice wherein an investigation by the Inspection Panel required approval from the Executive Board is essentially gone[115]; similarly, the IFC's Compliance Advisor Ombudsman (CAO) holds the power to decide an investigation and does not have to seek the Board's approval.[116] By contrast, Board approval power appears to remain in the AIIB.[117] The AIIB should learn from the World Bank and the IFC and change the approval power of the Board to no more than a formality (i.e., a judgement on the technical review criteria rather than on the merits of the claimant's request) in the next review of its PPM as another way of making 'incremental progress'.

Two specific aspects deserve close examination when comparing the accountability mechanisms of the AIIB and the World Bank. First, compliance review (or investigation) is carried out by a project-specific task force led by the Managing Director of the Complaints-resolution, Evaluation and Integrity Unit (CEIU) in the AIIB,[118] while in the World Bank, it is led by the Inspection Panel. The AIIB task force

[113] The World Bank initiated the first accountability mechanism of the kind among MDBs in 1993, under which the Inspection Panel has since been at the core, and compliance review was its single function until 2020 when the new service 'dispute resolution' was added. A succinct description of the establishment of the World Bank accountability mechanism in earlier years can be found in B Gu, *The Law and Governance of the Asian Infrastructure Investment Bank* (Wolters Kluwer 2019) 129.

[114] It means that the dispute resolution service is available only upon authorization of an Inspection Panel investigation. The World Bank Accountability Mechanism (n 110) paras 7, 9 and 11.

[115] 'If the Panel so recommends, the Executive Directors will authorize an investigation without making a judgment on the merits of the claimants' request' (The World Bank Inspection Panel Resolution (8 September 2020) para 29). The Board's exclusive authority to authorize or deny a full investigation led to significant politicization of the Panel process in the initial years; nevertheless, the Board has approved every Panel recommendation for an investigation since the 1999 Clarifications (paragraph 9 of which requiring the Board's approval). D Hunter, 'Using the World Bank Inspection Panel to Defend the Interests of Project-affected People' (2003) 201 Chicago Journal of International Law 206.

[116] In exceptional cases of doubt as to whether the technical review criteria have been met, IFC management may request that the Board of Directors review the CAO's decision to investigate. IFC/MIGA Independent Accountability Mechanism (n 111) para 107.

[117] 'If the PPM decides to recommend approval of the commencement of the Compliance Review or other appropriate course of action, it submits its recommendation to the Board for approval. ... If the Board approves a recommendation to commence the Compliance Review ....' Rules of Procedure of the PPM (n 109) para 6.7.3(d) and (g).

[118] The CEIU, a unique unit created within the AIIB, assists the non-resident Board in playing an oversight role to strengthen Bank accountability and effectiveness. The head of the CEIU (i.e. the Managing Director) advises management, while being independent and reporting directly to the Board of Directors. AIIB, 'Annual Report and Accounts' (2016) < https://www.aiib.org/en/news-events/annual-report/2016/home/index.html > 9.

is composed of outside experts and internal staff and functions on an ad hoc basis,[119] while the Inspection Panel is a standing body of three independent experts, supported by a secretariat.[120] The AIIB's CEIU secretariat, besides supporting compliance review, also supports the other two functions of the PPM (i.e., project processing queries and dispute resolution)[121]; in the World Bank, by comparison, an additional Accountability Mechanism Secretary, leading its own secretariat, is established to oversee the new function of dispute resolution,[122] and it is independent of the Inspection Panel's secretariat.[123] One may thus conclude that the compliance review function in the AIIB is informal, flexible and efficiency-oriented. While the arrangement reflects the trademark culture of 'leanness' within the AIIB, it may well elicit criticism for lacking elements of rule of law and formality. Furthermore, the Managing Director of the CEIU is burdened with three major responsibilities under one roof: project evaluations, the PPM and business sanctions.[124] One may doubt whether it is sufficiently well-resourced to live up to those complex mandates.[125]

Second is the matter of whether the accountability mechanism (the PPM in the case of the AIIB) is contingent upon the exhaustion of project-level remedies. Both the AIIB and the World Bank require their clients to establish a project-level remedy system, which is expected to facilitate the solution of most project-related disputes,

---

[119] Rules of Procedure of the PPM (n 109) Attachment 1 'Overview of the PPM' states, *inter alia*, that '[p]roject-specific Task Force members are selected with regard to the nature of the submission and the expertise required'.

[120] The Inspection Panel secretariat currently comprises nine devoted staff. For an overview, see < https://www.inspectionpanel.org/about-us/meet-panel > .

[121] Although 'the PPM is assisted by a Secretariat', as stipulated, the PPM secretariat seems inseparable from the CEIU secretariat because the former is headed by a staff of the latter. Further details about the PPM secretariat are lacking. Rules of Procedure of the PPM (n 109) Attachment 1 'Overview of the PPM'.

[122] See the description of the Accountability Mechanism Secretary and its secretariat, in The World Bank Accountability Mechanism (n 110) paras 3–5, 10.

[123] However, the Accountability Mechanism Secretary indeed plays a certain role with respect to the Inspection Panel, since a dispute resolution service is initiated in the context of the Inspection Panel. The World Bank Accountability Mechanism (n 110) para 8 (c) and (d).

[124] The three responsibilities of the CEIU are officially described as follows: For project evaluations, 'to selectively assess the quality and results (for completed projects) of the Bank's ongoing and completed portfolio'; for the PPM, 'to serve as the focal point for external requests or complaints regarding compliance with the AIIB's ESP under the PPM Policy'; and for business sanctions, 'to investigate project-related fraud and corruption cases under the Policy on Prohibited Practices'. Terms of Reference for the CEIU (10 July 2019) < https://www.aiib.org/en/about-aiib/governance/_common/_download/toR-for-the-CEIU.pdf > Section A.

[125] BY February 2022, the CEIU secretariat had no more than 10 staff, the number of which is expected to increase as Bank operations develop. The head of the CEIU also seems to have gained more importance in the AIIB's corporate hierarchy, since the position was initially titled Director General, as stated in AIIB, 'Policy on Prohibited Practices' (8 December 2016) < https://www.aiib.org/en/policies-strategies/operational-policies/prohibited-practices.html > Sect. 9.2, and has now been renamed and upgraded to Managing Director. Furthermore, potential conflict of interest exists between those mandates, as recognized in the Rules of Procedure of the PPM (n 109) Attachment 1 'Overview of the PPM', paras 7–9.

thereby conserving Bank-level resources for the most needed or difficult ones.[126] The AIIB explicitly puts forth that the PPM is available to project-affected people 'when their Project-related concerns cannot be addressed satisfactorily through Project-level [Grievance Redress Mechanisms, or GRMs] or the Bank's management processes'.[127] In other words, the complainant's submission must demonstrate good faith in trying to resolve the dispute locally before submitting to the PPM or, to the satisfaction of the PPM, why it has been unable to do so.[128] Thus, the AIIB generally adopts an approach of 'exhaustion of project-level remedies', which might nevertheless invite criticism over deprivation of freedom of choice for project-affected people and thus stain the credibility of the mechanism.[129] The World Bank, by contrast, does not require the exhaustion of project-level remedies prior to the procedure of the Inspection Panel,[130] relieving a complainant of the fear of retaliation (in appearance, at least), which is likely to be inflicted at the project level, but the complainant still needs to first address the concerns to the World Bank management, before turning to the Inspection Panel.[131] The Inspection Panel answers, after all, to the Executive Board and is the last resort for the complainant, as is the position of PPM within the AIIB. Another point to note is that the PPM considers a complaint '[related] to matters concurrently under arbitral or judicial review' as ineligible,[132] probably to avoid forum shopping or parallel pursuit of remedy by the complainant,

---

[126] AIIB ESF 2021 (n 42) ESP, para 71. The World Bank requires 'the Borrower to provide a grievance mechanism, process, or procedure to receive and facilitate resolution of concerns and grievances of project-affected parties arising in connection with the project'. IBRD ESF (n 84) ESP, para 60.

[127] AIIB ESF 2021 (n 42) ESP, para 72; Policy on the PPM (n 6) para 2.1.

[128] A submission is ineligible if '[t]he Requestors have not made good faith efforts to resolve the issues with the Project-level GRM and with Management or have not indicated to the satisfaction of the PPM why they have been unable to do so' (Policy on the PPM (n 6) para 5.1.8). The key terms here are 'good faith' and 'to the satisfaction of the PPM', which may refer to such particular reasons as non-functioning of the project-level system or a legitimate fear of retaliation for using the system, as stipulated in Rules of Procedure of the PPM (n 109) para 5.1.8.

[129] L Pike, '"China's World Bank" is Making it Easier to Complain' (China Dialogue, 19 February 2019). K Geary and D Schäfer, 'The Accountability Deficit: How the Asian Infrastructure Investment Bank's Complaints Mechanism Falls Short' (Recourse and Urgewald, October 2021) 16–17.

[130] See technical eligibility criteria for a submission under the Inspection Panel procedure: The World Bank Inspection Panel Resolution (8 September 2020) < https://www.inspectionpanel.org/sites/www.inspectionpanel.org/files/documents/InspectionPanelResolution.pdf > paras 13–15, 29.

[131] See IBRD ESF (n 84) ESP, para 61; The World Bank Inspection Panel Resolution (n 130) paras 14 and 29(c). These provisions stipulate a technical eligibility criterion of a submission under the Inspection Panel procedure, i.e. ask Bank management first. Admittedly, the criterion is essentially assertion-based and is easy for the complainant to meet.

[132] There are two points to note: first, as an exception, the Board of Directors may authorize the PPM to process the complaint; second, the requirement applies to requests for compliance review, irrelevant to project processing queries and requests for dispute resolution. Policy on the PPM (n 6) paras 5.2.4 and 6.8.5.

as well as to avoid conflict of resolution results.[133] It showcases the AIIB's willingness to cooperate with and even defer to other institutions (a sign of 'voluntarism and flexibility').[134] By comparison, the Inspection Panel of the World Bank is simply silent on this point during eligibility review.

The PPM is independent in nature, like any other independent accountability mechanism (IAM). It should be particularly so when the PPM carries out the compliance review function. That is why the PPM is formally independent from the Bank management, and the Managing Director of the CEIU reports to the Board of Directors. Meanwhile, the concept of independence does not mean that the PPM cannot work closely with management and staff. Instead, 'a cooperative working relationship between compliance function and business units should help to identify and manage compliance risks at an early stage'.[135] The PPM should lean toward the Oriental wisdom of advisory engagement, not the Western style of adversary checks, along the spectrum of oversight between the AIIB's non-resident Board and management that best suits the Asian gene of the Bank and its purposes.[136]

3.6 Indigenous Peoples: FPIC or FPICon?

Another highly contentious issue is whether the free, prior and informed consent (FPIC) of indigenous peoples is required if a Bank-financed project affects their land or other resources. FPIC is a specific right of indigenous peoples recognized in the United Nations Declaration on the Rights of Indigenous Peoples (UNDRIP),[137] a General Assembly resolution adopted in 2007 and serving as a guide for MDBs in implementing the FPIC process. With variants of the term, for example, 'free, prior

---

[133] However, critics have argued that the arrangement limits local people's freedom of choice. Geary and Schäfer (n 129) 19.

[134] In practice the PPM has not received a single complaint since its establishment in 2019. While the short existence of the PPM contributes to the status quo, eligibility is a big problem. Among other matters as discussed above, the alternative use of a co-financer's system is widespread in AIIB-financed projects, resulting in the ineligibility of the majority (72 out of the total 142 projects) for the PPM. Geary and Schäfer (n 129) 5, 11. To be sure, criticism of the accountability mechanism is not unique to the AIIB but is rather common among other IAMs. Another report reviewing 11 IAMs found that the eligibility process gets politicized, and fewer actual investigations have been made over the past 21 years; Center for International Environmental Law, 'Glass Half Full? The State of Accountability in Development Finance' (January 2016).

[135] M van Putten, *Policing the Banks: Accountability Mechanisms for the Financial Sector* (McGill-Queen's University Press 2008) 171, quoting the Basel Committee.

[136] For a detailed discussion of the AIIB Board's oversight power over management, see B Gu and C Xu, 'International Organizations and Corporate Governance: The Case of the AIIB' (2022) 30 Asia Pacific Law Review 309.

[137] 'Indigenous peoples shall not be forcibly removed from their lands or territories. No relocation shall take place without the *free, prior and informed consent* of the indigenous peoples concerned and after agreement on just and fair compensation and, where possible, with the option of return.' UNGA 'Declaration on the Rights of Indigenous Peoples' UN Doc A/RES/61/295 (2 October 2007) art 10 (emphasis added).

and informed consultation' (FPICon) for the AIIB and simply 'consent' for the ADB, the MDBs are never hesitant to define FPIC in their ESFs,[138] since the UNDRIP fails to offer a universally accepted definition. Those definitions are functionally equivalent, as they converge with more than they diverge from each other.[139]

The definitions of FPIC (including FPICon and consent) across MDBs generally comprise the following three indispensable elements: first, 'meaningful consultation', which allows for appropriate representation of Indigenous peoples, sufficient decision-making time for them and their effective participation in the lifecycle of the project[140]; second, 'broad (or collective) community support', entailing a majority of the affected Indigenous peoples and communities favoring the proposed activities, where no significant opposition exists[141]; and third, FPIC does not require unanimity and may be achieved even when some individuals or groups explicitly disagree with the project.[142] FPIC does not necessarily recognize a veto right of Indigenous people, as the MDBs accommodate the interests of borrowers.

If the criteria for establishing FPICon for the AIIB and FPIC for the World Bank, both specific to Indigenous peoples, are to be compared,[143] both apply to the project phases of preparation and implementation, as well as to outcomes; both build upon meaningful consultation and good faith negotiation; both document the negotiation process and results; and both have no unanimity requirement. Thus, one may find that they are functionally equivalent, if not identical. In the IFC's Sustainability

[138] For example, the EIB and the EBRD both define FPIC as the process whereby the affected community of Indigenous peoples arrives at a decision in accordance with their legal provisions, cultural traditions, customs and practices (World Bank (n 78) 35, 113). The ADB defines consent as 'a collective expression by the affected Indigenous Peoples communities, through individuals and/or their recognised representatives, of broad community support for the project activities. Such broad community support may exist even if some individuals or groups object to the project activities' (ADB, 'Safeguard Policy Statement' (July 2009) Glossary). The IFC defines FPIC as that which 'builds on and expands the process of [informed consultation and participation, ICP] and will be established through good faith negotiation between the client and the Affected Communities of Indigenous Peoples.' IFC (n 15) Performance Standard 7 ('Indigenous Peoples'), para 12.

[139] For example, the ADB holds that the combined requirements of meaningful consultation and broad community support are functionally equivalent to FPIC; and the EIB comments that the only difference between FPIC and 'free, prior and informed engagement', a term equivalent to FPICon as a standard for public consultation and participation, is that FPIC is specific to indigenous people as recognized in UNDRIP. World Bank (n 78) 20, 35, 114–115.

[140] For example, IBRD ESF (n 84) ESS7, para 23. An elaborate definition of 'meaningful consultation' is available in AIIB ESF 2021 (n 42) ESS1, para 23.

[141] If there is any significant opposition or major disagreement, it is resolved through good faith negotiations. ADB, 'Indigenous Peoples Safeguards: A Planning and Implementation Good Practice Sourcebook' (June 2013) 71.

[142] IBRD ESF (n 84) ESS7, para 25(d). AIIB ESF 2021 (n 42) ESP, para 69.2. AIIB President Jin Liqun commented as follows at the AIIB first annual meeting in 2016: 'Most people are rational; if 99 per cent of local households accept the compensation standard, then the 1 per cent dissenters have to pick up the money and move.' Quoted in B Gu, 'AIIB and Changing Standards in China' (The Straits Times, 28 July 2016).

[143] The criteria for establishing FPICon for the AIIB are found in the AIIB ESF 2021 (n 42) ESP, para 69.2, while the criteria for establishing FPIC for the World Bank are found in IBRD ESF (n 84) ESS7, paras 25–26.

Framework, for projects with adverse impacts on Indigenous peoples, 'informed consultation and participation' is normally sufficient[144]; FPIC is required only in a few special circumstances.[145] The criteria for establishing FPIC for the IFC are quite similar to those for the World Bank, emphasizing 'both process (i.e., good faith negotiation) and outcome (i.e., evidence of agreement)'[146] and also not requiring unanimity.

Finally, the AIIB explicitly acknowledges deferral to a FPIC system if its client so requires under national law,[147] once again exhibiting AIIB's respect for both high standards and national institutions. However, the different impact the requirement of FPICon in the AIIB ESF, in comparison with FPIC in other places, will make in actual practice remains to be seen. Nongovernmental and civil society organizations are, after all, still grumbling about the standard of FPIC in the World Bank ESF,[148] after winning the hard battle of helping to uplift the standard from FPICon,[149] as a symbol of enhanced safeguards for Indigenous peoples.

3.7 Concluding Remarks

The AIIB is at the forefront of environmental and social safeguards, along with other like-minded institutions in international development such as the World Bank and the IFC. Its ESF demonstrates both heritage and innovation, compared with that of the World Bank. It builds on more than three decades of law and practice in safeguards of the MDBs and blends it with the Asian wisdom of 'voluntarism, flexibility and incremental progress'.[150] Its innovation also lies in alternative uses of a co-financer's

---

[144] IFC (n 15) Performance Standard 1, para 32. 'Informed consultation and participation' is defined in ibid para 31.

[145] Those special circumstances are (i) impacts on lands and natural resources subject to traditional ownership or under customary use; (ii) relocation of Indigenous peoples from lands and natural resources subject to traditional ownership or under customary use; and (iii) where a project may significantly impact on critical cultural heritage; ibid Performance Standard 7, paras 13–17.

[146] IFC, 'Guidance Notes to Performance Standards on Environmental and Social Sustainability' (1 January 2012) < https://www.ifc.org/wps/wcm/connect/topics_ext_content/ifc_external_corporate_site/sustainability-at-ifc/publications/publications_policy_gn-2012 > 12.

[147] AIIB ESF 2021 (n 42) ESP, para 70.

[148] Critics have argued that FPIC is 'geared towards a negotiation in view of an agreement instead of the quest for an expression of self-determination. It does not allow for indigenous peoples to exercise dissent up front, nor to determine alone their decision-making process and their expression of consent .... FPIC really means "consultation-plus" rather than consent.' S de Moerloose, 'Indigenous Peoples' Free, Prior and Informed Consent (FPIC) and the World Bank Safeguards: Between Norm Emergence and Concept Appropriation' (2020) 53 World Comparative Law/VRU 237. See another critique of the World Bank's definition of FPIC in Ormaza and Ebert (n 83).

[149] FPICon was originally used in the World Bank's OP4.10 'Indigenous Peoples', a predecessor to the World Bank's 2016 ESF.

[150] A general criticism of the AIIB's innovative aspects can be found in Horta and Wang (n 47). The authors mainly advocate for more checks and balances and more transparency for the AIIB.

safeguards (and even accountability) system,[151] as well as that of a corporate client,[152] in lieu of its own in a spirit of collegiality and efficiency, provided that a 'material consistency' test is passed.

The institutions of both ESG portfolio investment and the UCS are 'escape clauses' in the AIIB's ESF, waiving the direct application of ESF standards. Specifically, on ESG portfolio investment, the AIIB should cooperate with its asset manager in carefully selecting and monitoring infrastructure-related green bonds by applying an operation-specific ESG framework that agrees with the AIIB ESF's 'spirit and vision'. ESG portfolio investment serves dual thematic priorities for the AIIB, i.e., green infrastructure and private capital mobilization, as stipulated in the Bank's Corporate Strategy of 2020.

On the other institution, the UCS, a general direction for the AIIB to pursue is to increase (and even mainstream) the use of national systems.[153] The UCS counts as a legal graduation strategy for borrower States with relatively strong domestic legal and administrative systems, while serving to enhance their project ownership and flexibility. Where the AIIB is to maintain a supervisory or monitoring role in the process of UCS, it should feature more of an advisory engagement in a bid to build the capacity of the client country, rather than imposing fervent checks and balances on the client. The AIIB is further advised to draw upon the World Bank's 'overview assessment' system, conditioning it on the request of the client and the AIIB's own feasibility study.

Indeed, the AIIB has been prudent in its practice of the UCS, since it is susceptible to criticism of deviation from Bank standards. The worry may be alleviated with the dispute resolution function in the PPM in place; in other words, the Bank-level grievance system is still available to complainants even in the UCS,[154] and high standards are bolstered accordingly. Where the AIIB may intervene in a dispute between a client and local people, this should be premised on the exhaustion of project-level remedies.

---

[151] 'Use of Co-financier's Independent Accountability Mechanism. If the Project is co-financed with another MDB, bilateral development organization or other development finance institution, and the Bank agrees to the application of the environmental and social policies and procedures of the co-financier (in lieu of the ESP) to the Project, the Bank may also agree to rely on the IAM of such co-financier (in lieu of the PPM) to handle submissions from Project-affected people.' AIIB ESF 2021 (n 42) ESP, para 73. Instead, the World Bank ESF states merely generally that '[w]here the Bank is jointly financing a project with other multilateral or bilateral funding agencies, the Bank will cooperate with such agencies and the Borrower in order to agree on a common approach for the assessment and management of environmental and social risks and impacts of the project'. IBRD ESF (n 84) ESP, para 9.

[152] By contrast, in the World Bank Group, only a country may be eligible for the UCS, while a private sector is not, since the IFC does not have a corresponding system in its Sustainability Framework.

[153] The governments of Brazil, China, India and South Africa all support and encourage the UCS to be a default choice, subject to the requirement of 'material consistency', as evidenced during the consultation phase leading up to the 2016 ESF of the World Bank.

[154] 'Use of a Client's systems ... does not preclude access of Project-affected people to the Project-level GRM or to the PPM.' AIIB ESF 2021 (n 42) ESP, para 59.3.

Both the World Bank and the AIIB deem the protection of human rights as non-binding in their respective ESF and condition it on non-intervention in member countries' domestic political affairs. The reading of the AIIB's new ESF easily reveals that the Bank is progressing in a delicate balance along the spectrum of Oriental wisdom regarding the 'role of law' at one end and Western wisdom of the 'rule of law' on the other for the general purpose of sustainable development, at the junction of which flexibility meets with formality and efficiency meets with justness. The observation is true with the AIIB, and it is even so for the World Bank, as it acknowledged in the *World Development Report* in 2017.[155] In this turbulent world, the development of the MDBs' environmental and social safeguards will be dynamic, with the destination of a *droit commun* still far away.[156]

---

[155] Featuring a rethinking of law and governance for effectiveness of development policies, the World Bank departs from its long-held manifesto, calling on the development community to think and do development differently from traditional technocratic approaches, and specifically to 'think not only about the *form* of institutions, but also about their *functions*; think not only about *capacity building*, but also about *power asymmetries*; think not only about *the rule of law*, but also about *the role of law*'. World Bank, 'World Development Report 2017: Governance and the Law' (2017) <https://www.worldbank.org/en/publication/wdr2017> 29, 71 and 279.

[156] While the safeguard systems demonstrate regulatory convergence across the MDBs, there are nuanced differences in many specific provisions. Specifically, discrepancies in the social sector seem even more significant than in the environmental sector, particularly with respect to the protection of human rights and Indigenous peoples' rights. On regulatory convergence and discrepancy across the MDBs' safeguards, see M Mbengue and S de Moerloose, 'Multilateral Development Banks and Sustainable Development: On Emulation, Fragmentation and a Common Law of Sustainable Development' (2017) 10 Law and Development Review 404.

Chapter 4
MCDF: A Multilateral Fund Administered by the AIIB

Summary The MCDF is an infant but prospectively important fund in international development finance, initiated by China at the inaugural Belt and Road Forum in 2017. The AIIB acts as the administrator of the MCDF financing facility, the host of the MCDF secretariat, as well as an implementing partner. Endorsed by eleven leading international development banks worldwide, the MCDF is expected to work closely with global agendas such as the BRI and the AIIB, as well as with other peer institutions including the GICA, the GI Hub, and the GIF, in pursuing their shared goals of promoting high-quality infrastructure and connectivity investment. This chapter endeavors to investigate some key institutional matters for the development of the MCDF; they are the structure of its Secretariat, the funding mechanism, and the designated functions. Along the spectrum of hardening soft law, the MCDF is expected to evolve as an independent international body, to be equipped with a charter as its constituent instrument. The prospect of China's role in the MCDF is predicated upon the understanding of Chinese culture and China's approach toward global governance, which has been consistently demonstrated during the development of the AIIB and the BRI. China will play a leadership role in the MCDF, while behaving responsibly to other participants, including to borrower countries.

This chapter originally appeared in *Journal of International Economic Law* (2020) 23 (3), entitled "MCDF:A New Beacon of Multilateralism in Development Finance"

B. Gu, *Chinese Multilateralism in the Asian Infrastructure Investment Bank (AIIB)*,
Modern China and International Economic Law,
https://doi.org/10.1007/978-981-97-1219-9_4

4.1 Introduction

China has been actively engaged in initiating a series of global public goods to the international community since the year 2013, under President Xi Jinping's appealing banner of "a community of shared future for mankind".[1] The Belt and Road Initiative (BRI), the Asian Infrastructure Investment Bank (AIIB), and the recent Multilateral Cooperation Center for Development Finance (MCDF) are most stellar of these efforts, which all happen to be in the area of infrastructure and connectivity investments.

The MCDF, compared with the BRI and the AIIB, is the youngest, and the least known to the public so far. It is a multilateral platform to foster high-quality infrastructure and connectivity for developing countries. To this end, the MCDF has three designated functions: to share information across development partners; to enhance relevant how-how and institutional capacity of developing countries; and to provide funding for project preparation, according to the MOU establishing the MCDF.[2] A major difference between the MCDF and the US-led Blue Dot Network is that the former has the money bags (with initial commitments of 180.3 million US dollars[3]), while the latter has all the brains, in particular by certifying infrastructure projects against certain benchmarks it designs.[4]

The MCDF activities are centered around the Finance Facility (responsible for capacity building and project preparation) and the Collaboration Platform (responsible for information sharing). The Governing Committee, the Finance Facility's decision-making body, comprises contributors who are either voting members (if they commit at least 10 million US dollars for a period of 5 years at most, currently China, Egypt, Hungary, and Saudi Arabia) or non-voting members (currently Cambodia,

---

[1] To understand China's perspective of world order featuring "a community of shared future for mankind", see President Xi Jinping's UN speech in 2015. Xi Jinping, "Working Together to Forge a New Partnership of Win-win Cooperation and Create a Community of Shared Future for Mankind", at the General Debate of the 70th Session of the UN General Assembly on September 28, 2015.

http://gadebate.un.org/sites/default/files/gastatements/70/70_ZH_en.pdf (visited December 23, 2019)

[2] The MOU's full name is "Memoranda of Understanding on Collaboration on Matters to Establish the Multilateral Cooperation Center for Development Finance" (dated March 25, 2019, hereinafter "the 2019 MOU of the MCDF"), and the text is available at https://www.aiib.org/en/about-aiib/who-we-are/partnership/_download/collaboration-on-matters.pdf (visited September 22, 2019).

[3] MCDF, "Partnering to advance high-quality infrastructure and connectivity" (2021 Annual Report) p.34.

[4] Blue Dot Network is "a multi-stakeholder initiative that brings together governments, the private sector, and civil society to promote high-quality, trusted standards for global infrastructure development in an open and inclusive framework", according to the US International Development Finance Corporation (DFC), i.e., the lead pusher behind the plan. Unveiled by the US Overseas Private Investment Corporation (OPIC, i.e., the predecessor of the DFC), Australia's Department of Foreign Affairs and Trade (DFAT), and Japan Bank for International Cooperation (JBIC) in November 2019, Blue Dot Network is considered as the US's major counteraction against the challenge of the BRI. DFC, "The Launch of Multi-Stakeholder Blue Dot Network", November 4, 2019, https://www.dfc.gov/media/opic-press-releases/launch-multi-stakeholder-blue-dot-network (visited March 6, 2020).

Lao PDR, and Philippines).[5] Decisions of the Governing Committee are made by consensus among the voting members.[6] On the other hand, the Coordination Committee, overseeing the Collaboration Platform, consists of 11 multilateral development bank (MDB) parties to the 2019 MOU of the MCDF and seven founding contributors to the MCDF Finance Facility. Decisions of the Coordination Committee are made by consensus among the members present at the meeting. Established in 2020, the MCDF is at an early stage of development.

This chapter focuses on this infant but prospectively important initiative in international development finance. In Sect. 4.2 it offers a brief introduction of the genesis of the MCDF. In Sect. 4.3 it discusses the MCDF's relationship with the BRI and the AIIB, arguing that they are compatible with, and conducive to, each other, according to the doctrine of implied powers or from a teleological legal perspective. Section 4.4 discusses the MCDF's relationship with three peer mechanisms, i.e., the GICA, the GI Hub, and the GIF, foreseeing a competitive cooperation relationship among them. Section 4.5 addresses some important institutional matters relating to the establishment of the MCDF, including: how the MCDF Secretariat is to be run; how the MCDF is to be funded; and how to carry out the functions as designated. Section 4.6 takes a forward look at the MCDF as an independent international body. In this section it discusses in particular a prospective constituent charter and China's role in the MCDF. Section 4.7 concludes.

4.2 Genesis of the MCDF

Globalization and multilateralism have been experiencing tremendous ups and downs in the aftermath of the 2008 Global Financial Crisis. China had learnt, in the wake of the Crisis, that overdependence on the traditional international institutions in trade and finance—dominated by the West, and mostly by the US—was dangerous. China decided to push for the reform of global economic governance by means of "walking on two legs":[7] while striving to realign the voting structure in traditional international organizations (such as the IMF and the World Bank) in favor of emerging powers and developing countries, it initiated new public goods ranging from the BRI and the AIIB in 2013, through to the MCDF in 2017.

China chose to start its contribution to global economic governance in the area of infrastructure and connectivity investments. Based upon its own success in over 40

[5] MCDF, "Partnering to advance high-quality infrastructure and connectivity" (2021 Annual Report) pp.11 and 34.

[6] Governing Instrument of the Finance Facility of the MCDF (May 15, 2020, hereinafter the "Governing Instrument") states in Article 9.2 that "Consensus shall be deemed to have been established in the absence of a request for a formal vote by any Voting Member. In the case of a formal vote, unanimity among Voting Members casting their votes shall be reached for all decisions otherwise requiring consensus."

[7] See my elaboration about China's strategy on "walk on two legs", Gu Bin, "Chinese Multilateralism in the AIIB", *Journal of International Economic Law* (2017) 20 (1), 137-158, at 143.

years of reform and opening up, where infrastructure building lays a solid ground, China is confident that infrastructure investment is vital to a country's economic development, and it is ready to project such experience into the international arena. Statistics indicate that infrastructure investment needs in Asia alone between the year 2016 and 2030 will be 26 trillion US dollars, equaling 1.7 trillion US dollars each year on average.[8] There is a large chunk of it yet to be met. But the key is not capital; rather it is to have institutions that can utilize capital effectively and efficiently. Those multilateral institutions led by China are committed to make it happen. In doing so China itself gets benefited as well, as it seeks to deepen domestic reforms by building a compatible international order.[9]

As early as the first Belt and Road Forum for International Cooperation (BRF), the BRI's top gathering event and held in Beijing in May 2017, an MOU under the BRI framework was signed among the Ministry of Finance of China and six leading MDBs: the Asian Development Bank (ADB), the AIIB, the European Bank for Reconstruction and Development (EBRD), the European Investment Bank (EIB), the New Development Bank (NDB), and the World Bank Group.[10] All signatory parties "agreed to work closely together to promote infrastructure and connectivity",[11] whereby China alone committed to establish the MCDF, regarding which China promised to "invite collaboration with the MDBs" in the MOU.[12] It marked the first time for the idea of the MCDF to float publicly, and the 2017 MOU was incorporated in the List of Deliverables of the inaugural BRF.[13]

The parties continued to discuss "actions to further the promotion of infrastructure and connectivity",[14] after the 2017 MOU of the BRI. Three more MDBs joined the discussion during the interval: the Corporación Andina de Fomento (CAF), the Inter-American Development Bank (IDB), and the International Fund for Agricultural Development (IFAD). But the NDB chose to drop out. Those parties, nine in total, signed the MOU establishing the MCDF on March 25, 2019, on the eve of the second BRF, which was held in Beijing in the next month. In that MOU, the MCDF's internal governance is sketched as thus: a Coordination Committee is responsible for providing strategic guidance to the MCDF, a Secretariat is to be established for the daily operation of the platform, and a funding facility is needed to support the

[8] AIIB Annual Report and Accounts 2016, at 7, quoting Asian Development Bank (ADB), "Meeting Asia's infrastructure needs" (2017).

[9] See my elaboration about the two-way impacts on China's domestic and international arena in infrastructure building, Gu Bin, *The Law and Governance of the Asian Infrastructure Investment Bank* (The Netherlands: Wolters Kluwer, 2019), at 11-14.

[10] The MOU's full name is "Memoranda of Understanding on Collaboration on Matters of Common Interest under the Belt and Road Initiative" (dated May 14, 2017, hereinafter "the 2017 MOU of the BRI"), and its text is available at https://www.ndb.int/wp-content/uploads/2018/09/MOU-on-BRI-signed.pdf (visited September 20, 2019).

[11] The quote is from the 2019 MOU of the MCDF, preamble.

[12] The 2017 MOU of the BRI, Article I.3.

[13] See the List of Deliverables of the First Belt and Road Forum for International Cooperation, http://www.xinhuanet.com/english/2017-05/15/c_136286376.htm (visited September 17, 2019).

[14] The quote is from the 2019 MOU of the MCDF, preamble.

MCDF's function. As expected, the establishment of the MCDF was endorsed by the second BRF and was incorporated in the List of Deliverables.[15] Later on, the NDB, the African Development Bank (AfDB), and the Islamic Development Bank (IsDB) joined the initiative, totaling eleven MDBs.[16]

The MCDF's Coordination Committee held its inaugural meeting in Washington D.C. on April 12, 2019, kicking off the formal establishment process.[17] A partnership seminar led by the Ministry of Finance of China was held in Beijing on January 15, 2020, and representatives from Britain, Jordan, Myanmar, and other countries, leading MDBs, international investment funds, and financial institutions of China attended it to learn more about the progress of the MCDF.[18] In May 2020, the MCDF Finance Facility was established based upon the Governing Instrument, which is the constituent instrument of the MCDF Finance Facility, as well as the MCDF in general, and the first contribution was made. In the following month, the AIIB Board of Directors approved for the AIIB to be the MCDF administrator and to establish and host the MCDF Secretariat.[19] In August 2021, the AIIB became the MCDF's first implementing partner, followed by the African Development Bank. By the end of 2021, the MCDF had approved its first three projects totaling 1.92 million US dollars.[20]

4.3 MCDF's Relationship with BRI and AIIB

As mentioned, the three important institutions—the BRI, the AIIB, and the MCDF—were all initiated by China. Respectively, the BRI is an international cooperative platform in a bid to enhance regional connectivity both within and between Asia, Europe, Africa, and other regions. The AIIB identifies two purposive elements in the

[15] See "List of Deliverables of the Second Belt and Road Forum for International Cooperation", April 27, 2019, http://www.beltandroadforum.org/english/n100/2019/0427/c36-1312.html (visited September 17, 2019).

[16] MCDF, "Partnering to advance high-quality infrastructure and connectivity" (2021 Annual Report) p.11. https://www.themcdf.org/en/what-we-do/annual-reports/2021/_common/pdf/MCDF-Report-2022-WEB.pdf (visited October 31, 2022).

[17] Ministry of Finance of China, "MCDF's Coordination Committee held its inaugural meeting in Washington D.C., USA" (in Chinese), April 12, 2019, http://gjs.mof.gov.cn/pindaoliebiao/gongzuodongtai/201904/t20190417_3227164.html (visited September 17, 2019).

[18] Ministry of Finance of China, "MCDF's Partnership Seminar was held in Beijing" (in Chinese), January 15, 2020, http://gjs.mof.gov.cn/gongzuodongtai2019/gongzuodongtai/202001/t20200121_3462976.htm (visited March 6, 2020).

[19] AIIB, "Directive on AIIB's Performance of its Role as the Administrator of the MCDF Finance Facility", February 5, 2021, https://www.aiib.org/en/about-aiib/who-we-are/role-of-law/.content/index/_download/Directive-on-AIIBs-Role-as-the-Administrator-of-the-MCDF-Finance-Facility.pdf (visited October 31, 2022).

[20] The timeline of MCDF development is available at MCDF, "Partnering to advance high-quality infrastructure and connectivity" (2021 Annual Report) p.15. https://www.themcdf.org/en/what-we-do/annual-reports/2021/_common/pdf/MCDF-Report-2022-WEB.pdf (visited October 31, 2022).

constituent instrument—Articles of Agreement (AOA): infrastructure connectivity and institutional cooperation.[21] And the MCDF vows to "serve as a platform to foster high-quality infrastructure and connectivity for developing countries".[22] Thus, the three international agendas do converge in purpose and mandate, all having their mandates focusing on one and the same area: infrastructure and connectivity investments.

In light of the shared object and purpose, it is sensible to argue that the three international institutions should be eligible to help and serve each other, given that there is no explicit provision against such cooperation. There are legal, theoretical, and historical grounds to support this argument.

Historically the teleological methodology, or the doctrine of implied powers, informed the constitutional development of a state, as well as that of an international organization. First, on the interpretation of a national constitution, one of the most telling examples is the early development of the US Constitution in the 18th century. Alexander Hamilton used the doctrine of implied powers masterfully to expand the powers of the federal government,including establishing a central bank, when he encountered a strong denial from James Madison, the chief architect of the Constitution, who argued that "Reviewing the Constitution…it was not possible to discover in it the power to incorporate a bank". Hamilton retorted by turning to Article 1.8 of the Constitution, a catchall clause giving Congress the right to pass any legislation deemed "necessary and proper" to exercise its listed powers, of which he argued for a liberal interpretation: "it is not denied that there are *implied* as well as *express* powers and that the former are as effectually delegated as the latter". Hamilton's interpretation won the support of both Congress and President Washington, ultimately giving birth to the Bank of the United States and making good on American early development.[23]

Second, the doctrine of implied powers also helps in understanding the constitution of an international organization. Take the creation of the International Center for Settlement of Investment Disputes (ICSID) by the World Bank during 1960s for example. The World Bank aims, among other purposes as designated in its charter, to promote private capital flow to developing countries.[24] But the charter is short of an explicit mandate to establish an independent dispute settlement institution focused on arbitrating disputes between foreign investors and host developing countries to help achieve such purpose. Aron Broches, then-General Counsel of the World Bank, used the doctrine of implied powers skillfully to make it happen, arguing that the cause of the ICSID would serve the Bank's purpose, and that the Bank's powers

---

[21] AIIB AOA Art. 1.1.

[22] Memoranda of Understanding on Collaboration on Matters to Establish the Multilateral Cooperation Center for Development Finance (March 25, 2019, hereinafter "the 2019 MOU of the MCDF"), Article I.1. The text of the MOU is available at https://www.aiib.org/en/about-aiib/who-we-are/partnership/_download/collaboration-on-matters.pdf (visited March 30, 2022).

[23] This story is best told by Ron Chernow, *Alexander Hamilton* (London: Head of Zeus, 2016), at 252, 350-355.

[24] International Bank for Reconstruction and Development (IBRD), AOA, Article 1.

were not limited to those that were granted in express terms.[25] Broches eventually persuaded the Bank's Executive Directors to pass a decision to establish the ICSID that eventually served to widen and deepen the flow of private capital to developing countries.

The Vienna Convention on the Law of Treaties (VCLT) of 1969 encompasses a wide variety of means of treaty interpretation, the foremost of which is that a treaty should be read according to the ordinary meaning in the context of purpose and object.[26] It is fair to say that a holistic interpretation, i.e., reading purpose into text, is appropriate, and the two possible extremes of textualism and purposivism are unacceptable. But when it comes to the interpretation of the constitution of an international organization, the element of purpose should, and tends to, be given more weight. This is because, enacted during the establishment of the international organization, a constitution cannot foresee all specific powers necessary to achieve the purpose stipulated in it, and thus it makes sense that the executive head of the organization be given sufficient discretion, provided that the exercise of such powers does not run counter to any explicit provision of the constitution. Even James Madison agreed that "For every new application of a general power, *the particular powers*, which are the means of attaining the *object* of the general power, must always necessarily vary with that object; and be often properly varied whilst the object remains the same."[27] Indeed, in each MDB's charter there is a standard provision to the effect that "the Bank shall be guided in all its decisions by the purposes ..."[28]

There is much support in doctrine, and in practice, for the view that "particular attention must be given to the object and purpose of the relevant constitution and the aims of the international organization concerned."[29] International court case studies find that strong support gives "a meaning to constitutional provisions that is most favorable for giving effect to the objectives of the organization".[30] For example, the International Court of Justice (ICJ) Judge Weeramantry stated that, in the interpretation of constitutions of international organizations, "particularly one which sets before itself certain sociological or humanitarian goals, the task of interpretation

[25] The position was expressed as follows by Broches in his 1959 lectures at the Hague Academy of International Law on The International Legal Aspects of the Operations of the World Bank:

...the Bank's powers are not limited to those that are granted in express terms. The fact that an operation or transaction is not expressly authorized or contemplated by a specific provision of the Articles, does not mean that the Bank has no power to undertake it. Whether it has or does not have a particular power must be determined in the light of the Bank's purposes, by which all the Bank's decisions must be guided.

Antonio R. Parra, *The History of ICSID* (Oxford: Oxford University Press, 2012), at 29 footnote 9, quoting Broches.

[26] The Vienna Convention on the Law of Treaties, Article 31.

[27] Alexander Hamilton, James Madison, and John Jay, *The Federalist Papers* (New York: Bantam Dell, 1982), *Federalist Papers*, No. 44, at 275.

[28] For example, IBRD AOA Art.1.

[29] Niels Blokker, "Constituent Instruments," in Jacob Katz Cogan, Ian Hurd, Ian Johnstone (eds.), *The Oxford Handbook of International Organizations* (New York: Oxford University Press, 2016), at 955.

[30] Ibid.

should be guided by the object and purpose… A literal interpretation, using strict method of anchoring interpretation to the letter rather than the spirit… would be inappropriate." [31] On another occasion the ICJ stated similarly that "when the Organization takes action which warrants the assertion that it was appropriate for the fulfillment of one of the stated purposes of the United Nations, the presumption is that action is not *ultra vires* the Organization."[32]

The teleological interpretation method, or alternatively the doctrine of implied powers, should be instructive for an appropriate understanding of the relationship between the AIIB and the BRI. Some people are concerned whether the AIIB, as an independent international organization, should serve the BRI, which they consider is China's own diplomatic strategy. Legal critics argue that since no legal clause of AIIB AOA refers explicitly to the BRI, the AIIB may not invest a dime in a BRI project, let alone acting as a BRI partner. Such an approach—characterized as legalistic and disfavoring the nexus between BRI and AIIB—is detrimental to the development of BRI, and even more so to that of AIIB. Such a choice of interpretation would risk managing global public goods in a fragmented and isolated manner, failing an optimal synergy between them.

Admittedly the term BRI does not appear in the AIIB Charter, nor in any of its internal legal documents so far. But this does not mean that the AIIB is not eligible to serve the BRI. Since the BRI is ostensibly conducive to the realization of the AIIB's objectives, i.e., "infrastructure connectivity and institutional cooperation" as prescribed in its AOA Article 1.1, the AIIB should not hesitate to invest BRI projects in order to achieve such designated purposes. The authorization of BRI investments may also be derived from AIIB AOA Article 16.9 which states "The Bank may exercise such other powers and establish such rules and regulations as may be *necessary or appropriate* in furtherance of its purpose and functions, consistent with the provisions of this Agreement". Those clauses are the very legal bases for the AIIB to serve the BRI. It is reasonable to argue that all AIIB-funded projects may be characterized as BRI projects, because they have so far all laid along the BRI routes.[33]

The MCDF's relationship with the BRI and the AIIB follows the same logic line. First, on the relationship between the MCDF and the BRI. The idea of the MCDF first appeared in the 2017 MOU of the BRI.[34] Thus, the MCDF has an inborn connection with the BRI, although the MCDF's mandate is not limited to the BRI; rather it may expand to serve other initiatives, such as the EU's connectivity plan for Eurasia. Indeed, the BRI is no more mentioned in the language of the 2019 MOU of the MCDF. Second, on the relationship between the MCDF and the AIIB. No doubt the AIIB has

[31] Ibid., quoting WHO Nuclear Weapons, Dissenting Opinion, ICJ Reports 1996, 148.

[32] Antonio R. Parra, *The History of ICSID* (Oxford: Oxford University Press, 2012), at 29 footnote 9, quoting Certain Expenses of the United Nations, 1949 ICJ Rep. 151, 168.

[33] See a complete list of AIIB approved projects, https://www.aiib.org/en/projects/list/index.html?status=Approved (visited June 14, 2022).

[34] The MOU's full name is "Memoranda of Understanding on Collaboration on Matters of Common Interest under the Belt and Road Initiative" (dated May 14, 2017). Its text is available at https://www.ndb.int/wp-content/uploads/2018/09/MOU-on-BRI-signed.pdf (visited June 14, 2022).

been a faithful support of the MCDF, as a signatory to both the 2017 and 2019 MOUs relating to the MCDF. The former AIIB Vice President Von Amsberg endorsed thus: "the MCDF is a timely initiative, as larger investment needs are demanding stronger coordination among stakeholders. By working with and through the development banks, the MCDF will promote a multilateral approach to connectivity initiatives and investments."[35] In 2020 the AIIB decided to host the MCDF, providing secretariat service for it and acting as the administer of MCDF funding facility.

4.4 MCDF's Relationship with the Peer Mechanisms

The MCDF is not the first multilateral platform to promote connectivity and infrastructure investments through the cooperation of the MDBs. There are three earlier similar mechanisms: The Global Infrastructure Connectivity Alliance (GICA), the Global Infrastructure Hub (GI Hub), and the Global Infrastructure Facility (GIF). The GICA was initially proposed by President Xi Jinping of China, as the host country of the Hangzhou G20 Summit in 2016, with a view to encouraging the MDBs to "give greater funds and intellectual support to infrastructure projects to speed up the process of global infrastructure connectivity."[36] The initiation was immediately endorsed by the G20 Leaders' Communique in a bid "to enhance the synergy and cooperation among various infrastructure connectivity programs in a holistic way".[37] The first GICA annual meeting was held in Paris two years later in January 2018, co-organized by the World Bank and the OECD.[38] The GICA Secretariat is hosted by the World Bank, specifically the Bank Hub for Infrastructure and Urban Development in Singapore. GICA membership comprises national governments, including China and Indonesia; MDBs, including Asian Development Bank(ADB), AIIB,[39] Eurasian Development Bank(EDB), and the World Bank; international organizations, such as OECD and UNCTAD; global institutions, such

[35] "Multilateral development banks key to connectivity: VP of AIIB", April 26, 2019 http://www.china.org.cn/business/2019-04/26/content_74725509.htm (visited March 30, 2021).

[36] "Full text: Xi's speech at B20 summit opening ceremony", September 5, 2016, available at http://www.china.org.cn/chinese/2016-09/05/content_39233599.htm (visited September 23, 2019).

[37] G20 Leaders' Communique Hangzhou Summit states in relevant part:

"We note that infrastructure connectivity is key to achieving sustainable development and shared prosperity. We endorse the Global Infrastructure Connectivity Alliance launched this year to enhance the synergy and cooperation among various infrastructure connectivity programs in a holistic way. We ask the WBG to serve as the Secretariat of the Alliance, working closely with the Global Infrastructure Hub, OECD, other MDBs, and interested G20 members to support its activities" (G20 Leaders' Communique, Hangzhou Summit, September 4-5, 2016, para.39.).

[38] "Highlights: First GICA Annual Meeting", March 6, 2018, https://www.gica.global/article/highlights-first-gica-annual-meeting (visited September 23, 2019).

[39] The GICA website reveals that AIIB is a member of GICA. GICA, "How to Participate in GICA", https://www.gica.global/about-us/how-participate-gica (visited September 23, 2019).

as the GI Hub; and international associations, such as the Long-Term Infrastructure Investors Association (LTIIA).[40]

The GI Hub, another G20 initiative established during the 2014 Brisbane G20 Summit and earlier than the GICA, aims to implement the G20 Global Infrastructure Initiative to support public and private investment in quality infrastructure.[41] It is mandated to develop "a knowledge-sharing platform and network between governments, the private sector, development banks and other international organisations," and to "foster collaboration among these groups to improve the functioning and financing of infrastructure markets".[42] The GI Hub is located in Sydney, operating as a public company limited by guarantee under Australian law.[43] The corporate Board has a minimum of three and no more than eight directors, comprising representatives of G20 countries as well as independent directors, which Australia chaired for the first four years.[44] A CEO, appointed by the Board, is responsible for providing executive management and leadership to the Hub,[45] and staff are infrastructure professionals from public and private sector backgrounds from around the world. The Hub is not a G20 institution, because any country, G20 or non-G20, may join the Hub as a member; nor is it a standard-setting body, or engaging in fee-earning advisory work, since any country may use the Hub's information "on a voluntary and non-binding basis".[46]

The GIF is a multidonor platform set up by the World Bank Group in an endeavor to find a new way, in particular through public-private partnerships (PPPs), for infrastructure investment in developing countries.[47] It was launched by the World Bank alongside other MDBs, donor nations, and private partners in 2014 and started operations in 2015 with an initial capitalization of USD 100 million. The GIF partnership is overseen by a Governing Council, co-chaired by the World Bank and a donor nation, and it comprises representatives from three types of partners: funding partners (to provide financial contributions to the GIF partnership, including the World Bank and donor nations like Australia, Canada, China, Japan, and Singapore); technical partners (i.e., MDBs, to lead the GIF project support activities); and beneficiary partners

---

[40] GICA membership is open to "G20 and non-G20 governments, MDBs, global and regional infrastructure programs, established associations and other international organizations actively involved in connectivity initiatives in infrastructure and related services." Memorandum of Understanding on Global Infrastructure Connectivity Alliance Membership: Common Terms, sec.2, January 18, 2018.

[41] The text of the G20 Global Infrastructure Initiative is available at https://cdn.gihub.org/uat-umbraco/media/1079/g20-note_global-infrastructure-hub-initiative_2014.pdf (visited September 23, 2019).

[42] G20 Leaders' Communique, Brisbane Summit, November 15-16, 2014, paras.5-6.

[43] See the Constitution of the GI Hub at https://cdn.gihub.org/uat-umbraco/media/1072/global-infrastructure-hub-constitution.pdf (visited September 23, 2019).

[44] Constitution of the GI Hub, sections 4.7-4.8; *also* G20 Global Infrastructure Initiative, para.18.

[45] Constitution of the GI Hub, section 13; *also* G20 Global Infrastructure Initiative, para.21.

[46] Constitution of the GI Hub, section 11; *also* G20 Global Infrastructure Initiative, para.10.

[47] GIF, "What is the GIF", https://www.globalinfrafacility.org/what-is-the-gif (visited March 9, 2020).

(i.e., emerging markets and developing economies). There is a fourth group of advisory partners, and they include institutional investors and commercial banks. This group, representing the voice of private sectors and together holding over USD12 trillion in assets under management, engages in early-stage discussions related to the GIF projects' design and use of risk instruments to ensure project bankability. The GIF's project support can cover the spectrum of design, preparation, structuring, and transaction implementation activities.

It may be enlightening to first look into the relationship between the GICA, the GI Hub, and the GIF, before we move to discuss an advisable relationship between the MCDF and those peer mechanisms. The GICA and the GI Hub signed an MOU in 2017, expressing interest in working together on goals and activities in infrastructure connectivity.[48] The GI Hub is a member of the GICA, providing in-kind contributions, i.e., assistance in knowledge and resources, instead of direct financing to the GICA Secretariat.[49] The GI Hub is also an advisory partner to the GIF.[50] In light of those, it is advisable that the four institutions—the MCDF, the GICA, the GI Hub, and the GIF—form a cooperative relationship in implementing their shared goals and activities in infrastructure connectivity.

Meanwhile, concerns may arise that those older institutions may be hostile to the new-comer MCDF. This is because they have a potentially competitive relationship in growing high-quality infrastructure projects. For example, the MCDF, the GICA, and the GI Hub are all based in the Asian and Oceania regions, where infrastructure markets are huge but bankable projects are limited. What is more, the leading shareholders behind them are different: behind the GI Hub is Australia, the lead advocate for the MCDF is China, and the GICA is based in Singapore and hosted by the World Bank. The relationship of the powers behind those institutions can be subtle and even confrontational in one way or another, affecting the relationship between those institutions themselves.

Such concerns have historical grounds. During the 1997 Asian Financial Crisis, Japan proposed the Asian Monetary Fund (AMF), an Asian version of the IMF, in order to prepare rescue funds in advance of a crisis, instead of raising them after a crisis stroke. The AMF plan successfully mobilized endorsement from Asian countries, but quickly encountered stringent opposition from the US and the IMF, which feared loss of control over Asia, and as a result, it was effectively demised later that year. The AMF lesson teaches us that the established institution tends to view a new comer as a threat, rather than partnership. The MCDF should be prepared for this and take preemptive actions to address it, by avoiding, mitigating, or transforming any element as may be perceived threatening.

---

[48] "GI Hub and Global Infrastructure Connectivity Alliance sign MoU", May 8, 2017 https://www.gihub.org/news/gi-hub-and-global-infrastructure-connectivity-alliance-sign-mou/ (visited September 23, 2019).

[49] "GICA Members," https://www.gica.global/about-us/members-and-contributors (visited September 23, 2019).

[50] GIF, "A list of partners", https://www.globalinfrafacility.org/partners (visited March 10, 2020).

The MCDF should take initiative to show a benign and cooperative attitude to its peer institutions, by working closely with them from day one. It became a technical partner of the GIF in June 2021, and two months later became the first official implementing partner of the AIIB.[51] Here are two further proposals. First, the MCDF should consult the GICA and become its member, providing in-kind contributions. Second, it should form formal partnership with the GI Hub, or sign an MOU with it, expressing interest in future collaboration. Those actions will not only do good to the external relations of the MCDF, but also will contribute to the success (both in terms of reputation and capability) of the MCDF itself. The optimal prospect is inspired by the strategically cooperative approach the AIIB chose to take, as an infant MDB, when it had to address possible discords with the World Bank and other peer institutions. Well before AIIB establishment in 2016, the Establishing Secretariat had engaged senior experts from those peer institutions in the work of preparing key legal instruments, including the AOA and the Environmental and Social Framework.[52] The AIIB has continued forging a sound collaborative relationship with peer institutions by exchanging knowledge, information and personnel, signing MOUs, and co-financing projects. Those efforts have successfully broken the rumor and speculation that the AIIB was meant to replace the World Bank and the ADB, which in turn must have been hostile to the new comer. Having learned this experience, the MCDF, the GICA, the GI Hub, and the GIF should go hand in hand in connecting the dots on global infrastructure connectivity, which is after all a huge and ambitious market.

4.5 Some Institutional Matters Under the MCDF

The MCDF's main structure is sketched in the 2019 MOU of the MCDF and detailed in the Governing Instrument of the Finance Facility of the MCDF in 2020. Yet, many specific institutional matters are unclear or have not been fully settled. Among them three matters are crucial. First, how will the Secretariat be run? Second, how will the MCDF be funded? Third, how will the three designated functions be carried out in practice? I will address them one by one and give my suggestions accordingly.

[51] The implementing partner of the MCDF must first be a technical partner of the GIF. Governing Instrument of the Finance Facility of the MCDF (May 15, 2020), Art. 3. AIIB, "AIIB, MCDF Partnership to Foster High-Quality Infrastructure Investments"(August 25, 2021) https://www.aiib.org/en/news-events/news/2021/AIIB-MCDF-Partnership-to-Foster-High-Quality-Infrastructure-Investments.html (visited October 21, 2021).

[52] There are two leading experts that shall never be forgot in the history of AIIB law development, who originally came from the World Bank and were engaged in drafting the AIIB's key legal documents in a stellar manner; they are Natalie Lichtenstein for the Articles of Agreement, and Stephen Lintner for the Environmental and Social Framework.

4.5.1 How Will the Secretariat Be Run?

The AIIB established the MCDF Secretariat in 2020 and has hosted it ever since. I advise that the hosting arrangement should be under a five-year renewable service agreement.[53] A major reason is that both the AIIB and China, the AIIB's largest shareholder, have fervently supported the MCDF. Technically this advice factors in economic and efficient considerations. The MCDF has benefited from the AIIB's good reputation, excellent personnel, and resources and is up and running in the first place.

The AIIB is not only able to accommodate the MCDF Secretariat in its new and grand permanent headquarters in Beijing, but also provides in part the Secretariat team for it. The GICA is an inspiration in this regard. All GICA Secretariat members are seconded from the World Bank. Specifically, two Work Bank staffs act as co-heads in the position of co-Secretaries in the GICA Secretariat, and 10 more or so World Bank staffs work as the Secretariat members.[54] These people have extensive experience in the transport, trade, private sector, and ICT sectors and work across regions and disciplines to promote global connectivity. I would argue that the MCDF personnel should not only be from the AIIB, but it is advisable to be open to the MCDF's broad membership base.[55] Such openness is conducive to the viability of the Secretariat. However, most Secretariat staff should be on secondment from the host AIIB, for the sake of cost, efficiency, and synergy between the two institutions. For example, the MCDF does not institute a separate legal team; instead it uses legal service provided by the AIIB Legal Department.

The Secretariat is led by Chief Executive Officer (CEO), known as Managing Director under the Governing Instrument. The inaugural CEO is Mr. Zhongjing Wang, who is appointed by the AIIB as the Administrator with the concurrence of the Governing Committee. The Secretariat staff are selected by the CEO and currently governed by the AIIB's human resources and administrative policies. It is noted that the Secretariat is administratively accountable to the AIIB, while functionally accountable to the Governing Committee.[56]

The Governing Instrument should sponsor an incremental expansion of the Secretariat.[57] An understaffed Secretariat is incapable to fulfill all of the MCDF's three core missions, which will be discussed in Section V.C. However, it does not mean that the MCDF needs a large bureaucracy. The MCDF should carry on its work in

[53] It is noted that there is a general provision under the Governing Instrument to the effect that the AIIB may terminate its role as Administrator at any time, after giving the Governing Committee six months' notice in writing. Governing Instrument of the Finance Facility of the MCDF (May 15, 2020), Article 14.3.

[54] "Meet the GICA Team", https://www.gica.global/about-us/team (visited September 27, 2019).

[55] MCDF membership is discussed later in Section VI.B "How to institutionalize the MCDF: a charter".

[56] Governing Instrument of the Finance Facility of the MCDF (May 15, 2020), Art. 15.

[57] This paragraph is mainly inspired by my proposal about an incrementally expanded Secretariat for the Financial Stability Board (FSB). Gu Bin and Liu Tong, "Enforcing International Financial Regulatory Reforms", *Journal of International Economic Law* (2014) 17 (1), 139-176, at 166-167.

collaboration with other international institutions, wherever possible, especially with the GICA, the GI Hub, and the GIF. This is not only to save resources, but also to avoid functional duplication among international institutions.

4.5.2 *How Will the MCDF Be Funded?*

The 2019 MOU of the MCDF provides that "a funding mechanism/facility is expected to be established to support the MCDF functions." The Governing Instrument of the Finance Facility of the MCDF delivered on this commitment in 2020. In real life, China committed 150 million US dollars; Egypt, Hungary, and Saudi Arabia each committed 10 million US dollars; and Cambodia, Lao PDR, and Philippines each committed 100 thousand US dollars.[58] Under the Governing Instrument, only those committing 10 million US dollars and honoring such commitment within five years are voting members, which are equal in the decision-making of the Governing Committee, regardless their difference in contributions.[59]

The MCDF's funding mechanism should fit the law and governance of the AIIB. AIIB law stipulates two types of funds: special funds and trust funds. Special funds mean that the funds are donated by outside parties and are owned and managed by the AIIB.[60] Trust funds, in contrast, are entrusted by outside parties, and fund ownership remains in the hands of the entrusting parties.[61] A basic difference between the two funds is whether ownership is transferred to the AIIB. The AIIB, an implementing partner, has categorized grants received from the MCDF as "MCDF Special Fund". However, it is unclear whether the MCDF Finance Facility, as administered by the AIIB, should be categorized as a trust fund, a special fund, or neither under AIIB law.

Featuring a close institutional relationship, the AIIB is the administrator and an implementing partner of the MCDF Finance Facility and the host of the MCDF Secretariat. But the MCDF is not an affiliate to the AIIB; rather it has an independent institutional standing.[62] The AIIB establishes and administers the MCDF funding

---

[58] MCDF, "Partnering to advance high-quality infrastructure and connectivity" (2021 Annual Report) p.34.

[59] Governing Instrument of the Finance Facility of the MCDF (May 15, 2020), Art. 7.1.

[60] AIIB AOA Art. 17.1 provides that "the Bank may accept Special Funds which are designed to serve the purpose and come within the functions of the Bank; such Special Funds shall be resources of the Bank. The full cost of administering any Special Fund shall be charged to that Special Fund."

[61] AIIB AOA Art. 16.7 provides that "the Bank may establish and administer funds held in trust for other parties, provided such trust funds are designed to serve the purpose and come within the functions of the Bank, under a trust fund framework which shall have been approved by the Board of Governors."

[62] Such institutional independence may be inferred from Article 14.3 of the Governing Instrument of the Finance Facility of the MCDF (May 15, 2020), where the AIIB may terminate its role as Administrator at any time.

mechanism, legally independent from that of the AIIB.[63] It seems that the funding mechanism should be a trust fund, not a special fund. If so, it would be the first trust fund for the AIIB. The AIIB charter requires that a trust fund be "designed to serve the purpose and come within the functions of the Bank".[64] This fund clearly meets the requirement, since it shares the AIIB's objectives in infrastructure connectivity investments.

However, the MCDF Finance Facility is an atypical trust fund of the AIIB at best—atypical in the following two aspects. First, a trust fund framework is prerequisite under AIIB law,[65] but is currently lacking, and the trust fund framework should have been approved by the AIIB Board of Governors by a decision of a majority of the votes cast.[66] It is expected that the trust fund framework should be in the form of a generally applied set of rules and regulations, blending specific agreements between the AIIB and a donor.[67] The agreements must address issues such as: decision-making by the Governing Committee on fund use, the donor's rights, cost of administering the fund, and other items relating to the rights and obligations of the signatory parties. Second, the MCDF Finance Facility is atypical in the sense that it is controlled by the donors through the Governing Committee, rather than by the AIIB as limited trustee. Such governing structure seems modeled upon the Global Environmental Facility (GEF), a landmark financial intermediary fund (FIF) administered by the World Bank.[68]

Who would be eligible to contribute to the trust fund? In principle, both national governments and private entities are eligible to contribute grant resources to the Finance Facility. When it comes to a private entity, the approval of the Governing Committee and the AIIB is required.[69] Such broad eligibility may be inspired by the AIIB Project Preparation Special Fund, a multidonor fund, which provides that an AIIB member or non-member, as well as any person approved by the President may

[63] Governing Instrument of the Finance Facility of the MCDF (May 15, 2020), Art. 20.

[64] AIIB AOA Art. 16.7.

[65] AIIB AOA Art. 16.7.

[66] The AIIB Board of Governors have three classes of decision-making, applying to different matters pending, mainly based on their degree of importance to the Bank. They are a super majority vote, a special majority vote, and a simple majority vote, in a decreased stringent order. The trust fund framework approval follows the third decision-making model, i.e., a simple majority vote.

[67] The proposal of blending general rules with specific agreements is learned from the practice of the AIIB Project Preparation Special Fund. Governing Instrument of the Finance Facility of the MCDF (May 15, 2020), Art. 14.1 provides that "The functions of the Administrator shall include …e) entering into contribution arrangements with Contributors."

[68] In the World Bank Group trust fund portfolio, the FIFs are distinct from trust funds, the latter being further divided into two categories: Bank-executed trust fund and recipient-executed trust fund. World Bank, "Trust Fund Annual Report 2018-2019", pp.6, and 90-95. On a detailed discussion of the GEF's governing structure, see Sophie Smyth, "A Practical Guide to Creating a Collective Financing Effort to Save the World: The Global Environmental Facility Experience", in Gerd Droesse (ed), *Funds for Development: Multilateral Channels for Concessional Financing* (Asian Development Bank 2011), pp.501-48.

[69] Governing Instrument of the Finance Facility of the MCDF (May 15, 2020), Art. 3.1.

be a contributor to the Fund.[70] A broad donor base tends to reduce chances of being maneuvered by particular donors and helps to reduce administrative costs, leading to improved development effectiveness. After all, the broad scope of eligibility would help in pooling sufficient resources, particularly when the MCDF carries out its funding function in project preparation, which will be discussed in Section V.C below.

As the MCDF grows, say after 5 to 8 years of development, the trust fund may be transferred and administered by the MCDF Secretariat itself. This would further enhance the independence of the MCDF's funding sources.

4.5.3 How to Carry Out the Functions as Designated?

The MCDF is mandated in the 2019 MOU to carry out three functions: information sharing,[71] capacity building,[72] and project preparation,[73] which are all key for development finance. Among those functions, information sharing is common to the MCDF, the GICA, the GI Hub, and the GIF, and there is a huge potential for the four institutions to cooperate. The second function, i.e., capacity building, is somewhat unique to the MCDF, since it must help borrower countries in "sustainable debt management",[74] which is to address the notorious debt-trap problems, incidental to development finance but having besieged some developing countries currently.

The third function, i.e., project preparation, is common to both the GIF and the MCDF, where the latter can learn from the former. With this function the MCDF needs to provide funding to upstream activities to identify bankable projects for its members. This function indeed establishes an image of "workshop", compared with the image of "talk-shop" as presented under other functions of the institution. It is estimated that the bulk of the MCDF's funding will be used in fulfilling this function. Since the AIIB Project Preparation Special Fund is designated with a similar function, the MCDF, as hosted by the AIIB, is expected to collaborate closely with the Bank in their common cause of identifying bankable projects.

The MCDF's three designated functions all spearhead high standards and quality in infrastructure investment. In applying the standards of international financial institutions (IFIs) as implementing partners in its projects, the MCDF is expected to

---

[70] Rules and Regulations of the AIIB Project Preparation Special Fund (June 24, 2016), section 2.02 (a).

[71] "Information sharing" means to "facilitate flow of information across the Parties and other development partners to avoid duplication and enhance collaboration." The 2019 MOU of the MCDF, Art. I.1.a.

[72] "Capacity building" means to "enhance relevant know-how and institutional capacity of developing countries and their development partners." The 2019 MOU of the MCDF, Art. I.1.b.

[73] "Project preparation" means to "finance upstream activities including but limited to pre-feasibility and feasibility studies, and environmental and social assessment." The 2019 MOU of the MCDF, Art. I.1.c.

[74] The 2019 MOU of the MCDF, Art. I.1.b.

assume a role of **standard harmonization** to facilitate collaboration among the MDBs and other development partners. Typically, the MDBs and state development banks each have their own environmental, social, and procurement policies or standards. Such divergence tends to create obstacles in their cooperation, particularly when an opportunity of co-financing arises. Endeavors have long been made toward *droit commun* among the MDBs, and with significant success; but efforts and achievements involving state development banks have been limited. It would be desirable for the MCDF to stand up to the challenge and make up for this loophole.

A promising and potentially landmark case in this regard is the MCDF project of enhancing China EXIM Bank's (CEXIM) environmental and social standards.[75] In 2022 the AIIB approved a loan of 200 million US dollars equivalent in Chinese Yuan to CEXIM, a major policy bank of China, which agreed to on-lend for green sub-projects such as renewable energy and ecosystem rehabilitation in China. And as stated, the loan aims to "strengthen the impact of CEXIM's green loan portfolio by enhancing CEXIM's ESMS [Environmental and Social Management Systems] through supporting its on-lending facility."[76] To complement and facilitate the efforts, the MCDF agreed the year before on a grant of 714 thousand US dollars (including an administration fee charged by the AIIB equal to 5% of the grant) to update CEXIM's environmental and social safeguards that should be compatible with AIIB standards.

Standard harmonization brings the following benefits. First, the MDBs' standards are instructive to state development banks and are expected to help the latter to improve governance and practice. They may even produce spillover, or extended effects in improving the relevant domestic standards within the country where the development partner is headquartered. For example, as stated in the CEXIM project, "The MCDF grant will also enable sharing lessons learnt and research with industry peers to support building a case study for the banking industry in China to take up similar approaches."[77] Second, the practice of state development banks will hopefully be enlightening to the MDBs, contributing to the MDBs' operations by making them efficient and effective. And third, a somewhat *droit commun* will be helpful for the

---

[75] MCDF, "China EXIM Bank Enhanced Environmental and Social Management Systems (ESMS)", https://www.themcdf.org/en/what-we-do/projects/2021/China-EXIM-Bank-Enhanced-Environmental-and-Social-Management-Systems.html.

[76] AIIB, "China: China EXIM Bank Green On-lending Facility", https://www.aiib.org/en/projects/details/2022/approved/China-EXIM-Bank-Green-On-lending-Facility.html.

[77] AIIB, "China EXIM Bank Enhanced Environmental and Social Management Systems (ESMS)" https://www.aiib.org/en/projects/details/2021/special-fund/China-EXIM-Bank-Enhanced-Environmental-and-Social-Management-Systems.html. Similarly, the MCDF stated thus: "CEXIM is a new partner in the MCDF context. The project will enable CEXIM to apply enhanced ESMS … and support the adoption of IFI standards by the wider banking sector in China." MCDF, "China EXIM Bank Enhanced Environmental and Social Management Systems (ESMS)", https://www.themcdf.org/en/what-we-do/projects/2021/China-EXIM-Bank-Enhanced-Environmental-and-Social-Management-Systems.html.

unity of the family of development partners, making their collaboration smooth and efficient, including through co-financing.[78]

The work of standard harmonization should aim both high *and* feasible.[79] The label of international best practice only shines when it follows the principles of stakeholder engagement (e.g., meaningful consultations with borrowers) and situation-specific implementation. AIIB law sets good examples in this regard, where its Environmental and Social Framework defines "good international practice" as employing the most appropriate technologies in the project-specific circumstances.[80]

The MCDF aims to foster high-quality infrastructure and connectivity investments. It must promote high environmental, social, and anti-corruption standards, while safeguarding debt sustainability as embodied in the official mandates in the Governing Instrument. The MCDF is expected to vigorously support the UN 2030 Agenda for Sustainable Development, the Sustainable Development Goals (SDGs), and the Paris Agreement on Climate Change.[81] As more development partners join in, the MCDF must consider harmonizing the different standards employed by each of its members. The sooner the better.

4.6 Institutionalization of the MCDF: A Prospect

I formulate four dimensions in hardening soft law in international financial regulation in my work *Enforcing International Financial Regulatory Reforms* in 2014: the dimensions of obligation,[82] stringency,[83] delegation,[84] and enforcement.[85] Among them, the third dimension—delegation to a third party the power of administering the execution of law—is essentially a process of institutionalization. The MCDF is a platform, or a mechanism at best, at this moment, far from an independent organization. It even does not have signature authority, which is instead exercised by

[78] There are a few cases of cooperation between multilateral and bilateral development partners, such as the MOU between New Development Bank and China Development Bank in 2017, in which cooperation in areas such as information exchange, personnel secondments, and co-financing is stipulated. The text of the MOU is available at https://www.ndb.int/wp-content/uploads/2019/09/19.-MOU_CDB_Memorandum-of-Understanding-between-New-Development-Bank-and-China-Development-Bank.pdf (visited October 1, 2019).

[79] *See* my elaboration on "high *and* feasible standards", Gu Bin, *The Law and Governance of the Asian Infrastructure Investment Bank* (The Netherlands: Wolters Kluwer, 2019), at 31-33.

[80] AIIB Environmental and Social Framework (approved February 2016, amended February 2019 and May 2021), at 82.

[81] It is inferred from the 2017 MOU of the BRI, Art. I.1 (v), as well as the Governing Instrument of the Finance Facility of the MCDF (May 15, 2020), "Introduction".

[82] Simply put, the dimension of "obligation" means a process of "legalization" into legally binding rules.

[83] "Stringency" focuses on a higher degree of quantitative restraint.

[84] "Delegation" refers to a third party authorized to administer the execution of law.

[85] "Enforcement" means that competent authorities take measures to apply legally binding rules.

the AIIB on behalf of it, for example, when it receives contributions from donors or gives grants to recipients.[86] Its legal bases are the Governing Instrument and the 2019 MOU of the MCDF, a form of soft law that "does not create any legal obligation or the incurrence of any liability on any Party".[87] Thus, it is at the very weak end along the spectrum of institutionalization of an international initiative. But does the MCDF have potential to develop into an international organization, or its law be hardened into a treaty? I will endeavor to address these questions, first discussing the rationale of institutionalization.

4.6.1 Rationale of Institutionalization

Almost no international organizations were born in the form as they are. Under the Bretton Woods system, the World Bank and the IMF were born as international organizations in 1940s. But at that time, they were much weaker and less bureaucratic than they are today. For example, the World Bank originated as a fund to reconstruct war-torn West Europe and gradually grew into a group of five independent institutions as business grew. The GATT, the predecessor of the WTO and a pillar of world economic governance, used to be an interim treaty executed largely by diplomatic means for almost five decades. Only by the end of the Uruguay Round negotiations from 1986 to 1994, the treaty was institutionalized as an international organization. The Financial Stability Board (FSB), a relatively recent example, originated from a much weaker platform—the Financial Stability Forum (FSF) in the aftermath of the Asian Financial Crisis of 1997, and is now an important international body, though the smallest.

History forces us to think an old question: what are the driving forces behind the development of those international economic and financial organizations? To answer it, three driving elements are considered: first, the importance of their mandates; second, the power and commitment of the advocator(s) behind them; and third, their relationship with peer institutions, particularly with those earlier, established ones. The first two elements will be elaborated below, while the third one will not lest duplication, since it has been elaborated above in Sect. 4.4.

First, the more important its mandate, the more likely an initiative gets institutionalized. For example, the IMF and the World Bank were international organizations from day one, because their mandates were considered important for world peace and stability, as the negotiators had learned from the economic causes of the outbreak of the past two world wars. Later, the World Bank were further developed into five

[86] An actual example is the implementing partner agreement between the MCDF and AIIB, where both parties are represented by the AIIB, because the MCDF is administered by the AIIB and has no signature authority. AIIB, "Implementing Partner Agreement between AIIB as Implementing Partner of the MCDF Finance Facility and AIIB as Administrator of the MCDF Finance Facility", August 9, 2021, https://www.aiib.org/en/about-aiib/who-we-are/partnership/_download/MCDF-IP-Agreement_Final-Executed_09-08-2021.pdf (visited October 31, 2022).

[87] The 2019 MOU of the MCDF, Art. V.1.

international organizations, because of the need to mobilize private capital to fulfill its mandates of reducing poverty and boosting prosperity.[88] The evolution of the FSF to the FSB was thanks to major financial crises one after another, which brought the importance of financial stability to an ever new high.

The importance of an initiative is not static. Rather, it may change. There can be both subjective (e.g., awareness of relevant stakeholders) and objective reasons (depending on situational context) behind such change. Take the history of the FSB for example. The 2008 Financial Crisis prompted the FSB to become "the fourth pillar of global economic governance", as then-US Treasury Secretary Geithner vowed. But the oath quickly slipped away from people's mind, as the crisis faded and the Wall Street took on deregulation campaigns.

The second driving force behind the institutionalization of an initiative is the power and commitment of its advocator. At the end of WWII, the US had the power to lead and build a new international economic order. And it had long committed to the order, which has since contributed to world peace and prosperity generally. But since the 2008 financial crisis, in particular since the Trump administration, the US has been relinquishing its leadership in global governance, as its power relatively declines. It has been effectively destroying the world order it helped to shape many decades ago, by showing a fervent desire to retreat from multilateralism, withdrawing or threatening to withdraw from international treaties and organizations, while unliterally initiating a global trade war.

Meanwhile, China decided to stand up to this increasingly looming leadership vacuum in world order and meticulously chose infrastructure connectivity investments as its way to reform global governance. Chinese leadership believed that "infrastructure building is the path to prosperity", which laid a solid foundation for China's own success,[89] and it is ready to share the success with the underdeveloped world. For this reason, China first initiated the BRI and the AIIB, and now the MCDF. More and more countries and international organizations have now realized the importance of infrastructure connectivity and have jumped on board. By the second Belt and Road Forum in April 2019, a total of 126 countries and 29 international organizations had signed MOUs with China endorsing the BRI; and three years later (i.e., by the end of 2022), the number had increased to 149 and 32, respectively.[90] The BRI has truly become a multilateral platform, and its further

---

[88] Under the World Bank Group, three organizations—MIGA, IFC, ICSID—are all dedicated to promoting private capital investment in developing countries.

[89] Deng Xiaoping, China's Chief Designer of reform and opening up, stated that economic modernization should start from transport and telecommunication investments, drawing the experience of Japan. He also commented that, in order to lay a solid foundation for economic development, four areas were important, among which were energy and transport. "A talk during a visit to Tianjing", August 19-21, 1986, and "A long-term view is advisable for the development of the Sino-Japan relationship", March 25, 1984, in Deng Xiaoping, *Selected Works of Deng Xiaoping* (邓小平文选, in Chinese) (Beijing: People's Publishing House, 1993) Volume 3, at 165, 54. *Also* Li Lanqing, *Breakthrough: When the National Gate First Opens* (突围:国门初开的岁月, in Chinese) (Beijing: Central Literature Press, 2008), at 277-316.

[90] "The official list of Belt and Road participatory countries" (in Chinese), available at https://www.yidaiyilu.gov.cn/xwzx/roll/77298.htm (visited November 4, 2022).

institutionalization cannot be excluded. It may soon need an independent Secretariat and even a third-party international body for administrative purposes in the future.[91]

4.6.2 *How to Institutionalize the MCDF: A Charter*

The MCDF is expected to be moving along the dimension of institutionalization, starting from the constitution of a Collaboration Platform, a Finance Facility, an Administrator, and a Secretariat.[92] It will probably end up to be a legally independent international body, to be blessed with a formal but not legally binding charter. The charter may provide for the MCDF's purpose, function, membership, organization, decision-making, funding, and operational issues, among others. Here, two items will be specifically discussed: MCDF membership and its organization.

First, in terms of membership, all parties to the 2019 MOU of the MCDF, as well as other development partners (including contributors and recipients), should be eligible to be MCDF members. In other words, MCDF membership is to be very broad, at least including four categories: sovereign members of IFIs, such as the Chinese Ministry of Finance as representing China; the IFIs, such as the World Bank and the AIIB; other international organizations, such as UNCTAD; and state development partners ("New Partners"), such as the China EXIM Bank, the China Development Bank, and the Silk Road Fund.[93] All those categories appear in the GICA membership list, save the fourth one (i.e., state development partners, or, bilateral development financiers) which nevertheless should be invited in the MCDF, since these institutions have been major players in development finance. The 2019 MOU provides that "other parties may execute this MOU and become Parties under this MOU… subject to the unanimous written consent of the Parties."[94] This clause sheds light on how to become an MCDF member: an applicant must secure unanimous written consent of all existing members of the MCDF.

Second, in terms of organization,[95] the Governing Instrument makes explicit four organs for the MCDF: The Governing Committee, the Coordination Committee, the

---

[91] A list of possible model choices for the institutional development of the BRI is available at "Belt and Road Cooperation: For A Better World—Report on the Findings and Recommendations from the First Meeting of the Advisory Council of the Belt and Road Forum for International Cooperation", with rapporteurs Shamshad Akhtar and Justin Yifu Lin, Chapter 5 on Strengthening the Architecture and Capacity Building for the Belt and Road Cooperation, at 31-35. Those considered models are the Boao Forum for Asia, the G20 architecture, an OECD model, the World Economic Forum, and the Financial Stability Board (FSB). The Report's full text is available at https://www.fmprc.gov.cn/web/wjbxw_673019/t1657185.shtml (visited October 3, 2019).

[92] Governing Instrument of the Finance Facility of the MCDF (May 15, 2020), Art. 2.

[93] Another possible category is private entities, as covered in the Governance Instrument, Art.3.

[94] The 2019 MOU of the MCDF, Art. V.2.

[95] My proposals about the MCDF organization are mainly inspired by the Charter of the Financial Stability Board (June 2012), among others.

Secretariat, and the Administrator (i.e., the AIIB).[96] The development of the Coordination Committee, which is yet in a primitive stage, deserves elaboration here. Made up of all representatives of MCDF membership, the Committee should be expanded, establishing at least four Standing Sub-Committees responsible for, respectively, the MCDF's three designated functions (i.e., information sharing, capacity building, and project preparation), and budget and resources mainly relating to the Secretariat. The Committee should also establish various Regional Consultative Groups, dedicated to infrastructure connectivity in Asia, Africa, Europe, Latin-America, and so on, as the case requires. And these groups should collaborate closely with each other on certain issues such as Eurasian connectivity. The Committee may establish working groups as necessary, pertaining to its designated functions. Both the Regional Consultative Groups and working groups may include representatives of non-MCDF members.

The charter should be reviewed and revised, after a period of, say, three to five years, as the MCDF develops. If the MCDF's contributor membership increases to a significant number by that time, say over 30, then a Plenary may be established to replace the Governing Committee as the sole decision-making body. And the Governing Committee, remaining small, will change its role to provide operational guidance between the Plenary meetings to carry forward the directions of the MCDF.

4.6.3 China's Role in the MCDF

As regards China's leadership role in the MCDF, it sounds logical to fear that China would seek hegemony in it. But the fear is groundless if we observe (1) from the angle of Chinese culture and China's approach toward global governance; and (2) historical cases that involved China's participation in international cooperation when China became a more powerful state, in particular since the turn of the new millennium.

First, in its cultural gene, China is not a missionary society; it chooses to influence others more by inducing respect than by conversion,[97] which contrasts a hegemon's intention to seek predominance over other countries.[98] Since they were all initiated by China, alongside with other emerging powers, it is sensible that the three institutions—the BRI, the AIIB, and the MCDF—are embedded with some degrees of "*Chinese* multilateralism", different from what is typically expected in a US-dominated international organization. *Chinese* multilateralism holds that the label of international best practice only shines when it follows the principles of stakeholder engagement (e.g., meaningful consultations with borrowers) and situation-specific implementation. It is expected that in a China-led international organization,

[96] Governing Instrument of the Finance Facility of the MCDF (May 15, 2020), Art. 2.

[97] As Confucius said, "If people from afar do not submit, influence them to do so by means of virtue and civil culture" ("远人不服，则修文德以来之" in Chinese) . An excellent exposition of China's cultural mentality in the western literature is seen in Henry A. Kissinger, *World Order* (New York: Penguin Books, 2015), pp. 213-33.

[98] Bin Gu, "China, the US and what it means to be a hegemon", *The Straits Times*, July 16, 2022.

for purposes of decision-making, consultations are taken more often than forceful imposition by voting based on capital shareholding.

Second, historical cases consistently echoed the spirit of *Chinese* multilateralism. For example, in the 100 billion US-dollar Contingency Reserve Arrangement (CRA) of the BRICS,[99] which aims to provide emergency credit to BRICS members in financial duress—the same function as that of the IMF globally, China pledged 41 billion US dollars, while asking drawing rights of 20 billion only. In the Chiang Mai Initiative (CMI), a similar arrangement among Asian countries in the aftermath of the Asian financial crisis, China contributed 77 billion US dollars, while voluntarily limiting its drawing rights as well.[100] In AIIB operations, China as the biggest shareholder keeps advocating the principle of "extensive consultation, joint contribution, and shared benefits", or alternatively "to achieve shared growth through discussion and collaboration", with no intention to abuse veto power.[101] China's position regarding the BRI is similar to that regarding the AIIB, while both institutions are compared to two engines, serving one aircraft of "a community of shared future for mankind". China is no exception in the development of the MCDF, playing a leadership role in it, while behaving responsibly to its partners. As the Chinese saying goes, "if we all chip in and add wood to bonfire, the flames will be much higher." Those case studies prove China as a self-restrained and benign power in international cooperation.

4.7 Conclusion

The MCDF has the potential to be a new propeller for global governance, amid a time when international cooperation has been severely threatened by nationalism and unilateralism. The MCDF agrees with the BRI and the AIIB on their purposes and object, i.e., infrastructure and connectivity investment, and they should go hand in hand in both business development and institutional building. It is estimated that the MCDF may form a competitive cooperation relationship with three other peer institutions, i.e., the GICA, the GI Hub, and the GIF.

The agreement of the AIIB to host the MCDF is reminiscent of both practices of the World Bank hosting the GICA (plus the GEF), and the BIS hosting the FSB, and is helpful for both the AIIB and the MCDF to save cost, increase efficiency, and build synergy in governance and operations. MCDF membership should be open to all development partners, including state development financiers such as China EXIM

---

[99] Kai He and Huiyun Feng, "Leadership Transition and Global Governance: Role Conception, Institutional Balancing, and the AIIB", The Chinese Journal of International Politics, 2019, Vol.12, No.2, at 172.

[100] Ibid.

[101] Regarding China's veto power in the AIIB, see below Section 4.3. Also see Bin Gu & Tong Liu, "Shareholding Formulas in International Financial Institutions: Learning from the Asian Infrastructure Investment Bank", Journal of International Economic Law, 2022, Vol.25, Issue 4, at 6-7. https://academic.oup.com/jiel/advance-article-abstract/doi/10.1093/jiel/jgac035/6696844?redirectedFrom=fulltext

Bank. The MCDF, mandated with three important functions, should spearhead high standards and quality by coordinating different standards of development partners. The purpose of doing so is to harmonize them into high and feasible standards, ultimately developing into *droit commun* in the future.

The MCDF is expected to be institutionalized, thanks to the importance of its mandates, and the power and commitment of its lead advocator. As a formal but not legally binding basis, an MCDF charter is necessary and should build upon the Governing Instrument of 2020. The charter must elaborate on the MCDF's purpose, function, membership, structure, decision-making, funding, and operational issues, among others. China, the lead advocator of the MCDF, is not expected to be a hegemon in the institution. Rather, it will play a leadership role in it, while behaving responsibly to other participants, including to borrower countries.

Chapter 5
The Issue of SOEs: Perspectives of AIIB and Other Institutions

Summary The treatment standards of state-owned enterprises (SOEs) as public entities have far-reaching and significant implications against the background of China's rise and the reform of global economic governance. The relevant standards have been abundantly debated and tested in three areas of international economic law: international financial law, represented by AIIB and other multilateral development banks; international investment law, represented by law of the International Centre for Settlement of Investment Disputes; and international trade law, represented by law of the World Trade Organization. After reviewing those areas of international law, the chapter concludes that a function-based approach has generally been observed in conducting the relevant examination, but some deviations, featuring an ownership-based approach, do exist. This finding is meaningful for the development of future international law, as well as for China's domestic SOE reform. Broadly, it is instructive on whether China's unique economic system, guided by a strong government, will be accepted by the international community, and if yes on what condition.

5.1 Introduction

Are the state-owned enterprises (SOEs) public entities or private ones? This question becomes increasingly important for the international community against the rise of China in particular, which maintains a significant number of powerful SOEs and commits a leadership role for them in the economy.[1] A lot of concerns have been

This chapter originally appeared in *Hong Kong Law Journal* (2020)50(3), entitled "Treatment Standards of State-Owned Enterprises as Public Entities: A Clash or Convergence across International Economic Laws", coauthor Ms. Chengjin Xu.

[1] Some people describe China's economic system by using the term "state capitalism", which is defined as "a system in which the state functions as the leading economic actor and uses markets primarily for political gain". "Political gain" in turn means "not for maximizing economic growth but for maximizing the state's power and the leadership's chances of survival". Ming Du, "China's State Capitalism and World Trade Law" (2014) 63 *Int'l & Comp LQ* 409, 410, quoting Bremmer. These people imagine that China's state capitalism enables it to operate as China Inc., but the fact is that

B. Gu, *Chinese Multilateralism in the Asian Infrastructure Investment Bank (AIIB)*, Modern China and International Economic Law,
https://doi.org/10.1007/978-981-97-1219-9_5

aroused over China's possible political motives or goals when the SOEs go global and take over foreign investments, under the Belt and Road Initiative, for example. The SOEs have also stimulated concerns over market distortion and fair competition, because of the presumed support by their government. Thus, the question is far more than conceptually, theoretically, or strategically important; it has a strong effect of market application and must be examined case by case in order to appropriately address it.

There are three areas of international economy where the SOEs are active market players, that is, international trade, international investment, and international finance. And it is optimal to provide a comprehensive and even holistic review of the relevant law governing those areas in the endeavor to address the question. This chapter commits to the job.[2] Specifically, in the area of international finance, the law of the multilateral development banks (MDBs) is reviewed; in the area of international investment, the law of investment arbitration, represented by the International Centre for Settlement of Investment Disputes (ICSID), is reviewed; and in international trade, the World Trade Organization (WTO) law is reviewed. By threading those three laws together in this one article, we endeavor to dig out the common ground underlying the treatment standards of SOEs as public entities or private ones, as well as the possible clashes existing within each law and across them.

In each of the three laws, there are debates about two contrasting treatment standards of SOEs, that is, function-based and ownership-based. The function-based standard means that one has to examine the specific act of the SOE in question, while the ownership-based standard means that it is sufficient to examine the SOE's capital structure, purpose, and its relationship with the government, in the work of deciding an SOE as a public or a private entity. In other words, the function-based standard looks into the entity's *behavior*, while the ownership-based standard focuses on the *entity* making that behavior. Admittedly this is a rough distinction, but it is instructive for a preliminary understanding of the important question.

In this chapter, Sect. 5.2 addresses the MDB law, finding common grounds in the treatment standards of SOEs as private entities across different MDBs. In particular, the procurement laws of the leading MDBs, including the veteran World Bank and the young Asian Infrastructure Investment Bank (AIIB), as well as relevant business sanction decisions by the World Bank, are examined, respectively, in this section. Section 5.3 discusses the ICSID case law, finding the decisive role played by the

private firms generate the lion's share of the Chinese economy, accounting for over 50 percent of tax revenue, 60 percent of gross domestic product growth and 70 percent of technological innovation, as well as providing 80 percent of jobs. Bin Gu, "Five Myths about China Must Be Debunked before the Trade War with the US Can End", *South China Morning Post*, 15 June 2019.

[2] As Professor Julien Chaisse rightly put it, "[I]n an increasingly interconnected world, simply discriminating [SOEs] on a political basis is no longer acceptable"; we must look into laws and their application with respect to this issue. Julien Chaisse, "Untangling the Triangle: Issues for State-controlled Entities in Trade, Investment, and Competition Law" in Julien Chaisse and Tsai-Yu Lin (eds), *International Economic Law and Governance: Essays in Honour of Mitsuo Matsushita* (Oxford: Oxford University Press, 2016) p 235.

Broches test and the International Law Commission's Draft Articles on Responsibility of States for Internationally Wrongful Acts (*ILC Articles*) in some leading ICSID arbitral decisions, including the *BUCG* case in 2017, while in another case a significant deviation appears, creating inconsistency and confusion in investment arbitration. Section 5.4 looks into the WTO law, in particular relating to the Agreement on Subsidy and Countervailing Measures (*SCM Agreement*). In this section, two Appellate Body reports are examined, both involving the Chinese SOEs. The conclusion is that the Appellate Body adopted different treatment standards of SOEs in the two cases, thus having created clashes from within the WTO's dispute settlement system. Section 5.5 concludes the chapter.

5.2 International Finance: MDB Law

The MDBs generally lend to both governments and private entities in developing countries. But their lending priorities vary: the International Bank for Reconstruction and Development (IBRD) focuses on lending to governments and public entities, while the International Financial Corporation, a sister institution of the IBRD under the World Bank Group, lends to private entities. The European Bank for Reconstruction and Development (EBRD) mainly lends to private entities, but also to developing-country governments. In contrast, the Asian Development Bank, the Inter-America Development Bank, the African Development Bank, and the AIIB, which are similar in their investment profile, mainly fund the governments' projects but also those of private entities.

Lending priorities are significant for the MDBs. Since public entities in developing countries generally have their government's credit support, lending to them is deemed safe and sound for the MDBs. It not only helps with respect to Bank loan sustainability, but it also contributes to good credit ratings for a new MDB. This is important because a new MDB is highly motivated to establish itself, while often seeking opportunity to issue bonds in international capital markets. No wonder the clients of the AIIB were overwhelmingly developing-country governments or public entities in the first few years of Bank operations.[3] But each coin has two sides. A major problem about lending to government is the so-called debt-trap issue, which has posed risks to borrowing governments these years, and the MDBs have promised to address it.[4]

---

[3] A list of approved projects by the AIIB is available at https://www.aiib.org/en/projects/approved/index.html (visited October 14, 2019).

[4] One important endeavor in this regard is the establishment of the Multilateral Cooperation Center for Development Finance (MCDF) in 2020, initiated by China and supported by eleven leading MDBs, including the World Bank and the AIIB. The MCDF's mandate explicitly includes safeguarding debt sustainability for developing countries. "Memoranda of Understanding on Collaboration on Matters to Establish the Multilateral Cooperation Center for Development Finance", art I.1. Full text is available at https://www.aiib.org/en/about-aiib/who-we-are/partnership/_download/collaboration-on-matters.pdf (visited September 22, 2019).

Under MDB law, the distinction between a public and a private entity is meaningful in MDB-financed procurement markets, specifically from three perspectives: the choice of procurement methods; eligibility to bid for contracts; and eligibility to be governed by MDB sanctions law.

First, a public entity and a private one, acting as borrowers, apply different procurement methods. In the case of public entities as loan recipients, the procurement process follows the formal international open competitive tendering norm in principle,[5] which is an icon of high standards and thus the preferred method of procurement for an MDB.[6] In contrast, private entity borrowers only need to follow other established commercial practices to satisfy their lenders.[7] Compared with the former (competitive tendering methods), the latter (alternative commercial practices, such as direct contracting) tends to save time, reduce cost, and increase efficiency. For loan recipients, this advantage is meaningful.

Second, a private entity in the borrower country is eligible to compete and be awarded MDB-financed contracts. But a public entity, as an affiliate of the borrower government,[8] is not qualified to participate in the tender.[9] The distinction is significant

---

[5] For example, the AIIB has the following requirement on Bank-financed contracts procured by public entities:

"An international open competitive tender process is the normal method of procurement conducted for a Bank-financed contract. Alternative methods may be applied, provided the Recipient demonstrates to the Bank's satisfaction that the alternative method is the best strategic procurement approach for the Project and that it adequately reflects the Core Procurement Principles" (AIIB Procurement Policy (January 2016) para 5.6).

[6] For example, AIIB Interim Operational Directive on Procurement Instructions for Recipients (June 2, 2016) s II.10.1. World Bank Procurement Regulation s VI, para 6.11.

[7] For example, the AIIB has the following requirement on Bank-financed contracts procured by private entities:

"The Bank's concerns for the appropriate use of funds, with due consideration from economy and efficiency, apply equally to Bank-financed contracts procured by Private Entities. Private Entity Recipients often meet these concerns by following established private sector or commercial practices other than formal international open competitive tendering for their procurement. Nevertheless, whenever the Bank deems appropriate, it may require the use of competitive tendering methods by Private Entities, particularly for large contracts" (AIIB Procurement Policy (January 2016) para 6.1).

The EBRD similarly encourages the use of competitive tendering methods by its private sector clients, particularly for large contracts. EBRD Procurement Policies and Rules (revised October 2014) s 4.1.

[8] A public entity is considered as part of the "government". For example, the AIIB defines "government" to include its Member's political and administrative subdivisions and all other public entities. See AIIB Operational Policy on Financing (January 2016) s II.2.1(e). Similarly, in WTO law, the term "public body" shares certain attributes of the "government". Appellate Body Report, United States—Definitive Anti-Dumping and Countervailing Duties on Certain Products from China (*US Anti-Dumping and Countervailing Duties (China)*), WT/DS379/AB/R (March 11, 2011) para 317.

[9] For example, AIIB Interim Operational Directive on Procurement Instructions for Recipients (June 2, 2016) s II.4.10.1 provides as follows:

> "No affiliate of the Recipient, or of a procurement agent engaged by the Recipient, is eligible to participate in a tender or RFP [request for proposals] in any capacity whatsoever, unless the Recipient demonstrates to the satisfaction of the Bank that there is no significant degree

for SOEs operating in the borrower country: only when the SOEs are deemed as private entities are they able to compete in the bidding for an MDB-financed contract.

Third, the MDBs' sanctions law punishes the "firms and individuals" that have committed fraud or corruption during the procurement contract bidding or execution. The definition of "firms and individuals" is confined to private parties and does not extend to government officials or public entities. Thus, SOEs as private entities are normally subject to the sanctions law, but they are not, however, when acting in public capacity.[10]

The underlying question of the above discussion is how to identify a private vis-à-vis a public entity in MDB law. After reviewing the legal standards used in MDB law, and their application in individual sanctions cases, the conclusion is consistent and clear: the criteria of the distinction is more functional than otherwise (such as ownership-based).

5.2.1 Legal Standards in MDB Law[11]

The World Bank has new Procurement Framework and Regulations,[12] applying to all new lending operations after July 1, 2016, after an overhaul of its procurement system from 2012 to 2015. The overhaul does not alter the legal standards of a private entity, and the eligibility requirements for participating in the World Bank-funded procurement activities are consistent with the past practice of the Bank.[13] Under the new law, the SOEs in the borrower country are eligible for bidding, only if they meet the following criteria in a manner acceptable to the Bank: they (1) are legally and financially autonomous, (2) operate under commercial law, and (3) are not under

of common ownership, influence or control between the Recipient on the one hand, and the Recipient's agent and the affiliate on the other."

[10] Advisory Opinion on Certain Issues Arising in Connection with Recent Sanctions Cases, No. 2010/1 (Legal Vice Presidency of the World Bank, November 15, 2010) ("Advisory Opinion") para 129.

[11] This part is heavily borrowed from Bin Gu, *The Law and Governance of the Asian Infrastructure Investment Bank* (The Netherlands: Wolters Kluwer, 2019), pp 50–51.

[12] The revision enables the World Bank procurement policy to evolve from a traditional one-size-fits-all policy to a fit-for-purpose policy. See the key innovations of the new Procurement Framework at http://www.worldbank.org/en/projects-operations/products-and-services/brief/procurement-new-framework (visited November 1, 2019).

[13] The SOEs were termed as "government-owned enterprises" in the World Bank's past procurement policy, which stated in the relevant part as follows: "Government-owned enterprises in the Borrower's country may participate only if they can establish that they (i) are legally and financially autonomous, (ii) operate under commercial law, and (iii) are not dependent agencies of the Borrower or Sub- Borrower". See World Bank, "Guidelines: Procurement under IBRD Loans and IDA Credits" (January 1995, revised January and August 1996, September 1997 and January 1999) para 1.8(c); World Bank, "Guidelines: Procurement under IBRD Loans and IDA Credits" (May 2004, revised October 1, 2006, and May 1, 2010) para 1.8(c).

supervision by the agency contracting them.[14] But in practice, it is a *prima facie* case across the MDBs (including the Word Bank) that an SOE meets their relevant criteria and thus is qualified to compete in the bidding. In other words, an SOE has no obligation to take initiative to prove its private entity status, unless evidence proving opposite is produced.

The EBRD procurement law explicitly defines what constitutes a private entity: (1) the entity in question operates autonomously in a competitive market environment; and (2) it is subject to bankruptcy or insolvency law.[15] The legal criteria are clearly irrelevant to ownership but rather reveal an essentially functional test.

The European Investment Bank (EIB)[16] defines a public entity in its procurement law based on three criteria[17]: (1) it is established for the specific purpose of meeting needs in the general interest, not having an industrial or commercial character; (2) it has legal personality; and (3) it is financed in most part by public authorities or is subject to management supervision by public authorities or has an administrative, managerial, or supervisory Board in which more than half of the members are appointed by public authorities. An enterprise "operating in markets which are not liberalized" is also deemed as a public entity.[18]

AIIB procurement law distinguishes "public entity" from "private entity", in a much more straightforward manner than laws of peer institutions. It provides that any entity that is not a private entity will be a public entity. A private entity, in turn, is defined as follows[19]:

"Private Entity means any natural or legal person, whether publicly or privately owned:

(i) which is carrying out or is established for a business purpose, and is operating on a commercial basis;
(ii) which is financially and managerially autonomous from the government; and
(iii) whose day-to-day management is not controlled by the government."

It is thus clear that ownership is irrelevant in distinguishing a public entity and a private entity under AIIB procurement law. Instead, "commercial", "autonomous", and "uncontrol" are all the three magical words which constitute a comprehensive legal standard corpus for identifying a private entity. Since the AIIB chooses not to

[14] The World Bank Procurement Regulations for Investment Procurement Financing (IPF) Borrowers (July 2016, revised August 2018), s 3.23 (b).

[15] EBRD Procurement Policies and Rules (revised October 2014) s 3.2(c).

[16] The EIB is an atypical MDB in the sense that it is the bank of the European Union and regulated by EU law. It is the largest international long-term public lending institution.

[17] The EIB terms the concept "public entities" as "bodies governed by public law". EIB, Guide to Procurement (June 2011), Annex V.

[18] This provision applies in the specific case of gas; heat; electricity; water; transport; exploration for, or extraction of, oil, gas, coal, or other solid fuels; ports and airports; telecommunications; and postal services. EIB, Guide to Procurement (June 2011), Annex V.2.

[19] AIIB Procurement Policy (January 2016) s 2.1(b). Also, AIIB Environmental and Social Framework (February 2016) pp 24, 31 and 36, wherein a project established or carried out by "a private entity" is named "a private-sector project".

define a private entity on the basis of ownership, it enables an SOE as a private entity to compete in the AIIB-financed contracts. Other AIIB law also treats a commercial SOE as equivalent to a private enterprise.[20]

5.2.2 *Law Application in MDB Sanctions Cases*

When firms and individuals are suspected to be involved in business fraud and corruption in a World Bank-funded project, they would be investigated by a World Bank department (i.e., the Integrity Vice Presidency, or INT) and, in appropriate instances, a sanctions decision would be issued by the sanctions officer (the first tier), or by the Sanctions Board (the second and ultimate decision-maker) upon appeal.[21] However, the World Bank sanctions law normally does not apply to government officials and other public entities involved in the case. The rationale for such arrangement lies in the cooperative relationship the World Bank wishes to maintain with its Members, including the borrower State, and also because the World Bank must respect their sovereignty.[22] In particular, cases against high officials or political appointees must not run afoul of the "political prohibition" as contained in the Articles of Agreement of the World Bank.

It does not mean, however, that these public suspects will be clear of bearing any legal responsibility. Alternative means are available to address these cases; in particular, the borrower State has the obligation to take timely and appropriate action against these people, and the World Bank is able to exercise remedies under the financing contract, such as suspending or withdrawing loans, if the borrower State fails to act.[23]

Meanwhile, in a few cases, the suspected government officials or public entities may be acting in private capacity when they commit the prohibited practices. And they are treated as private entities and are subject to World Bank sanctions. Thus, the exemption that the World Bank affords to public entities is functional in nature.[24] The judgment is affirmed in the following World Bank sanctions cases.

---

[20] For example, AIIB Policy on Prohibited Practices (December 8, 2016) s 2.1, Definition 19 (equating a state-owned commercial entity to a private enterprise) reads as follows:

> "Non-sovereign-backed Financing means any Financing extended by the Bank that is not a Sovereign-backed Financing; it includes any Financing to or for the benefit of a private enterprise, or a state-owned or sub-sovereign owned commercial entity that is not backed by a guarantee or counter-guarantee and indemnity provided by the Member to the Bank."

[21] With respect to the process of investigating and reviewing a sanctions case, see Gu (n 11 above) pp 149–151.

[22] The World Bank Group's Sanctions Regime: Information Note (November 2011) p 19.

[23] *Ibid.*

[24] *Ibid.*, pp 19–20.

In Sanctions Board Decision No. 118 (2019), the Individual Respondent initially argued that he is a government official for purposes of INT's allegations, and that the Sanctions Board therefore does not have jurisdiction over him. However, the Individual Respondent later stated at the hearing that "the immunity argument is not one we're pursuing". Considering that the Individual Respondent drops the jurisdictional argument, and consistent with past precedent (referring to Sanctions Board Decision No. 115), the Sanctions Board affirmed jurisdiction over him with respect to conduct allegedly performed in his private capacity as a representative of the Respondent Firm.[25]

In Sanctions Board Decision No. 115 (2019), the Individual Respondent acted as a representative of an entity that competed for a Bank-financed contract, while allegedly using his position as a government official to further a collusive scheme. After examining the Individual Respondent's dual role, the Sanctions Board found that the Bank may exercise jurisdiction over the Individual Respondent with respect to conduct allegedly performed in his private capacity as a representative of the Respondent Firm.[26]

In Sanctions Board Decision No. 88 (2016), the Sanctions Board held that INT's designation of a wholly owned subsidiary of a state-owned entity as the Respondent does not run counter to the Bank's general policy that "governments and government officials should not be sanctioned when acting in their official capacity", because this policy does not extend to SOEs that operate autonomously and are thus eligible to bid on Bank-financed contracts.[27]

---

[25] World Bank Sanctions Board Decision No. 118 (2019) para 38.

[26] World Bank Sanctions Board Decision No. 115 (2019) paras 29–33. It is noted that, in an earlier case, the Sanctions Board distinguished the term "public official" from "government official", stating that the former bears a meaning within the context of the Bank's sanctions framework that is not equivalent to the latter for purposes of the general policy excluding government officials from sanctions (Sanctions Board Decision No. 78 (2015) para 45). The effort of making such distinction then revealed the Bank's reluctance to subject government officials to sanction, regardless in their official or private capacity when committing prohibited practices. The attitude obviously changed in the present case No. 115.

[27] World Bank Sanctions Board Decision No. 88 (2016) para 21. It is noted that the same reasoning regarding an SOE as respondent, using similar if not identical language, appears in Sanctions Board Decision No. 66 (2014) para 18, which states:

> "INT's designation of a majority state-owned entity as the Respondent, which INT alleges to be liable for the acts of the State-Owned Corporation in regard to the Contract, does not contradict the Bank's general policy that governments and government officials should not be sanctioned when acting in their official capacity, because this policy does not extend to state-owned enterprises that operate autonomously and are thus eligible to bid on Bank-financed contracts."

5.2.3 *A Little Comment*

The review of World Bank sanctions cases, as above, exemplifies the MDBs' general endorsement of a function-based approach: a person or entity acting in a private capacity is subject to MDB sanctions law, whether or not that person or entity wears a cap of government, government official or an SOE, at the time of being involved in business fraud and corruption. The function-based approach is consistent with the eligibility criteria for an SOE to be able to compete for an MDB-financed contract, as discussed in Sect. 5.2(a) above. What is more, in practice, it is a *prime facie* case that the SOE is a private entity, until proved otherwise. In MDB-funded procurement markets, the SOEs compete just like any other private party and are accordingly subject to sanctions when getting involved in illegal practice.

5.3 International Investment: ICSID Law

SOEs have been playing an important role in international investment activities today, and their evolvement in investment dispute settlement has become more and more prominent. In light of the central role that the ICSID plays in resolving investor–state disputes, more chances emerge that the SOEs would sue the hosting states through the jurisdiction of the ICSID.

Under ICSID Convention art 25(1), the jurisdiction of the ICSID is confined to two particular parties, that is, "between a Contracting State and a national of another Contracting State". In the case of an SOE as a potential claimant before the ICSID, the key is to make clear whether the SOE in question fulfills the role of "a national of another Contracting State",[28] in order to pass the jurisdictional threshold test. In other words, the SOE should be a private entity enjoying autonomy from the government for eligibility of an ICSID claim.[29] If, otherwise, the SOE is considered as an agent for the state, then the case would turn into a state-to-state dispute, of which the ICSID clearly lacks jurisdiction according to art 25(1) of the Convention.

Thus, whether the SOE is a private entity, or a public one, is a key issue in international investment law. There have been opposing views on this issue in the development history of ICSID law. In this section we will review these varied views

[28] The concept of "national", as used in art 25(1), is declared in art 25(2) to include both natural and juridical persons, but none of the terms is defined further in the Convention. However, the legislative history of the Convention indicates that the term "juridical persons" as employed in art 25 and, hence, the concept of "national" was not intended to be limited to privately owned companies but to embrace also wholly or partially government-owned companies. This interpretation has found general acceptance. *Ceskoslovenska Obchodni Banka, AS v The Slovak Republic*, ICSID Case No. ARB/97/4, Decision of the Tribunal on Objections to Jurisdiction (May 24, 1999) (*CSOB*), para.16.

[29] ICSID has no jurisdiction to arbitrate disputes between two States nor between two private entities. Its main jurisdictional feature is to decide disputes between a private investor and a State. Aron Broches, "The Convention on the Settlement of Investment Disputes: Some Observations on Jurisdiction" (1966) 5(2) *Columbia Journal of Transnational Law* 267.

and thereby endeavor to uncover the common ground in this important area of international economic law.

In the very early days of the ICSID, the development of a mixed public and private economy had already become a phenomenon and had caught attention from the organization. Aron Broches, the first secretary-general of the ICSID and one of the principal drafters of the ICSID Convention, commented thus in 1972[30]:

> "[I]n today's world the classical distinction between private and public investment, based on the source of the capital, is no longer meaningful, if not outdated. There are many companies which combine capital from private and governmental sources and corporations all of whose shares are owned by the government, but who are practically indistinguishable from the completely privately-owned enterprise both in their legal characteristics and in their activities. It would seem, therefore, that for purposes of the Convention a mixed economy company or government-owned corporation should not be disqualified as a 'national of another Contracting State' unless it is acting as an agent for the government or is discharging an essentially governmental function."

The *Broches* test, as so dubbed, sets up the criterion whether an SOE is qualified as a "national of another Contracting State" and thus may or may not proceed a case before the ICSID. The criterion is, simply put, whether the SOE "is acting as an agent for the government or is discharging an essentially governmental function". Here are two points to make.

First, the test uses the present progressive tense, demonstrating that it must point to a particular instance from where the legal dispute arises directly. It is consistent with art 5 of the *ILC Articles*, which examines whether "the person or entity is acting in [the government authority] capacity in the particular instance", for the purpose of judging whether the conduct of a private entity is attributable to the state. The *ILC Articles*, reflecting customary international law,[31] echoes the *Broches* test in using the present progressive tense, and in examining "the particular instance". No wonder the *Broches* test is alternatively known as the mirror image of art 5 of the *ILC Articles*.[32] Second, which is no less important, the test focuses on government authority or function. And the concept of government authority will be examined in detail in Sect. 5.4(a)(i), in conjunction with art 5 of the *ILC Articles*.

In examining the criterion set up by the *Broches* test, one may consider whether the SOEs "are practically indistinguishable from the completely privately-owned enterprise both in their legal characteristics and in their activities". If the SOEs are not different from private firms "in their legal characteristics and in their activities", then they are private entities and not agents for the government. Here are another two points to make.

---

[30] *Beijing Urban Construction Group Co Ltd v Republic of Yemen*, ICSID Case No. ARB/14/30, Decision on Jurisdiction (May 31, 2017) (*BUCG*), para. 33, quoting *Broches*.

[31] Tribunals and commentators alike consider that "[w]hile those Draft Articles are not binding, they are widely regarded as a codification of customary international law". Michael Feit, "Responsibility of the State Under International Law for the Breach of Contract Committed by a State-Owned Entity" (2010) 28 *Berkley J Int'l L* 1, 142, 146, quoting *Noble Ventures, Inc v Romania*, Award, ICSID Case No. ARB/01/11 (October 12, 2005), para.69.

[32] *BUCG* (n 30 above), para.34.

First, it is a comparison between the SOEs and typical private players, in terms of whether they behave similarly. And the comparison is instructive in judging the nature of the SOEs. Second, in specific, with respect to their "legal characteristics", the SOEs must be independent legal persons, having independent legal capacity in carrying out business activities. The word "activities" in the phrase involves a fact-specific connotation and context, rather than a pre-made judgment before looking into their business activities.

The *Broches* test, widely recognized in international investment arbitration, is clearly a function-based test, rather than an ownership-based one. ICSID tribunals have cited the *Broches* test in adjudicating many cases for decades, on which both complainants and respondents agreed,[33] only proving the everlasting validity of the *Broches* test. The early *CSOB* in 1999 and the recent *BUCG* in 2017 are two such milestone cases.

5.3.1 CSOB Case

This case involves the privatization of a state-owned bank, that is, CSOB, in the Czech Republic in 1990s, following the Velvet Revolution in 1989.[34] In light of Czech's new policy orientation from command economy toward market economy, CSOB adopted measures to enable it to function as an independent commercial bank. In particular, CSOB took measures to remove from its books those non-performing receivables resulting from its earlier lending activities during the state's non-market economy period, in order to improve its balance and consolidate its financial position.

CSOB was an SOE with 65 percent of its shares owned by Czech and some 24 percent by Slovak.[35] CSOB claimed that Slovak had breached an agreement, which was concluded among Czech, Slovak, and CSOB in an effort to facilitate the privatization of CSOB and its operation in Czech and Slovak after their separation.[36] CSOB brought the dispute to the ICSID, and as an initial step to establish jurisdiction, it needed to prove its private party status to fulfill the requirement of a "national of another Contracting State" under art 25(1) of the ICSID Convention.

The Tribunal established two important legal standards in the case. First, it should examine the behaviors of the two subjects, that is, the government and the enterprise, separately, rather than in a mixed way, however they are related to each other. It is no doubt that Czech's decision to transform its economic system involves the exercise of governmental functions. But it does not follow that the SOE is performing state functions "when it takes advantage of these State policies and proceeds to restructure

---

[33] For example, *CSOB* (28 above), para.17; *BUCG* (n 30 above), para.33.

[34] *CSOB* (n 28 above), para.21.

[35] *Ibid.*, para. 18.

[36] *Ibid.*, paras. 1–2.

itself'[37] nor does it mean that the measures taken by the SOE to achieve the objective involve the performance of state or governmental functions.

The second legal standard established in the case is that, in determining whether a party is public or private, the key is to examine the nature of the party's act, rather than the motive, purpose, or reason behind it. The Tribunal held that it did not matter whether the measure taken by CSOB was "driven by or was part of the privatization process instituted by the Government or whether it was the result largely of CSOB's unrelated business decision to strengthen its financial position".[38] It was true that CSOB's ability to take favorable measures in the case had benefited from both the Czech and Slovak governments, which had an interest in seeing CSOB become a competitive market entity.[39] But this would not turn an otherwise commercial transaction into a government act. Rather, what matters is the nature of the act per se in question.[40]

How to decide the nature of a said act then? The *CSOB* Tribunal stated as follows: "In the instant case, the steps taken by CSOB to solidify its financial position in order to attract private capital for its restructured banking enterprise do not differ in their nature from measures a private bank might take to strengthen its financial position".[41] The Tribunal thus compared the nature of the acts taken respectively by an SOE and by a typical private entity, in order to determine the commercial nature of the SOE's act, which then lead to a decision on the private party status of the SOE itself.

Aligning with such comparisons, another often-quoted, hypothetical case deserves to be mentioned here. In Louis Henkin's classic textbook *International Law*,[42] it illustrates thus, "When a foreign state purchases shoes for its army from a US supplier, the purpose of the transaction is public, but the nature of the transaction is of the kind that private persons undertake (e.g., buying shoes)". In this case the foreign state is not entitled to immunity, because it acts as a private person in the particular transaction, possessing no governmental function.

In sum, the legal standards for an SOE to be a private entity are best summarized in the arbitral award of the *CSOB* case, which is quoted as follows[43]:

> "[I]t cannot be denied that for much of its existence, CSOB acted on behalf of the State in facilitating or executing the international banking transactions and foreign commercial

---

[37] *Ibid.*, para.23.

[38] *Ibid.*, para.24.

[39] *Ibid.*, para.25.

[40] It is noted that there is criticism over the *CSOB* Tribunal's reliance on the nature of, not the purpose of, the specific act. For example, Feldman criticizes that the *CSOB* Tribunal "accorded weight only to the nature ('commercial'), and not the purpose ('promoting the governmental policy or purposes of the State'), of a State-owned bank's activities when determining whether the bank's ICSID claim gave rise to a State-to-State dispute". Mark Feldman, "State-Owned Enterprises as Claimants in International Investment Arbitration" (2016) 31(1) *ICSID Review* 34.

[41] *CSOB* (n 28 above), para.25.

[42] Lori Fisler Damrosch et al., *International Law: Cases and Materials* (Minnesota: Thomson Reuters, 5th ed., 2009) p 882.

[43] *CSOB* (n 28 above), para.20.

operations the State wished to support and that the State's control of CSOB required it to do the State's bidding in that regard. But **in determining whether CSOB, in discharging these functions, exercised governmental functions, the focus must be on the nature of these activities and not their purpose**. While it cannot be doubted that in performing the above-mentioned activities, CSOB was promoting the governmental policies or purposes of the State, **the activities themselves were essentially commercial rather than governmental in nature**."

5.3.2 *BUCG Case*

BUCG is a recent case, whose arbitral award was released in 2017, almost 20 years after the *CSOB* case. In this case, BUCG, as a Chinese SOE, was responsible for building an airport terminal in Yemen under a construction contract with the Yemen government. BUCG's investment interest was impaired when Yemen's military forces intervened in the construction work. BUCG filed the case against Yemen before the ICSID. Yemen disputed the ICSID jurisdiction, arguing that BUCG was an inappropriate claimant under art 25(1) of the Convention, since it was exercising governmental functions when performing its work on the airport site.

In particular, as Yemen argued, BUCG was subject to the overall direction of a Board that was the "representative of the state interests and the operation decision making organ", and it must "accept the supervision and inspection of Beijing State-owned Assets Supervision and Administration Bureau and Beijing Finance Bureau".[44] Moreover, the Party committee in BUCG must not only focus on supervising human resources, finance, and materials but are also responsible for "monitoring the implementation of the scientific concepts of development and national policies, to promote enterprises to play a leading role in carrying out political and social responsibility".[45] Thus, examples that could be seen as government agent were more or less similar in *BUCG* as in *CSOB*.[46] Yemen basically argued that BUCG was expected to advance China's national interest.

Of these evidences, the Tribunal agreed with Yemen that "[t]hese corporate controls and mechanisms are not surprising in the context of PRC State-owned corporations".[47] But the Tribunal disapproved Yemen's argument, holding that "[t]he Respondent's positioning of BUCG in the broad context of the PRC State-controlled economy is convincing but largely irrelevant"[48]; rather, the focus should be on the functions of BUCG "in the particular instance", that is, the construction of the airport

---

[44] *BUCG* (n 30 above), para.37.

[45] *Ibid.*, para.38.

[46] In *CSOB*, the Tribunal found that "for much of its existence", the claimant, a State-owned bank, "acted on behalf of the State in facilitating or executing the international banking transactions and foreign commercial operations the State wishes to support and... the State's control of CSOB required it to do the State's bidding in that regard" (*CSOB* (n 28 above)), para.20.

[47] *BUCG* (n 30 above), para.39.

[48] *Ibid.*, para.42.

terminal project.[49] For the Tribunal, the assertion that "the Chinese State is the ultimate decision maker" over BUCG is too remote from the facts of the airport terminal project to be relevant.[50]

Thus, the Tribunal looked into the evidentiary record disclosing the commercial nature of the airport terminal project[51] and concluded that BUCG was not acting as an agent of the Chinese government. After all, the independent legal characteristics (i.e., a term used in the *Broches* test) of BUCG is explicitly acknowledged in its Articles of Association, in particular art 7, which reads:

> "The Company is entitled to all corporate property rights formed by the investor and lawful civil rights as well as civil liabilities; the Company independently operates, assumes sole responsibility for profits and losses, performs independent accounting, pays taxes in accordance with the regulations, and assumes liability for debts of the Company with all its assets."[52]

Indeed, the *BUCG* Tribunal upheld the function-based test, just as the *CSOB* Tribunal did almost 20 years ago, for purposes of deciding whether an SOE is an agent of the government and discharging a governmental function. The two cases offer consistent endorsement in practice for the *Broches* test and art 5 of the *ILC Articles*.

5.3.3 Some Deviations

The function-based test has not always been respected in the ICSID case law history, however. The case *Maffezini v Spain*, done in 2000, is such an exception.[53] The Tribunal formulated a two-pronged test in deciding whether SODIGA (a regional development agency in Spain) is a State entity.[54] The first test is the structural or formal test, which examines factors such as ownership, control, purpose, and objective of the corporation in question.[55] In case the first test is insufficient to

---

[49] *Ibid.*

[50] *Ibid.*, para.43.

[51] *Ibid.*, para.40.

[52] *Ibid.*, para.39, footnote 19.

[53] ICSID Case No. ARB/97/7, Decision of the Tribunal on Objections to Jurisdiction (January 25, 2000) (*Maffezini v Spain*, English Translation from Spanish Original). This case is different from *CSOB* and *BUCG* in the sense that the Tribunal was to decide jurisdiction based on the judgment whether SODIGA's action is attributable to Spain as respondent.

[54] The Tribunal stated that "the structural test by itself may not always be a conclusive determination whether an entity is an organ of the State.... An additional test has been developed, a functional test", and "[i]t is difficult to determine, a priori, whether these various tests and standards need necessarily be cumulative. It is likely that there are circumstances when they need not be". *Maffezini v Spain* (n 53 above) paras.79–81.

[55] *Ibid.*, para.77.

make a conclusion, then comes the second—the functional test—"which looks to the functions or role to be performed by the entity".[56]

With respect to the two-pronged test as applied in *Maffezini v Spain*, it is appropriate to make the following three comments. First, the formally different roles of the two tests are not clearly defined; instead, they largely converge in content in that case. The two-pronged test largely concentrates on the following factors: ownership, motive, purpose, and generally designated functions with regard to (the establishment of) the party in question.[57]

Second, those factors considered in *Maffezini v Spain*, as quoted above, are explicitly dismissed as being "largely irrelevant" by the later *BUCG* Tribunal in making similar judgments,[58] holding that "the issue is not the corporate framework of the State-owned enterprise, but whether it *functions* as an agent of the State in the fact-specific context" (original emphasis).[59]

Third, the "functional test" was applied in *Maffezini v Spain* in a distorted and mistaken manner, different from what was endorsed by the *BUCG* and *CSOB* tribunals. In specific, the term "functional test" referred to the generally designated functions to SODIGA[60]; it failed to apply correctly to the specific act of SODIGA, which lead to the claimant's injuries and the ensuing dispute at issue, and which should have fallen into the scope of the functional test.

Thus, the Tribunal in *Maffezini v Spain* clearly deviated from the established legal standards as endorsed by *CSOB*, *BUCG*, the *ILC Articles,* and the *Broches* test, although it chose not to openly defy the function-based test. Actually, the later *BUCG* Tribunal simply walked away from *Maffezini v Spain,* when the respondent sought to rely on it for support.[61]

Opponents might seek support from the Commentaries on art 5 of the *ILC Articles*,[62] which, speaking of the scope of "governmental authority", states that "[o]f particular importance will be not just the content of the powers, but the way they are conferred on an entity, the purposes for which they are to be exercised and

---

[56] *Ibid.*, para.79.

[57] *Ibid.*, paras.77–89.

[58] *BUCG* (n 30 above) para.42.

[59] *Ibid.*, para.39.

[60] *Maffezini v Spain* (n 53 above) para.86.

[61] *BUCG*, paras.38–39. The respondent in *BUCG* cited the following paragraph in *Maffezini v Spain* for support, which the *BUCG* Tribunal dismissed diplomatically but without hesitation.

> "[T]he test that has been developed [to establish whether a particular entity is a state body] looks to various factors, such as ownership, control, the nature, *purposes and objectives* of the entity whose actions are under scrutiny, and to the character of the actions taken." (Emphasis added by the respondent)

[62] Draft Articles on Responsibility of States for Internationally Wrongful Acts, with Commentaries, *in* Report of the International Law Commission on the Work of Its 53rd Session, UN Doc A/56/10 (2001) (*ILC Articles*).

the extent to which the entity is accountable to government for their exercise".[63] But "the purposes" here is mentioned as an evidentiary standard in judging governmental authority and not a legal standard as explicitly stipulated in the text of art 5.

After all, a purpose-oriented approach is not workable.[64] First, the purpose of an SOE investor is often multitasking,[65] mixed with both public and commercial elements. Uncertainty and even internal conflicts tend to emerge accordingly in such situations. Second, some ultimate purpose with a public nature, as designated by the State shareholder, may be too remote to be considered in examining the nature of the specific act, as held by the *BUCG* Tribunal. Third, a dual consideration of both the purpose and nature of the said act may possibly lead to conflicting conclusions, and if so, the nature-of-the-act approach must prevail. That is, the legal standard prevails over an evidentiary standard. Consider the case of military shoe purchase, as quoted above. The purpose of the purchase is public, but the nature of the transaction itself is commercial; in such instance, the state organ is not carrying out "governmental authority" when acting as shoe buyer in the transaction. Indeed, as the Commentaries on the *ILC Articles* notes, "These are essentially questions of the application of a general standard to varied circumstances",[66] and we must look into the nature of the specific act.

5.4 International Trade: WTO Law

The legal battle about an SOE's identification as a private entity is most heated, controversial and unsettled in the WTO, compared with the debates in fora of the MDBs and the ICSID. Specifically, all controversies arise from the architecture of art 1.1 of the *SCM Agreement* and the interpretation thereof. The provision contemplates two principal categories of entities whose conduct may be attributable to a WTO member: the first type is a government or "a public body", and[67] the second type is "a private body" that demonstrates an affirmative link of "entrust or direct" between the government (or a public body) and the specific conduct of the private body.[68] If an SOE constitutes a public body, what it grants to a business firm may well qualify

[63] Commentaries on the *ILC Articles*, art 5, p 43.

[64] This viewpoint will be reiterated and reinforced at the end of the following Sect. 5.4(a)(ii).

[65] Be mindful of those important concepts such as environmental, social, and governance and corporate social responsibility. In August 18, 2019, a large and powerful US business group (i.e., the Business Roundtable) redefined the corporate purposes as multiple. Available at https://corpgov.law.harvard.edu/2019/08/21/legal-implications-of-the-business-roundtable-statement-on-corporate-purpose/ (visited August 29, 2019).

[66] Commentaries on the *ILC Articles*, art 5, p 43.

[67] The collective reference of "a government or any public body" as "government" under art 1.1 of the *SCM Agreement* suggests a certain degree of commonality or overlap in their essential characteristics.

[68] Appellate Body Report, *US Countervailing Measures (China) (Article 21.5)* para 5.94; Appellate Body Report, *US Anti-Dumping and Countervailing Duties (China)* para 284.

to be subsidy, as stipulated under art 1.1 of the *SCM Agreement*, and thus is subject to countervailing measures. The term SOE, although never appearing in the *SCM Agreement*, weighs significantly in it.

Two milestone WTO cases, involving Chinese SOEs, have so far discussed the legal criteria of a public body and whether an SOE constitutes a public body under art 1.1 of the *SCM Agreement*. The two cases are *US Anti-Dumping and Countervailing Duties (China)*, or *DS379*, done in 2011,[69] and *US Countervailing Measures (China) (Article 21.5)*, or *DS437*, done in 2019.[70] The Appellate Body in both cases endorsed a basic legal standard: a public body must possess, exercise, or be vested with governmental authority.[71] The legal standard renders the term "governmental authority" of paramount importance. This section will first review what constitutes government authority or government function alternatively, pursuant to the two cases and international law in general.

5.4.1 What is Government Authority?

In *DS379*, the Appellate Body figured out several criteria that may assist in deciding "whether an entity is vested with authority to exercise governmental functions".[72] First is the legal instruments "expressly vest[ing] authority in the entity concerned".[73] Second is about the actions of the said entity,[74] which requires investigating the function of the entity. Third, one can look into whether the government exercises meaningful control over the said entity.[75] By comparison, the first criterion is a straightforward exercise, requiring searching for relevant legal texts only, but the second and third criteria are more controversial and complicated. With respect to the second criterion specifically, in order to determine the governmental nature of the function in question, one must address an underlying question, that is, what

---

[69] United States Definitive Anti-Dumping and Countervailing Duties on Certain Products from China (*US Anti-Dumping and Countervailing Duties (China)*) WT/DS379/AB/R (March 11, 2011).

[70] United States Countervailing Duty Measures on Certain Products from China (*US Countervailing Duties (China)*) recourse to art 21.5 of the DSU by China, WT/DS437/AB/RW (July 16, 2019).

[71] Appellate Body Report, *US Anti-Dumping and Countervailing Duties (China)* para 317; Appellate Body Report, *US Countervailing Measures (China) (Article 21.5)* para 5.95.

[72] Appellate Body Report, *US Anti-Dumping and Countervailing Duties (China)* para 318.

[73] "In some cases, such as when a statute or other legal instrument expressly vests authority in the entity concerned, determining that such entity is a public body may be a straightforward exercise." Appellate Body Report, *US Anti-Dumping and Countervailing Duties (China)* para 318.

[74] "Evidence that an entity is, in fact, exercising governmental functions may serve as evidence that it possesses or has been vested with governmental authority, particularly where such evidence points to a sustained and systematic practice." Appellate Body Report, *US Anti-Dumping and Countervailing Duties (China)* para 318.

[75] "It follows, in our view, that evidence that a government exercises meaningful control over an entity and its conduct may serve, in certain circumstances, as evidence that the relevant entity possesses governmental authority and exercises such authority in the performance of governmental functions." Appellate Body Report, *US Anti-Dumping and Countervailing Duties (China)* para 318.

constitutes governmental authority or function; with respect to the third criterion, one must look into the relationship between the entity and the government and find out indicia of "meaningful control".

5.4.1.1 Government Authority

The legal characteristics of government authority are bound to differ from State to State, "depend[ing] on the particular society, its history and traditions", as the Commentaries on the *ILC Articles* notes.[76] That said, the term "government" does share a certain common ground across States. Perhaps that is why the definition of government authority requires a review of the legal order of the relevant member,[77] as well as "the classification and functions of entities within WTO Members generally".[78] In a similar vein, in determining criteria for distinguishing commercial versus public act, it is recognized that "national law may be used to draw the distinction, but may not deviate from the views of the preponderance of states as to what belongs to the region of state authority in its narrow and proper sense".[79] To be clear, the WTO Appellate Body defines the term "government" as the "continuous exercise of authority over subjects; authoritative direction or regulation and control", and the essence of government is that "it enjoys the effective power to regulate, control, or supervise individuals, or otherwise restrain their conduct, through the exercise of lawful authority".[80] Thus, the WTO adjudicating body should have power to make an objective review of whether government authority exists in a particular case.

The Commentaries on art 5 of the *ILC Articles* offer some telling examples of government functions, which then are used to decide the legal characteristics of the entities that carry those functions. "The conduct of a railway company to which certain police powers have been granted will be regarded as an act of the State under international law, if it concerns the exercise of those powers, but not if it concerns other activities (e.g. the sale of tickets or the purchase of rolling stock)". Public powers such as powers of detention and discipline, if contracted to private security firms acting in the capacity of prison guards, may turn them into public entities in the exercise of those powers. Powers in relation to immigration control or quarantine, as delegated to private or state-owned airlines, similarly turn those enterprises into public entities in the exercise of those powers. Those examples reveal that a public body inquiry in the *ILC Articles* is essentially a function-based test.

However, the Appellate Body in *DS437* took a different approach. Rather, it stated that "once it has been established that an entity is a public body, then '*all* conduct' of that entity shall be attributable to the Members" (original emphasis).[81] This features

[76] Commentaries on the *ILC Articles*, art 5, p 43.

[77] Appellate Body Report, *US Anti-Dumping and Countervailing Duties (China)* para 297.

[78] Appellate Body Report, *US Countervailing Measures (China) (Article 21.5)* paras 5.95–5.96.

[79] Damrosch et al. (n 42 above) p 882.

[80] Appellate Body Report, *US Anti-Dumping and Countervailing Duties (China)* para 290.

[81] Appellate Body Report, *US Countervailing Measures (China) (Article 21.5)* para 5.100.

an entity-based approach whereby identity decides all. It runs counter to the *ILCs Articles'* approach and deviates from the Appellate Body's earlier holding in *DS379* that "[t]he same entity may possess certain features suggesting it is a public body, and others that suggest that it is a private body".[82] As a third party in *DS437*, the European Union (EU) formulated an "exceptional scenario" where an entity engages in two distinct areas of activity and "such an entity may be seen as acting as a public body when engaged in one of those areas, but not in the other".[83] The EU's viewpoints are indeed in line with those examples in the Commentaries on art 5 of the *ILC Articles*, as quoted above. The cases of such an "exceptional scenario" are noticeably increasing nowadays, only to blur the distinction between private and public bodies. Think about Facebook's plan to issue digital currency Libra,[84] a traditionally governmental function and rarely carried out by commercial entities. Surely Facebook would have to be treated and governed as a public body in exercising such function.[85]

5.4.1.2 "Meaningful Control"

Another important criterion in a public body inquiry is "meaningful control" by a government. The Appellate Body held that manifold indicia of meaningful control "may permit an inference that the entity concerned is exercising governmental authority".[86] As a matter of principle, meaningful control must be observed in daily operation and must exist in specific act, rather than being generally concluded from the shareholder relationship.[87] Meaningful control may infer elements of government authority, but it does not mean that one may conflate "meaningful control" directly with government authority, by way of simply defining the term as "control related to the possession or exercise of governmental authority and governmental

---

[82] Appellate Body Report, *US Anti-Dumping and Countervailing Duties (China)* para 318. To enhance this holding, the Appellate Body added a footnote in the same place, stating that "the analysis of whether the conduct of a particular entity is conduct of the government or a public body or conduct of a private body is indeed multi-faceted and that an entity may display characteristics pointing into different directions".

[83] Appellate Body Report, *US Countervailing Measures (China) (Article 21.5)* para 5.88.

[84] Peter Morici, "In Search of Stable Digital Money", *The Washington Times*, July 8, 2019.

[85] As Backer wisely commented, "The character of the action, rather than the status of the actor, ought to be the basis of legal systems where the object is to regulate actors who intervene in areas once deemed to be the sole preserve of states". Larry Cata Backer, "Sovereign Investing in Times of Crisis: Global Regulation of Sovereign Wealth Funds, State-Owned Enterprises, and the Chinese Experience" (2010) 19 *Transnat'l L & Contemp Probs* 3, 144.

[86] Appellate Body Report, *US Anti-Dumping and Countervailing Duties (China)* para 318.

[87] The term "meaningful control" was first used by the Appellate Body in *DS379*, nevertheless, with no clear definition; only in the later *DS436* the Appellate Body gave the term an act-specific connotation. Appellate Body Report, *US Carbon Steel (India)* paras 4.37, 4.40, 4.43–4.44.

functions",[88] as the United States twisted the criterion in its Public Bodies Memorandum.[89] According to the Public Bodies Memorandum, Chinese SOEs, as well as some Chinese private entities, are all overwhelmed by indicia of "meaningful control" by the Chinese government and the Communist Party of China.[90] Thus, they may all be public bodies.

The Public Bodies Memorandum represents the US government's understanding of, and approach to, Chinese SOEs, the essence of which was endorsed later by the Appellate Body in *DS437*. In *DS437*, an entity's generally designated purpose (including its relationship with government), rather than its specific function, prevails in deciding the nature of the entity. Once the entity agrees, endorses, or serves the purpose of the government, which is a major source of indicia of "meaningful control" as interpreted in the Public Bodies Memorandum,[91] then the entity is characterized as a public entity. On the other hand, the dimension of measuring the specific function of the entity, as commonly recognized in other places such as in *DS379*, is dwindled to none in *DS437*.[92]

The approach in *DS437* essentially agrees with the Public Bodies Memorandum, which describes China's governmental function as to "maintain and uphold the

---

[88] Appellate Body Report, *US Countervailing Measures (China) (Article 21.5)* para 5.55, quoting the Public Bodies Memorandum. Regrettably, the Appellate Body failed to explain in what logic the two terms "meaningful control" and "governmental authority" are connected.

[89] The Public Bodies Memorandum refers to: US Department of Commerce (USDOC)'s Memorandum dated 18 May 2012 for Sect. 129 Determination of the Countervailing Duty Investigation of Circular Welded Carbon Quality Steel Pipe; Light-Walled Rectangular Pipe and Tube; Laminated Woven Sacks; and Off-the-Road Tires from the People's Republic of China: An Analysis of Public Bodies in the People's Republic of China in Accordance with the WTO Appellate Body's Findings in WTO *DS379*; and USDOC Memorandum dated May 18, 2012 on the relevance of the Chinese Communist Party for the limited purpose of determining whether particular enterprises should be considered to be "public bodies" within the context of a countervailing duty investigation.

[90] Appellate Body Report, *US Countervailing Measures (China) (Article 21.5)* paras 5.56–5.57, quoting the Public Bodies Memorandum.

[91] The Public Bodies Memorandum lists seven such indicia, almost none of which point to any specific act of the SOE (Appellate Body Report, *US Countervailing Measures (China) (Article 21.5)* para 5.56). The seventh indicium, for example, is "the presence of CCP [ie, China Communist Party] groups and committees within enterprises", which is also the most controversial and debated among them. To understand this indicium, the key is not the presence of CCP in the enterprise, but what the CCP does there in practice. Here is a quote perfectly addressing the question:

"What does the Party committee, established as required by law, do in a company? Here is an illustrative analogy. The Party in China is like God among Christians, while its Party committee is like a church. The church calls upon congregation to be helpful to neighbors, while the Party committee asks members to be role model for corporate codes compliance. In daily operations, Chinese companies perform commercially and autonomously, uncontrolled by the Party; just like a Christian CEO doing business on his own, free from God's intervention." (Bin Gu, "Western Fears of Party Influence on Chinese Companies Are Overblown", *Financial Times*, February 18, 2019. Also, Bin Gu, "Five Myths about China Must Be Debunked before the Trade War with the US Can End", *South China Morning Post*, June 15, 2019.).

[92] Evidence is thus: "Rather, the relevant inquiry hinges on the *entity* engaging in that conduct, its core characteristics, and its relationship with government". Appellate Body Report, *US Countervailing Measures (China) (Article 21.5)* para 5.100.

socialist market economy", including maintaining a leading role for the state sector in the economy.[93] And the Chinese SOEs are "instrumentalities to effectuate the governmental purpose of maintaining the predominant role of the state sector in the economy and upholding the socialist market economy",[94] and while in serving such governmental purpose, they are deemed as public bodies. What the United States described here is more of governmental purpose than governmental function, which by definition is authority over individuals, as quoted above in Sect. 5.4(a)(i), in the Appellate Body report in *DS379*. Further, such description of Chinese government purpose is incomplete, because it intentionally ignores China's commitment to nourishing a fair market competition environment, by encouraging and promoting non-state economies as well as state ones.[95]

This purpose-oriented shift runs afoul of common sense unfortunately. For example, the controversial National Endowment for Democracy (NED), funded by the US government, serves the governmental purpose of promoting Western values and democracy worldwide, but no doubt the NED is a private entity and runs independently. The shift may render confusion and chaos in the free market as well. For example, the Trump administration is committed to "Make America Again", and all firms in the United States, including those from China originally, are expected to contribute to the grand agenda. It would be ridiculous to argue that all these firms are public bodies just because they endorse the Trump dream. On August 18, 2019, a large and powerful US business group, the Business Roundtable, publicized the *Statement on the Purpose of a Corporation*, which breaks away from the long-dominating principle that a corporation's sole or primary purpose is to maximize shareholder value and that other stakeholders' interests are only "relevant as a derivative of the duty to stockholders". Rather, the *Statement on the Purpose of a Corporation* commits to (1) delivering value to its *customers*, (2) investing in its *employees*, (3) dealing fairly and ethically with its *suppliers*, (4) supporting the *communities* in which it works, and (5) generating long-term *shareholder* value.[96] The redefinition of the corporate purposes as multiple makes it even unpredictable and thus ridiculous to rely on a purposed-oriented approach, as discussed in the previous section of ICSID law.

---

[93] *Ibid.*, para 5.56.

[94] *Ibid.*, para 5.56.

[95] Chengjin Xu and Bin Gu, "A Review of State-Owned Enterprises from WTO Law Perspective" (《WTO法视野下的国有企业法律定性问题》) (May 2016) 23(3) *Journal of SUIBE* 18, quoting China's Constitution Law, Property Law, and the Decision of 18th CCP Central Committee Third Plenary Session.

[96] The *Statement of Purpose* text is available at https://corpgov.law.harvard.edu/2019/08/21/legal-implications-of-the-business-roundtable-statement-on-corporate-purpose/ (visited August 29, 2019).

5.4.2 The Criteria of "Ownership" in a Public Body Inquiry

The role of "state ownership" presents nuanced differences in deciding a public body across different Appellate Body decisions as well as in the US Public Bodies Memorandum. It is clear in *DS379* that control through majority government ownership is unlikely to establish either "meaningful control" or the necessary possession of governmental authority; more indicia is needed to make it.[97] The Appellate Body emphasized in that case that "meaningful control" is something more than mere formal links such as majority ownership.[98] One may well envision an entity that is "controlled" by government as a major shareholder, but is autonomous in daily operations, and thus constitutes a private rather than a public body. The Tribunal in a commercial arbitration case, *Al-Kharafi & Sons Co v Libya*, splendidly echoed this, and we will quote here as support of the Appellate Body in *DS379*:

> "In certain circumstances, the separate personality of an entity fully controlled by a state can be discarded and the state considered bound by the terms of a contract entered into by such an entity . . . . Such a conclusion, however can only be drawn if this entity acted as an instrument of the state."[99]

However, the US Public Bodies Memorandum clearly deviates, by increasing the weight of "state ownership" in deciding a public body, even though the Memorandum was supposed to be an implementary document as to the Appellate Body's finding in *DS379*.[100] For example, the Memorandum states: "[A]ny enterprise in China in which the government has a full or controlling ownership interest is found to be a public body".[101] Even though the Memorandum emphasizes that the judgment is made "in the institutional and SIE-focused policy setting of China",[102] trying to conceal inconsistency with the Appellate Body in *DS379*, it still amounts to an

---

[97] Appellate Body Report, *US Anti-Dumping and Countervailing Duties (China)* para 318.

[98] "We stress, however, that, apart from an express delegation of authority in a legal instrument, the existence of mere formal links between an entity and government in the narrow sense is unlikely to suffice to establish the necessary possession of governmental authority. Thus, for example, the mere fact that a government is the majority shareholder of an entity does not demonstrate that the government exercises meaningful control over the conduct of that entity, much less that the government has bestowed it with governmental authority." (Appellate Body Report, *US Anti-Dumping and Countervailing Duties (China)* para 318).

[99] *Al-Kharafi & Sons Co v Libya*, Final Arbitral Award, 22 March 2013, 263, quoting GB Born. The quote proves that attributability of the act of an entity to a state is stringently conditional; one must pass the tests of "full control" and "acting as an instrument of the state" to make it happen.

[100] The relationship between the Memorandum and *DS379* is demonstrated in the title of the Memorandum: "Sect. 129 Determination of the Countervailing Duty Investigation of Circular Welded Carbon Quality Steel Pipe; Light-Walled Rectangular Pipe and Tube; Laminated Woven Sacks; and Off-the Road Tires from the People's Republic of China: An Analysis of Public Bodies in the People's Republic of China in Accordance with the WTO Appellate Body's Finding in WTO DS379" (Department of Commerce, May 18, 2012).

[101] Appellate Body Report, *US Countervailing Measures (China) (Article 21.5)* para 5.57, quoting the US Public Bodies Memorandum.

[102] SIE, short for state-invested enterprise, is used interchangeably as SOE in the US Public Bodies Memorandum.

automatic recognition of an entity as a public body based on state ownership solely, while ignoring the specific act of the entity in question.

In the later *DS437*, the Appellate Body seemed to turn to embrace the United States' position, however, explicitly endorsing an entity-based approach in a public body inquiry. Under this approach, the relevant inquiry focuses on "*the entity* engaging in that conduct, its core characteristics, and its relationship with government".[103] It is reasonable to assume that under this approach, state ownership plays an even important role in a public body inquiry, as indicated in the Appellate Body's statement: "[G]overnment ownership of an entity, while not a decisive criterion, may serve... as evidence".[104] This statement infers a somewhat more positive and favorable inclination toward evidence of state ownership, compared with the criteria established in the earlier *DS379*.[105] Although the Appellate Body in *DS437* ostensibly reiterated a comprehensive investigation of all evidences,[106] it actually placed disproportionate weight on state ownership. In contrast, the importance of the specific-conduct element dwindled in *DS437*, and it lost its status as a virtually separate legal criterion in a public body inquiry. Instead, it functioned merely as evidence of the entity's core characteristics, according to the United States.[107] The Appellate Body in *DS437* even held that the specific-conduct element is irrelevant in a public body inquiry,[108] about which we will elaborate below.

---

[103] Appellate Body Report, *US Countervailing Measures (China) (Article 21.5)* para 5.100.

[104] *Ibid*., para 5.97.

[105] Appellate Body Report, *US Anti-Dumping and Countervailing Duties (China)* paras 343–346. In the dispute, the Appellate Body also reviewed the USDOC's public body determinations in respect to *other* SOEs than SOCBs (i.e., state-owned commercial banks), namely "producers of steel, rubber and petrochemical inputs" that sold such inputs to downstream producers. The Appellate Body ultimately found those determinations to be WTO-inconsistent, because the USDOC had relied "principally" on government ownership.

> "In our view, this is not sufficient because evidence of government ownership, in itself, is not evidence of meaningful control of an entity by government and cannot, without more, serve as a basis for establishing that the entity is vested with authority to perform a governmental function. Accordingly, such evidence, alone, cannot support a finding that an entity is a public body."

[106] Appellate Body Report, *US Countervailing Measures (China) (Article 21.5)* para 5.97.

[107] *Ibid*., paras 5.101, 5.104. Indeed, as the Appellate Body commented, "while the USDOC did take into account evidence relating to the conduct of SOCBs, it did so within the framework of its inquiry into the core characteristics of those entities and their relationship with the GOC [ie, Government of China]".

[108] Appellate Body Report, *US Countervailing Measures (China) (Article 21.5)* para 5.84.

5.4.3 "Private Body" in Art 1.1(a)(1)(Iv) of the SCM Agreement

The Appellate Body in *DS379* found that, in order to establish a financial contribution by a private body in art 1.1(a)(1)(iv), an additional link between the government and the conduct of the private body in question must be "established by a showing of entrustment or direction".[109] In other words, it "requires an affirmative demonstration of the link between the government and the specific *conduct*".[110] The finding was paraphrased later by the United States in *DS437* that "a focus on the conduct of an entity is relevant when examining the entrustment or direction of a private body", but it is irrelevant in a public body inquiry.[111] The Appellate Body in *DS437* seemed to agree with the United States, holding that an examination of the specific conduct in a public body inquiry, which China had firmly advocated, "would unduly blur the distinction between, on the one hand, a public body inquiry and, on the other hand, an 'entrustment or direction' inquiry".[112] In other words, the specific-conduct element is unique to an "entrustment or direction" inquiry, and the introduction of it into a public body inquiry would make it redundant, violating "the principle of effective treaty interpretation".[113]

Meanwhile, in a manner of self-contradiction, the Appellate Body expressed that the conduct of an entity is relevant in a public body inquiry. In *DS379*, for example, it considered the examination of the conduct of the entity in question as a major criterion for deciding "whether an entity is vested with authority to exercise governmental functions".[114] The Appellate Body favored a view that "whether the functions or conduct are of a kind that are ordinarily classified as governmental in the legal order of the relevant Member may be a relevant consideration for determining whether or not a specific entity is a public body",[115] which clearly falls in the function-based test. Even in *DS437*, the Appellate Body noted that both the state-owned commercial banks' (SOCBs) specific act per se, that is, making loans in the case, and the SOCBs' broader relationship with the government should be "taken together" in consideration.[116]

Thus, the fact the Appellate Body in *DS437* dismissed outright the specific-conduct element in a public body inquiry is not only self-conflicting within the report itself but it also contradicts the earlier *DS379* report. And the conflict results from a misread of the nexus between a public body and a private body in the "entrustment or

---

[109] Appellate Body Report, *US Anti-Dumping and Countervailing Duties (China)* para 285.

[110] *Ibid.*, para 285.

[111] Appellate Body Report, *US Countervailing Measures (China) (Article 21.5)* para 5.84, quoting the United States.

[112] *Ibid.*, paras 5.84, 5.103.

[113] *Ibid.*, para 5.84.

[114] Appellate Body Report, *US Anti-Dumping and Countervailing Duties (China)* para 318.

[115] *Ibid.*, para 297.

[116] Appellate Body Report, *US Countervailing Measures (China) (Article 21.5)* paras 5.85, 5.101, 5.104.

direction" inquiry. Instead in this inquiry, one should look into the additional element of link through "entrustment or direction" by a public body to a private body, instead of a misplaced focus on "conduct".

A positive case is thus: an SOE is presumed as a private body, and when it is entrusted or directed by a government in a particular conduct, the conduct in question transforms the SOE into a public body or government. This legal scenario is based on art 1.1(a)(1)(iv) of the *SCM Agreement* and is consonant with art 8 of the *ILC Articles*.[117] Alternatively, the SOE is a presumed public body, to the extent that it "possesses, exercises, or be vested with government authority" under internal law. This legal scenario is based on the treatment of public body equivalent to government in art 1.1(a)(1) of the *SCM Agreement* and consonant with art 5 of the *ILC Articles*.

To be sure, China is frustrated about the Appellate Body's decision regarding a public body inquiry in *DS437*. The legal effect of the decision is thus: by judging the core characteristic of the SOE in question, as well as its relationship with the government in the narrow sense, a Chinese SOE would be a public body inherently possessing government authority or function. In other words, the market behavior of the SOE becomes largely irrelevant in a pubic body inquiry, which clearly runs afoul of common sense again and must be discarded.

5.4.4 Comments on Different Standards in a Public Body Inquiry in DS379 and DS437

In *DS379* and *DS437*, the Appellate Body adopted distinct lines of thinking about the nature of an SOE. Respectively, the Appellate Body in *DS379* took a conduct-focused approach in judging whether an SOE is a public or a private body, while in *DS437* it took an entity-based approach in addressing the issue. The difference between the two approaches is thus: the former answers whether the *conduct* under art 1.1(a)(1) is governmental, while the latter addresses whether the *entity* engaging in the conduct is governmental.

Specifically, a conduct-focused approach is two pronged: the first prong is to see whether the conduct in question has elements of governmental authority; to do so, an appropriate understanding of the term "governmental authority" is a precondition. As discussed, "governmental authority" varies across WTO Members, even though there may be some common ground such as tax collection (referring to art 1.1(a) (1)(ii) of the *SCM Agreement*), which tends to be recognized universally as "governmental authority". The second prong of the conduct-focused approach points to "meaningful

---

[117] Article 8 of the *ILC Articles* states as follows:

> "The conduct of a person or group of persons shall be considered an act of a State under international law if the person or group of persons is in fact acting on the instructions of, or under the direction or control of, that State in carrying out the conduct."

control", equivalent to "entrust or direct" in art 1.1(a)(1)(iv) of the *SCM Agreement*, by the government (including a public body) over a private body's specific conduct, regardless of the conduct being commercial or not. In such situation, the conduct of a private body (including an SOE) is attributable to the government, and in the exercise of the conduct, the private body is elevated to be a "public body" accordingly. As in *DS379*, certain Chinese SOCBs were deemed as public bodies, on evidence that those SOCBs were meaningfully controlled by the government in the exercise of their functions, that is, making loans.[118]

In contrast, an entity-based approach follows a different line of thinking. Instead of rattling over those dynamic but seemingly unsettled concepts such as "governmental authority" and "meaningful control", as featured above, the entity-based approach is rather normative and thus linear and clear-cut. It focuses on the core features of the entity and its relationship with the government. In this line, since ownership plays a critical role, the SOE tends to be presumed as a public body, regardless of its specific conduct at issue. This line of thinking is best illustrated in the US Public Bodies Memorandum, which categorizes three different types of enterprises; among them, an enterprise in which the State owns majority shares is automatically deemed a public body. The Appellate Body in *DS437* endorsed this Memorandum by explicitly denying its inconsistency with the *SCM Agreement* and past precedents; in other words, it effectively endorsed the entity-based approach. An individual opinion by an adjudicating Appellate Body member in *DS437*, as attached to the Appellate Body report, dared to go thus far as to deny the link between a public body and government authority,[119] which is the established legal standard everybody first quotes when discussing the topic.

Admittedly, in carrying out a conduct-focused approach, the Appellate Body in *DS379* considered other "extensive evidence" furnished by the United States, speaking to the core characteristics of those *entities* and their relationship with the Chinese government.[120] On the other hand, the Appellate Body in *DS437*, in carrying out an entity-based approach, did not deny altogether the relevance of evidence of an entity's conduct or practice to a public body inquiry.[121] To be fair, thus, if a public body inquiry is to be carried out along a spectrum with "entity" (its ownership, purpose and relationship with government) on one extreme[122] and with "conduct" on the other, then the Appellate Body in *DS379* stands somewhere nearing the extreme of "conduct", while in *DS437* it stands somewhere nearby the extreme of "entity".

---

[118] Appellate Body Report, *US Countervailing Measures (China) (Article 21.5)* para 5.80, quoting Appellate Body Report, *US Anti-Dumping and Countervailing Duties (China)* para 355.

[119] The anonymous Appellate Body member states: "There is no requirement for an investigating authority to determine in each case whether the investigated entity 'possesses, exercises or is vested with governmental authority'". Appellate Body Report, *US Countervailing Measures (China) (Article 21.5)* para 5.248.

[120] Appellate Body Report, *US Anti-Dumping and Countervailing Duties (China)* para 355.

[121] Appellate Body Report, *US Countervailing Measures (China) (Article 21.5)* para 5.101.

[122] Such focus on entity is alternatively termed as "formal indicia of control". Appellate Body Report, *US Carbon Steel (India)* para 4.43.

The entity-based approach, surely a simplified and perhaps simple-minded approach, departs greatly from customary international law, which tends to hinge on a particular act or conduct, for the purpose of judging the characteristics (public or private) of an entity other than governmental organ, as reflected in arts 5 and 8 of the *ILC Articles* and in the *Broches* test. Following the entity-based approach, the term "public body" is daringly instilled with a brand new connotation, one that undoubtedly brings about confusion and even chaos in the international law community. The deviation is unnecessary, without a cogent reason.

5.5 Conclusion and Prospect

The question of treatment standards of an SOE as a public or a private entity can be dated back over half a century ago at least, when the *Broches* test first appeared. A function-based (or conduct-focused) approach has largely been observed in conducting the examination. It means that one must look into the specific act of the entity in question, rather than dwell merely superficially on the so-called core characteristics of the entity per se. The standard is affirmed in examining three areas of law in international economic activities, that is, international finance, international investment, and international trade.

In law of international finance, represented by MDB law, the SOE is consistently treated as a private party in the MDB-funded procurement market, enjoying various rights and bearing various responsibilities that apply to a typical private entity. In law of international investment, represented by the ICSID law, the SOE is eligible to initiate an investor-state arbitral case, which is an acknowledgment of the SOE's legal status as a private investor rather than as part of the government. In law of international trade, represented by the WTO law, the recognized legal standard is that "a public body must possess, exercise or be vested with governmental authority". Thus, the SOE must bear government authority in order to qualify as a public body; state ownership or capital structure alone is insufficient to prove it as a public body.

However, the examination above does reveal some deviations. Those deviations may appear in different narratives and in different forms, and they may be termed roughly as an ownership-based (or entity-based) approach. The WTO Appellate Body's ruling in *US Countervailing Measures (China) (Article 21.5)* represents the latest and most extreme development in that direction. Following that approach, such factors as the entity's capital structure, its relationship with the government, its purpose, and its generally designated mandate become decisive in examining whether an SOE is a public or private entity, regardless of the specific behavior of the entity.

The development of such deviations comes with no coincidence at the juncture of China's rise on the world stage, and it has far-reaching and significant implications. It means whether a market economy with Chinese characteristics will be accepted by the international community, and if yes on what condition.

First, Chinese SOEs have no original sin.[123] The ownership-based approach, as advocated by the United States and a few others, constitutes prejudice over state ownership superficially, while prejudice over nationality (i.e., the Chinese system) in essence. Article 345 of The Treaty on the Functioning of the European Union (TFEU) stipulates: "The Treaties shall in no way prejudice the rules in Member States governing the system of property ownership".[124] And the EU-China Comprehensive Agreement on Investment (CAI) requires both parties to treat all enterprises impartially, regardless of private or public ownership.[125] Those laws exemplify the principle of ownership-neutrality as endorsed by the international community. China must promote such legal clause in international rule-making negotiations, particularly at a time of request to join the CPTPP,[126] to defeat the United States' relentless efforts to stigmatize its economic system.

Second, Chinese SOEs are not controlled by the Party or the government.[127] They act not as an instrument or agent of the state; rather they act just like any other private business seeking profits in operations. Regarding the Party's role in the economy, here is an illustrative analogy[128]: the Party is to China what God is to Christians, and a Party committee is a church. Just as a church calls upon worshippers to love their neighbors, a Party committee asks members to be role models with regard to corporate codes of conduct. In daily operations, Chinese companies run commercially

---

[123] However, not all agree to treat an SOE as a private party, and it seems even insurmountable for some of them to accept such treatment ideologically. One may sense such flavor from this characteristic statement:

"The current scenario is technically favorable to [SOEs], and it shows that they can now operate like any other private investor. Further, the whole ICSID and investment regime was designed for the promotion of foreign private investment. However, the [SOEs] have now become significant players who are treated like any private investors.... It is a paradox that the system states designed to promote private investment is being gradually penetrated and reshaped by state capitalism without much difficulty." (Julien Chaisse, "State Capitalism on the Ascent: Stress, Shock, and Adaptation of the International Law on Foreign Investment" (2018) 27 *Minn J Int'l L* 339, 404–405.).

[124] However, admittedly TFEU art 65(1)(b) may allow de facto prejudice over state ownership "on grounds of public order or public security". As for a suggestion on avoiding an extensive use of TFEU art 65, see Julien Chaisse, "The Regulation of Sovereign Wealth Funds in the European Union: Can the Supranational Level Limit the Rise of National Protectionism?" in Karl P Sauvant et al. (eds), *Sovereign Investment: Concerns and Policy Reactions* (Oxford University Press, 2012) pp 485–486.

[125] EU-China Comprehensive Agreement on Investment (concluded but not yet ratified), January 22, 2021, Section II, art. 3ter.

[126] MOFCOM, "China officially applies to join the Comprehensive and Progressive Agreement for Trans-Pacific Partnership (CPTPP)", September 18, 2021. http://english.mofcom.gov.cn/article/newsrelease/significantnews/202109/20210903201113.shtml (visited November 5, 2022).

[127] The term "control" here should not be interpreted loosely, but there seem wrong tendencies to overstretch it to mean "influence", "guide", "regulate", or even "exercise of shareholder rights", whereby the term risks being meaningless, because one cannot imagine a single firm uncontrolled by a state in this sense. For example, the Trump administration uses laws of export control and entity list to block American and other firms from doing business with Huawei and other Chinese firms; it does not mean that the US "controls" its firms, however. Rather "control" is a technical legal term, narrowly meaning "meaningful (or full) control" as discussed above in the article.

[128] Gu, "Western Fears of Party Influence on Chinese Companies Are Overblown" (n 91 above).

and autonomously, uncontrolled by the Party, just as a Christian CEO does business on his own, free from God's intervention.

Third, Chinese SOEs must quicken the pace of reform in the direction of gaining more independence from government and being more market-oriented.[129] The reform should be two pronged: in terms of corporate governance, a diversified Board of Directors is paramount. To make it happen, a mechanism facilitating private and foreign investments in an SOE is the key.[130] The other prong is the introduction of competitive neutrality in the economy, in order to level the playing field between an SOE and other business enterprises. In particular, they should be treated equally in terms of raw material supply and financing rates.

Chinese SOEs must be allowed to compete fairly in international markets. This is consistent with the tradition of international economic law and will be meaningful for the future development of international law. That being said, it is predicable that the legal battle of treatment standards of SOEs will continue and can only be fiercer in future.

---

[129] China has recently passed a key three-year plan of SOE reforms, which has not been made public at the time of writing, for implementing the Decision of 19th CCP Central Committee Fourth Plenary Session (党的十九届四中全会《决定》). The latter Decision, passed on October 31, 2019, and in the relevant sector of SOE reform, focuses on both "mixed ownership" and "corporate governance". The original text of the CCP Decision is available in Chinese at https://china.huanqiu.com/article/9CaKrnKnC4J (visited August 29, 2020). Also see my earlier comments and proposals about China's SOE reform, Bin Gu, "Corporate Governance Pivotal Part of State-Owned Enterprise Reforms", *The Global Times*, November 25, 2013.

[130] The proposal aims to make the Board diversified and dynamic, by having different Board members representing interests of different shareholders. The reform is different from privatization in purpose, in the sense that "whether privatization is a necessary condition for improving the efficiency of the SOEs cannot be determined a priori. Fundamentally, for any large modern corporation,... there are no owners in any meaningful sense." Justin Yifu Lin et al., "Competition, Policy Burdens, and State-Owned Enterprise Reform" (1998) 88 *Am Econ Rev* 422, 427.

Annex A
My Columns on AIIB, China, and the World

Three Lessons Learned from the Pickard Betrayal for Better Management of an International Organization

The Asian Infrastructure Investment Bank (AIIB, or the Bank), the China-led global development bank, survived its first ever crisis in leadership reputation, following the release of an authoritative investigation report July 7th. The report, all-embracing with 36 pages and evidence- and rules-based, reaffirms the Bank's strong governance.

The crisis arose upon the resignation of the Bank's global communications chief, Mr. Bob Pickard on June 12th. He immediately blamed the Bank for its toxic culture under the control of Communist party members, and Canada, his home country and an important member of the Bank, announced to "immediately halt all government led activity at the bank" and probe into his allegations. Canada also sought its allies' support in the AIIB but failed.

The incident of the Pickard betrayal presents three major lessons for better management of an international organization, as well as for the training and education in international civil service.

Lesson 1 is to develop best practice in crisis management. Appropriate crisis management tests the noble mind, genuine heart and problem-solving wisdom on the part of an organization and its leadership. The Bank was very responsive to the investigating demand of the Canadian government as a 1% shareholder, announcing full cooperation with it. Its Board of Directors additionally initiated an internal review, chaired by the Dean whose institutional mandate of overseeing the President was put into a major test for the first time. This July 7th report officially concludes the internal review.

This dual track of actions demonstrates a consideration of propriety by the Bank, rather than required by law. It is a token of sincerity to maintain trust and smooth relationships with its member countries. To tackle any defamation, the best method is to maintain transparency—in Benjamin Franklin's words, "to be concerned in no affairs I should blush to have made public, and to do nothing but what spies

B. Gu, *Chinese Multilateralism in the Asian Infrastructure Investment Bank (AIIB)*, Modern China and International Economic Law,
https://doi.org/10.1007/978-981-97-1219-9

may see and welcome". The crisis has been turned into an opportunity of affirming good governance, since the Bank has "nothing to hide", and the internal review recommends instituting a crisis response and communications plan.

Management crisis is not rare these days across international organizations. Kristalina Georgieva of the IMF in 2021, Roberto Azevêdo of the WTO in 2020, and David Malpass of the World Bank in 2022 all used to face distrust and criticisms by big shareholder countries during their tenure, with the latter two even being forced to resign early before their term end. Although Pickard's allegations "were cast in broad terms and no evidence was provided to substantiate them", as the internal review concludes, and the incident also proves much less severe in nature (some call a storm in a cup), a deficit of trust has been felt acutely again amid intense global geopolitical rift.

Lesson 2 is to develop best practice in personnel conduct. International civil servants should adhere to the code of conduct—be loyal only to their organization, and to no other authority in the discharge of their duties. Pickard's stated motive of betrayal—"As a patriotic Canadian, [resignation] was my only course.... I don't believe that my country's interests are served by its AIIB membership"—reflects how contradictory internally this unhappy gentleman was during his short, 15-month service in the AIIB, where he had to swear upon appointment to "regulate my conduct with the interests of the AIIB only in view".

Instead, the internal review only proves Pickard as unprofessional and irresponsible during his tenure, and accordingly recommends strengthening the Bank's pre-recruitment screening processes for leadership positions.

Indeed, being loyal to the organization does not have to compromise one's own sense of patriotism. The two lofty sentiments do not have to be of a relationship of dichotomy. Instead, they can be reconciled, and even mutually enhanced, if one is open, tolerant and collegial in an international environment. Indeed, staffs should uphold only the banner of development mission for the Bank.

In special instances, loyalty to the organization appears conflicting patriotism. For example, a government might seek to instruct international civil servants of its nationality, or to influence him in the discharge of his duty. If so, it poses risks of violating international law on the part of the government, while, for the staff, violating his code of conduct, thus sabotaging the interests or reputation of both. In this light, to maintain independence from government influence safeguards interests of both, and thus serves patriotism.

Lesson 3 is the need for appropriate understanding of the role of staff who are also CPC members. Another motive of the Pickard betrayal, as alleged, is that the Communist Party of China (CPC) runs or controls the Bank in "one of the most toxic cultures imaginable", and he does not "want to be a useful idiot". Pickard's language reflects a wide and deep bias towards the role of CPC members in a community, besides implicating insults unwisely to his former colleagues in the Bank. Indeed, Sir Danny Alexander, AIIB vice president, refuted that this language did not reflect his own experience working in the Bank since 2016.

The function of CPC membership in a community is comparable to that of Christianity in a neighborhood. Communist faith motivates one to be a role model in business, just as a Christian does well by doing good and loves his neighbors. In daily operations, Party members perform autonomously, and uncontrolled by the Party; just like a Christian acting on his own, free from God's intervention. Indeed, CPC membership is common both in the international organizations led by China and those where China acts as an ordinary participant.

The AIIB is open to theists as well as atheists, while the World Bank should not discriminate among the Evangelical, the Puritan, the Deist, and a Communist believer. Indeed, the personnel codes of conduct of those international organizations all condemn discrimination by virtue of political or religious affiliation. In them a culture of harmony in diversity is the prime, which may be summed up thus: "Find your beauty, and that of others, share the beauty, and achieve unity."

(This article, in an edited form, appeared on *South China Morning Post*, July 16, 2023.)

Is Canada Meddling in Development Bank's Affairs?

Bob Pickard, a Canadian national and officer of the Asian Infrastructure Investment Bank (AIIB), claimed earlier this week that he found the secrecy of CPC running the Bank, thus decided to resign, and fled China immediately for personal safety. He might have a heroic Snowden in his mind on his fleeing flight to Tokyo, but he is in the wrong.

Pickard based his claims on the mere fact that there are many CPC members in the Bank, according to his own public comments. It proves that he is ignorant of China, where the Bank is headquartered and whose elites are more than often party members. He should know that CPC has nearly 100 million members, 2.5 times of the total population of Canada.

The function of CPC membership in a community is no more than that of Christianity in a neighborhood. One's faith in communism motivates him to be a role model in business, just as a Christian is expected to do good to others. The AIIB is open to theists as well as atheists, while the World Bank should never discriminate a CPC staff.

On the other hand, these international civil servants should adhere to their code of conduct— be loyal to their organizations, be impartial in countries' political affairs, and be independent from government influence. Regrettably Pickard revealed a strong political and ideological bias in his words and deeds.

Pickard, if not ignorant, was imprudent about his career choice when he joined the Bank merely 15 months ago. He fled after so brief a span of time in the Bank, where he had been treated well but ungratefully accused his employer of "toxic culture". The Bank, instead, has been proud of nourishing a "lean, clean and green" culture since its founding in 2015.

This unhappy gentleman is a grown-up, seems experienced, and should be responsible. He knowingly leaves himself a notorious record of unprofessional conduct, which is backbiting betrayal in essence and deplorable in international civil service, no less elsewhere on this globe.

One has to wonder why he decided to join the Bank in the first place? If he is not a spy fleeing with the Bank's internal, commercially sensitive documents, there is no reason for him to fear being detained like his imprisoned fellow citizens in China, as he publicly concerned.

Indeed, the Canadian government immediately avowed a review of Mr. Pickard's allegations, and threatened to take any action against the Bank. The collusion between the Canadian government and person was conducted in a seamless manner.

An almost blind follower of US policy, will Canada repeat the American plot of accusing Kristalina Georgieva, the IMF boss, of her bias in favor of China in ranking countries' business climate in 2021? It may, for example, seek to discredit AIIB President Jin as an instrument of CPC in the Bank, on a similarly baseless ground. The Canadian coup plot may also implicate the selection of a new president for the AIIB in 2025.

In the Bank charter, its 106 members including Canada agree that they shall all respect the Bank's international character and "refrain from any attempt to influence" or intervene in Bank affairs. To be clear, the identification of party membership among Bank staffs is a distinct legal issue from the allegation that CPC controls or runs the Bank. Canada's threat may well cross the line, and have broken international law.

What is expected next? Canadian financial minister Freeland threatened to "immediately halt all government led activity at the bank". If she means what she said, Canada will fail to fulfill its obligations to the Bank. Then the Bank may respond by moving to suspend Canadian membership. Then Canada may be kicked out of the Bank after one year of such suspension. Is Canada ready to play fire? It simply backfires on the nation's reputation.

Ms. Freeland added that the investigation would be expeditious, and "I am not ruling out any outcome following its completion", which implicitly indicates a voluntary withdrawal. The prospect of withdrawal, be it compulsory or voluntary, is indeed slim, because such issue is rare in the history of international organizations, and certainly does not serve either Canada's or AIIB's interests. But be prepared in order to prevent it.

(This article, in an edited form, appeared on *China Daily*, June 19, 2023.)

It Is Divine to Promote Best Practices for the Belt and Road Initiative at Ten

When there was "taxation without representation", there was a revolution. That is the story of the American Revolution in the eighteenth century. Today in international relations, there is a similar dismay of "contribution without representation" among China and other emerging economies: they have long represented the bulk of global

GDP growth, but lack a comparable position in global governance. Such disparity brings evolution, not revolution, *luckily*.

The reforms of global economic governance have caught on for decades, but American hegemony delays the process, frustrating emerging powers. Specifically, the WTO has largely been paralyzed both in terms of negotiation and dispute settlement, the World Bank has been crying for capital inadequacy, and the IMF lacks a credible quota formula to reflect the changed landscape.

Since the reform of those old institutions has been difficult, China decides to walk on a new path of multilateralism, i.e., establishing new institutions that secure the voice, as well as catering for the needs, of the most. They include the Belt and Road Initiative (BRI, since 2013), the Asian Infrastructure Investment Bank (AIIB) and New Development Bank (NDB, both since 2015), and the most recent Multilateral Cooperation Center for Development Finance (MCDF, since 2020). All of them have focused on one sector— infrastructure, revealing China's commitment to share its story of success, i.e., "roads and dams lead to prosperity", a household saying in China.

Luckily, as I said, the new institutions unequivocally uphold international best practices. For example, the BRI summit in 2019 vowed zero tolerance for corruption, and promotion of debt sustainability by promulgating a BRI-devoted debt sustainability analysis framework, drawing upon the IMF/World Bank practice while avoiding the latter's anti-investment bias. The Chinese government has prohibited overseas investment in new coal power starting 2022. The AIIB recently revised its energy policy, explicitly banning coal mining and coal power investment; as a matter of fact, it has not invested a dime in coal since day one. The China-led institutions are all determined to be clean and green.

The BRI surprisingly embraces the promotion of high standards, amid popular criticisms of environmental deterioration, human rights violation, and China's debt trap diplomacy. The Export and Import Bank of China (CEXIM), the lead bank in BRI investments, upgraded its environmental and social standards last year, to be fully consistent with those of international financial institutions. In other words, each dime the Chinese bank invests thereafter should agree to international best practices.

China's top diplomat Wang Yi stated in 2016, 'We are not trying to build a rival system; on the contrary, we are trying to play a bigger role in the existing international order.' Over the years this language has revealed its truth—i.e., *Chinese* multilateralism is built upon *American* multilateralism, inheriting the latter's pros (i.e., a rules-based system and upholding best practices) and dropping its cons (i.e., overly bureaucratic; and one size fits all, neglecting local condition).

Will *Chinese* multilateralism lead to Chinese hegemony, as were the cases of UK and US in history? The UK tried to cling to imperial preferences when the US surpassed it in 1940s; and since the end of WWII, the US has never hesitated to kick away the ladder when Germany, Japan and now China as newcomers climb it.

However, power and hegemony are different, and one does not necessarily lead to the other. As a world power historically, China expanded not by conquest but by osmosis. It now induces respect and admiration, seeing others come to it. As Confucius said:"If people from afar do not submit, influence them to do so by means of virtue and civil culture." The missionary culture, in contrast, tends to convert and impose one's will upon another; when it comes to international relations, it tends to intervene, and even to overthrow foreign governments by force.

These days the US behaves in a detrimental manner to multilateralism. Both the CHIPS Act and the Inflation Reduction Act, appropriating subsidies contingent upon local manufacturing of semiconductor and electric vehicles (EV), serve the American version of forced technology transfer, as showcased in the Ford-CATL EV battery deal, and they trample the law and spirit of free and fair trade. It is American unilateralism, practiced consistently by the Trump and Biden administrations, that is defeating multilateralism as built by their forefathers.

(This article, in an edited form, appeared on *South China Morning Post*, May 10, 2023.)

Seven Myths About China's Approach to Global Governance

China has been unprecedentedly active on the world stage since President Xi Jinping's rise to power. It is historically amazing, given that the West had been urging China to become a "responsible stakeholder" not long before. Now many people are curious: What would the world look like if China actually led the world? Seven misunderstandings regarding this transition must be debunked to understand China's approach toward global governance.

First, American multilateralism versus Chinese multilateralism. During the past decade, China has initiated a series of public goods in infrastructure connectivity, including the Belt and Road Initiative (BRI), Asian Infrastructure Investment Bank (AIIB), and Multilateral Cooperation Center for Development Finance (MCDF). Does *Chinese* multilateralism, as so dubbed, require decoupling from *American* multilateralism? Or alternatively, if China advocates *Chinese* multilateralism, whereas the West still has faith in *American* multilateralism, is it really possible for them to cooperate and coordinate on world matters?

American multilateralism contributed to world peace and prosperity, but the developing world has unfortunately been ignored or little heard. Failure to produce the hoped-for results backfires on the reputation of *American* multilateralism. *Chinese* multilateralism builds upon *American* multilateralism, and it is well positioned to correct the latter's defects by being responsive to the particular needs of developing countries, while maintaining a rules-based, high-standard system, as exhibited by the success of its development initiatives.

Second, hegemony versus self-restraint. Consensus is a preferred decision-making method in the Bretton Woods institutions, as well as in the AIIB and the BRI. Meanwhile, both the United States and China manifestly hold veto power in those institutions. In the World Bank, the United States has been blocking shareholder realignment reforms in favor of emerging economies, delaying the implementation of the official shareholding formula known as the 2016 Dynamic Formula. For example, China would have held over 12% of shares under that formula, instead of merely

6 percent now. Similarly, in the International Monetary Fund (IMF), negotiations over a new shareholder formula that is supposed to increase the voice of emerging economies, including China and other BRICS countries, have dragged on for over a decade.

A hegemon has two composite elements: it must be powerful (that is a prerequisite) and then based on its power, impose its will on others. Holding a veto power is one thing; to abuse it is another. In its cultural gene, China is not a missionary society and it chooses to influence others by inducing respect rather than by conversion. Featuring voluntarism and self-restraint, the Chinese approach toward global governance contrasts with a hegemon's mentality to impose its will and seek predominance over others.

Third, high versus feasible standards. A major characteristic of *Chinese* multilateralism is the promotion of high *and* feasible standards. High standards are integral in the operations of a top-notch development institution. There used to be concerns over what standards the AIIB would apply, which have nevertheless been relieved because the Bank has instituted environmental, social, and governance standards (ESG) both in text and in practice.

On the other hand, the standards must be feasible. While offering a leading role for the Bank's clients in project preparation and implementation, AIIB standards are open to exploring greater flexibility for the benefit of borrowing countries, for example, by relying on their system for standard compliance while conforming to AIIB's core principles and standards.

Fourth, rule of law versus role of law. The development community has been urged to think differently about aid, in particular, to think not only about *the rule of law* but also about *the role of law*. For finding that an institution has power, it is enough that the exercise of the power may further the purpose of the institution, and that it is not inconsistent with existing law.

This, dubbed a teleological methodology, enables an international organization to adapt to new environments by flexibly interpreting its laws. The methodology empowered the AIIB to combat the Covid-19 pandemic through a $20 billion crisis recovery facility, as well as to embrace the BRI and administer MCDF.

Fifth, adversary checks versus advisory engagement. Good corporate governance is integral to the success of an institution. The AIIB has a built-in oversight mechanism "to ensure proper checks and balances" between its non-resident board and management. To find out where the degree of "properness" lies along a spectrum is key.

Facing ever-changing circumstances, the AIIB needs to rely upon a pragmatic executive branch to take any bold but necessary actions to promote the interests of the Bank. It is advisable, therefore, to lean towards the Oriental wisdom of advisory engagement, rather than the Western style of adversary checks, along the spectrum of oversight that best suits the Asian gene of the Bank and its purposes.

Sixth, competition versus cooperation. Forging a cooperative external relationship, particularly with those established ones, is key to the success of a newcomer. The failure of Japan's proposal to establish the Asian Monetary Fund, a replica of the

International Monetary Fund in 1997, proves that the established institution tends to view a newcomer as a threat, rather than a partner.

The AIIB has forged a sound collaborative relationship with peer institutions by sharing knowledge, signing memorandums of understanding, and co-financing projects. Drawing upon the AIIB, the MCDF took initiative to engage with peer institutions in a benign and cooperative manner. The approach also helps a newcomer make rapid progress in reputation and capacity-building.

Seventh, alliance versus partnership. China has persevered with its goal of "rejuvenating the nation." To make this happen, it tends to concentrate on continuous self-improvement while avoiding making enemies. The Chinese dream is predestined on a harmonious world environment, contrasting the U.S.-branded hegemony— "either with us or against us." China's mentality decides the mantra of its diplomacy as looking for "partnerships rather than alliances."

Traditionally China considers its bond with developing countries as the bedrock of its diplomacy and treats the European Union as a trusted partner in upholding multilateralism. While China and Russia coordinate closely in world affairs, attesting to their "no-ceiling" cooperation, they are not allies, as has been proved saliently in the ongoing Russo-Ukrainian War. China is with everybody and against nobody.

(This article appeared on *The National Interest*, July 25, 2022.)

China, the US and What It Means to Be a Hegemon

China has been unprecedentedly active on the world stage under Xi Jinping's leadership. Prior to that, the West had been urging China to become a "responsible stakeholder" in global matters. But now questions are being asked as to China's intent given its ascent. Specifically: Will China act like a hegemon like the US when it leads the world?

There is no doubt about the legitimacy of the concern, if one considers the international initiatives that China launched in the past decade. For example, in some international financial institutions such as the Asian Infrastructure Investment Bank (AIIB), China holds a veto power. In others, such as the Belt and Road Initiative (BRI) and the Multilateral Cooperation Center for Development Finance (MCDF), China is also dominant, and has de facto veto power.

If a country is to be a hegemon, there are two defining elements. One is that it must be a recognised power; the other is that, by utilising its power, the country imposes what it alone decides or wishes for upon others, heedless of their feelings or interest.

China is an economic power, surpassing the US if measured in terms of GDP at purchasing power parity (PPP) rates. China has also quickly become a military power, with its third and most advanced aircraft carrier launched recently. China no longer feels shy to exercise power and its right of veto.

But holding and wielding veto power and abusing it are two different things.

In the case of AIIB, China's veto power is derived from a unique shareholding formula, with GDP as the only variable and the requirement that 75% of shareholdings is retained within Asia. In other words, the right to veto, whether China exercises it or not, is rules-based.

But will China abuse its veto power to pursue its interest at the expense of others, that is, act like a hegemon?

In the short term, the possibility is zero. As a growing power, China is still in the phase of establishing itself before the international community. It has been taking prudent and meticulous steps to win trust and cooperation from others, including from the established powers. All the while it is clear that the country is under intense scrutiny, not to mention attacks motivated by Western bias.

In a highly competitive and even hostile environment, China has to behave as a benign and self-restrained power in global economic governance. There is not the slightest chance for China to abuse its veto power and exercise hegemony, either in the BRI, the AIIB or the MCDF.

Over the longer term, it is also very unlikely that China will wield its powers like a hegemon. One reason for it is cultural. China is not a missionary society. It prefers to win others over by inducing respect than by conversion. As Confucius said: "If people from afar do not submit, influence them to do so by means of virtue and civil culture." ("If people from afar are dissatisfied, then they should cultivate literature and morality and come back to them"). This reliance on influence, to get others to come over to your side or point of view willingly, stands in contrast to a hegemon's mentality, which is to impose its will and seek predominance over others.

This Chinese cultural mindset explains China's so-called golden rule of "extensive consultation, joint contribution, and shared benefits" in its interactions within traditional international institutions, as well as in the new ones where it dominates. Case in point: China's moderating role in the bitter fight over Covid-19 vaccine patent rights helped the World Trade Organisation pull off a limited waiver deal recently, a success that provided a boost to the WTO as an institution as well.

Contrast this with the way the US asserts its weight in the Bretton Woods institutions, stopping or stalling much-needed reforms in them. For example, there has been no agreement on revising the quotas which determine voting power and borrowing capacity at the International Monetary Fund despite a decade of tortuous negotiations. Similarly the World Bank has long delayed implementation of its shareholding formula. The US blocks reforms to suppress China's rising influence. It does not hesitate to use the dominance of the dollar and its sway over international financial institutions to sanction anybody it dislikes, while sending out a chilling warning to others.

Regrettably these US hegemonic actions risk undermining the legitimacy of these institutions and American multilateralism. The US has gone a step further by sabotaging Chinese multilateralism, as represented by the BRI and the AIIB. It has sought to stigmatise those institutions with accusations of low standards, and by coercing its allies from signing up to them.

Shared values are a prerequisite for a sustainable world order. China aspires to "a shared future for mankind", one characterised by harmony in diversity across civilisations. To make it happen, China should keep in mind a key lesson drawn from the US: Chinese multilateralism only shines when veto power does not slip into hegemony.

(This article appeared in *The Straits Times*, July 16, 2022).

International Organizations Are at Risk as They Are Being Forced to Take Sides in the Ukraine War

Amidst the war launched by Russia in Ukraine, which is a regrettable tragedy, the US is launching another invisible war against multilateralism within major international economic organizations, forcing them to take political sides. The US's actions put the international character of those organizations at risk, trampling their Charters and international rule of law.

In the IMF, the US, UK and Canada managed to suspend the Russian representative as the dean of the Board. The move successfully killed two birds with one stone: a token of punishing Russia while revenging against the officer for non-cooperation in his deanship capacity during the US's campaign to discredit the IMF managing director Georgieva last year, when she was accused to be involved in business data manipulation in favor of China during her time in the World Bank. The US also sought to strip Russia of the opportunity to convert its 17 billion US dollar-equivalent special drawing rights (SDRs) to hard currencies, a legitimate and legal right of any member state under the IMF Charter.

In the WTO, the US led the West in a fervent move to halt their most-favored nation (MFN) obligation towards Russia, the bedrock of the world trading system. And they did so by citing the WTO's national security clause, which nevertheless applies only when members' own national security is threatened, and this is hard to prove. The US congress even attempted to suspend Russia's WTO membership, which is nevertheless a lawless action per se, because WTO law is silent on membership suspension.

International organizations (IOs) exhibited nuanced differences in their statements on the war, responding to the US's maneuver to push them to take sides and isolate Russia. The IMF and the World Bank both vowed to "support Ukraine on the financing and policy fronts". By comparison, the director-general of WTO, headquartered outside the US, was able to be prudent and maintain her neutral position. The China-led Asian Infrastructure Investment Bank (AIIB) took a similar stance as the WTO.

The Charters of these IOs require that "only economic considerations shall be relevant to their decisions", and political activity is prohibited. But the World Bank's David Malpass went much further, explicitly siding with the Ukrainian president and expressing admiration of his heroism, resembling a mouthpiece of US government. The suspension of Russian deanship in the IMF only politicized, and even poisoned the integrity of, the organization.

Besides, each country has the obligation to respect the international character of officers and staff in the IOs, refraining from meddling in the discharge of their duties.

The US expelled 12 diplomats in the Russian mission to the UN and one Russian staff in the UN, grossly violating its own commitment under the UN headquarters agreement. Espionage has become a standard excuse for the US to harass and expel those international servants it dislikes, which rekindles the discussion of moving those IOs outside the US.

Regrettably, this is not the first time for the US to discredit multilateralism. The previous Trump administration took a fervent approach to retreat from multilateralism, by withdrawing—or threatening to withdraw—from international treaties and organizations. What is different this time is that it goes to the length of isolating Russia, not leaving by itself. What is common is that multilateralism is again at risk, and people with zeal for multilateralism must be alert, and rise to hardship.

The path of multilateralism has never been smooth for the larger part of the past two decades. The Bretton Woods institutions are for long losing relevancy and legitimacy, as the US persistently exercises the tactic of delay in the much-needed governance and voice reforms in them. For example, the negotiations on a new quota formula are committed to increasing the voice and representation of emerging economies in the IMF, but have experienced over a decade of fruitless talk. China's shareholding of 6% in the World Bank is fundamentally misaligned under the 2016 Dynamic Formula, and should be increased to over 12% at least.

The US's hypocrisy exhibited in the tactic of delay forced China and a few others to embark on a new path, initiating the Belt and Road and the AIIB in 2013, and the Multilateral Cooperation Center for Development Finance (MCDF) in 2017. *Chinese* multilateralism, as so dubbed, features a relationship of heritage and innovation with respect to *American* multilateralism. In specific, *Chinese* multilateralism is built upon *American* multilateralism, being rules-based and showing respect for international best practices. Meanwhile, it embraces Asian wisdom of "voluntarism, flexibility and incremental progress", emphasizing on consensus building, rather than hegemony in the IOs.

However, even the remote AIIB feels the chill of sanctions by the US and the West, and has to adjust its operations accordingly. It immediately put all three infrastructure or COVID-19 relief projects in Russia, and two others in Belarus, on hold on March 3. As a founding member of AIIB, Iran paid in 300 million US dollars in capital, but has not been able to benefit and get a single project, lest the Bank suffer business risks due to the US's sanctions over the country. One must be clear that AIIB did so solely on the ground of economic consideration and in conformity with its Charter, rather than as a token of political stance.

We surely stand with the Ukrainian people. But let it be clear that we should also stand with the Russian people. A rampant, herd-like boycott of Russian businesses, sports and arts across Europe is wrong; Tchaikovsky, Swan Lake, and the performers are innocent. Bullying those who disagree, or refuse to take sides, is not a wise policy choice. At the heart of an unprecedented crisis on the European continent since WWII and with its full consequences yet to be seen, Europeans must be assured that sanctions are truly a double-edged sword; they work no more than suicide.

(This article, in its edited version, appeared in *South China Morning Post*, March 28, 2022).

The Global South Needs More Options from the IMF

The International Monetary Fund (IMF) annual meeting on October 16 witnessed the operationalization of a major trust fund, the Resilient and Sustainable Trust (RST), established in part to reallocate special drawing right (SDR), following a historic SDR allocation in August last year. Yet, over thirteen months have passed, and no single SDR out of the allocation of $650 billion has yet been recycled to a low-income country, depressing the original motive of the allocation to help poor and vulnerable countries combat Covid-19 and debt distress.

SDR may be exchanged for any of the five hard currencies in the SDR basket: the U.S. dollar, euro, Chinese renminbi, Japanese yen, and British pound. What is magical is that SDR was created with the stroke of a pen. With such a windfall, IMF members may meet liquidity needs to import vaccines and PPEs, repay external debts, or simply buffer their existing reserves. The only condition of the SDR use is to preserve its reserve asset status.

Under IMF law, countries are entitled to SDRs in proportion to their quotas in the IMF—whoever has shall be given more. Therefore, the G7 countries received almost half of the new allocation, while the seventy-plus low-income countries only received 3%. With such a deep disequilibrium, finding viable voluntary recycling methods from the rich to the poor has become paramount.

The IMF has two trust funds ready for SDR recycling. One is the Poverty-Reduction and Growth Trust (PRGT), which lends exclusively to designated low-income countries and mainly for short-term balance of payments needs. The other is the RST, mentioned at the beginning of this piece, to complement the time-honored PRGT. This fund expands to serve all low- and middle-income countries and to meet longer-term structural challenges, such as climate change and pandemic preparedness.

There are two other SDR recycling choices outside of the IMF. One is to recycle through multilateral development banks (MDBs). The African Development Bank, for example, which has a strained balance sheet amid global crises, badly needs to enhance its lending capacity, either by borrowing rich countries' SDRs and on-lending them or by using the SDRs to enhance its capital base. The other is to recycle the SDRs directly from rich countries to the poor, waiving the route of any financial intermediary.

Regrettably, recycling choices outside of the IMF have received little discussion due to major opposition from the European Central Bank and the IMF itself. Those opponents' argument is that the reserve-asset nature of SDR does not allow it to be used for development purposes. This ideology, however, is old-fashioned and should be changed.

By definition, a reserve asset is readily available with high liquidity and credit quality. However, the definition has been evolving, and the reserve asset's characteristic gets rather more relative than absolute, given that central banks' foreign reserves are often seen to be invested in below-3A government bonds, and even in private corporate bonds. Those investments are considered to have preserved their reserve-asset character; the same should hold for SDR loan resources, including for development purposes.

In both outside-IMF modalities, the reserve asset status of the SDRs may be well maintained by technically drawing upon the encashment system and the reserve and deposit accounts designed to preserve the liquidity and soundness of the SDR lending through both IMF trust funds. Indeed, rarely, if ever, do rich countries need to encash their SDR claims, let alone those issuing freely usable currencies.

An untold reason for opposing the SDR reallocation beyond the IMF is political and difficult: more options bring more competition. The IMF lends with conditionality, imposing policy adjustments upon borrowers in exchange for financial resources, which is criticized as largely unworkable while overly intrusive. The new RST, claiming no conditionality, still requests a concurrent IMF program and policy reforms by the borrowing country. With more choices available, the IMF model can be less appealing to borrowers.

Following the new SDR allocation last year, the G20 committed to recycling $100 billion in SDRs. Among other donors, China alone promised to recycle $10 billion in SDRs to African countries, accounting for 23% of its allocation. PRGT and RST are ready for such recycling, but opening more channels is optimal for fully realizing the purposes of the SDR allocation, and for the welfare of the Global South.

(This article appeared on *The National Interest*, October 22, 2022).

China's Belt and Road Initiative Should Stop Financing New Coal Power

Last month, US President Joe Biden asked his G7 counterparts to back a worldwide infrastructure plan to rival China's Belt and Road Initiative (BRI). This marked the beginning of his campaign for international co-operation in the area of high-quality infrastructure, which may be viewed as a scaled-up, post Covid-19 version of the Trump-era Blue Dot Network. Nevertheless, Biden's call produced few concrete results.

The G7 meeting did, however, promise to stop using government funds to finance new international coal power plants by the end of 2021. This commitment should be noted by the BRI, which has been severely criticised for its impact on the environment since its launch in 2013.

Coal power generation is the single biggest source of greenhouse gas emissions. If BRI made coal-free commitments similar to the G7, it would help meet the Paris Agreement target of keeping global temperature rises at 2C, as well as improve its own reputation.

The Second Belt and Road Forum, held in Beijing in 2019, set out a central plank of constructing high quality infrastructure that was both clean and green. A commitment of no more coal would surely help in fulfilling this ambition.

Banning coal would be consistent with China's pledge of reaching a carbon peak by 2030 and carbon neutrality by 2060. The interval between these two timelines is already short. A coal ban would force major development financiers, such as the China Development Bank and China ExIm Bank as well as commercial banks, to adopt best practices. This in turn would accelerate the transition to a green future for those countries that borrow from BRI.

More than 30 major international institutions are official partners with BRI, including the United Nations, the IMF and the World Bank. These institutions prioritise international best practices. A coal-free BRI would help them to view the initiative's investments in a positive light.

According to the UN, more than 110 countries have pledged carbon neutrality by 2050. A low-carbon economy represents the greatest business opportunity of our time. Those who move resolutely and fast in that direction will benefit the most.

The BRI should be particularly watchful of, and responsive to, the policy changes at multilateral development banks. For example, the European Investment Bank will stop financing fossil fuel energy projects (including oil, gas and coal) next year. The Asian Development Bank has not funded a coal power plant since 2013, and banned coal formally in an energy policy proposal last May. The Asian Infrastructure Investment Bank is following the same path, and is expected to update its energy strategy with a ban on coal power later this year.

One hundred and forty countries have expressly endorsed BRI so far. Even some western countries, including Australia, Canada, the UK and Japan, have chosen to benefit from the initiative through the so-called third-party market co-operation. By declaring itself coal free, we might expect more countries to join this cheering squad.

I am not suggesting that BRI has been criticised solely because of its low standards around coal. It is stigmatised mainly because the US feels threatened by China's rise. By committing zero funding for new coal power plants, BRI can harvest good will from the west, in particular from western Europe. This will help undermine Biden's strategy of trying to isolate China.

In order to make a better world for all of us, green standards must be realistic. Asia has the richest coal deposits, representing 38% of world reserves. As it is cheap and accessible for many developing countries, coal constitutes some 40% of energy consumption in Asia, much higher than the world average of 29%. This fact must be acknowledged.

A coal-free BRI cannot mean no coal at all, nor an immediate cessation in its use. Instead, investments into "clean coal" technologies, such as carbon capture and storage, to make the dirty coal greener, should be encouraged for existing coal- power plants. This will enable them to phase it out gradually. And if there is to be an early coal-power retirement, alternatives must be available and attractive.

At a time of ever-increasing uncertainty and destabilisation, it is best to view BRI as a new corridor for China-west co-operation. Ending BRI's use of coal makes this possible.

(This article appeared in *The Financial Times*, July 5, 2021).

China's Example Shines

Long a symbol of human solidarity, the United Nations is currently experiencing dark times, as the COVID-19 pandemic casts its deadly shadow and the world economy tumbles. People are being divided. Countries are being decoupled. Hatred and blame are being spread. In a call to action during the celebration of the UN's 75th anniversary recently, President Xi Jinping of China urged unity in tackling this unprecedented crisis facing the world community.

History tells that when facing a global challenge, such as a financial crisis, climate change or terrorism, countries normally pull together to cooperate. They agree on a responsive international mechanism. Compared with modern history's other known crises, the global health emergency prompted by COVID-19 is unprecedented and guaranteed to fundamentally change the world order as we have known it.

First, global health security is so much more than a development issue, as it has been framed in the past. It was almost invariably poor and developing countries asking for assistance, as they lacked the wherewithal to treat diseases such as ebola and malaria. But COVID-19 for the first time forces us to think that public health security is a universal problem, respecting neither geographic borders nor socioeconomic status.

Worse still, many rich countries initially, and even recently, performed poorly in the fight against COVID-19. This was, and still is, especially true of the U.S., given its early knowledge about this plague and its leaders' denigration of public health and science. This is in stark contrast to the early leadership by China and the World Health Organization in containing the virus and warning of the need for immediate action. It is saddening to see that the arrogance has resulted in so much suffering and so many lives lost. The rich world should recognize China's positive performance, rather than stigmatizing it with racist names such as the "Chinese virus" or "Kungflu".

Second, we have never appreciated the economic impact of a virus as fully as we have with COVID-19. We thought narrowly that public health security, as with any development issue, only costs money for the rich donor nations while providing no benefit to them in return. Therefore, helping others may make less economic sense for them. That may explain why the amount contributed to the Global Fund, which was created in 2002 to fight epidemics, never collected the full amount pledged. But COVID-19 teaches us that without sustainable financing for public health, a contagious disease can immobilize the whole world.

Investing relatively little money in global health security today will most certainly pay huge dividends in saving lives and economies tomorrow. While it was timely to commit to spend swiftly and decisively at the extraordinary G20 leaders' summit in March, investments ideally must precede outbreaks to maximize the investment's potential impact.

The third ray of light emanating from COVID-19 is that mankind is indeed a community with a shared future, and no one is safe until everyone is safe, precisely as expressed by President Xi in his recent UN speech. China has indeed been grateful for the outpouring of assistance from the international community during the first two-months of its national war against COVID-19. In turn, China generously reciprocated when the pandemic was declared by the WHO on March 11. China sent out medical teams and supplies worldwide, while also sharing online its methods for testing, prevention and treatment.

In the multinational arena, China committed to increase funding for the WHO, the main international organization coordinating the fight against COVID-19, and it joined COVAX, a platform working for equitable global access to coronavirus vaccines. China also actively participated in the G20 debt suspension plan, which is critical for low-income countries in the fight against the pandemic. The Asian Infrastructure Investment Bank, a multilateral organization initiated by China that is now in its fifth year of operation, also made prompt funding commitments for public health infrastructure alongside peer institutions.

Each country has to address a difficult dilemma in the fight against COVID-19—containing the disease or saving its economy. Which comes first? China resolved to contain the disease before opening its economy, and the strategy proved a remarkable success. It is the only major economy projecting positive growth this year. In China's war to contain the virus, literally all its 1.4 billion people have been mobilized since late January. The dual success is no coincidence; the Chinese government has been transparent, resolute and consistent from day one. The tried-and-true best practices established by China should be applauded.

By contrast, President Donald Trump and other officials in the United States have repeatedly called COVID-19 the "Chinese virus" and "Kungflu," and some American media used the racist headline "China is the real sick man of Asia," a universally damning idiom that echoes in Chinese ears as a historical insult. Internationally, before the U.S. withdrew from the WHO, Trump ignored his country's solemn legal obligation to support the WHO, an organization he criticized as both corrupt and pro-China. The U.S. has effectively relinquished its leadership at this critical time for mankind.

Trump not only proved himself utterly incompetent in this crucial test, and his ineptitude and lack of crisis leadership devastated his re-election campaign. At the same time, he grievously injured his country, his allies and the world. Regardless of the results of the U.S. election, I believe that Trump, to his last day in office and perhaps even afterward, will continue to play politics over science, facts and law. He will continue to divide his people and mobilize his base of hate to shift blame onto others, possibly triggering even more domestic social unrest or even hot wars at home or abroad. This will surely be catastrophic for America and bad for the world. In doing so, however, Trump has inadvertently hastened the ultimate restructuring of the world order.

(This article appeared in *China-US Focus*, November 10, 2020).

BRI Is Not Revival of Ancient China's Tributary System

The Belt and Road Initiative (BRI) has grown rapidly into the most important global public in the new century. Having won the endorsement of 138 countries and 30 international organizations, more governments are now turning to the global connectivity program, hoping that it can help boost the world economy.

But as the BRI has been contributing to the fight against the pandemic, for example having aided Europe with countless life-saving medical supplies from China through the BRI-branded China–Europe freight trains, the British newspaper *The Economist* produced a very biased special report, composed of six articles, to strike a major disgrace upon the BRI.

The idea delivered in those articles is that China wants to revive the ancient tributary system through the BRI, and to ultimately regain its sphere of influence. With that idea, one may well foresee that China will confront, and even decouple itself from, the West. That idea, being so dangerous and wrong nevertheless, has been prevailing in the West for years, unfortunately. I must make a serious response by revealing the absurdity regarding the name and intention of the BRI, as represented in the special report, and tell how to best understand them.

First, the report wrongly explained the Chinese name of the program—Yidai Yilu (One Belt, One Road). Given the full name—"Silk Road Economic Belt and 21st Century Maritime Silk Road"—being too long to remember, Yidai Yilu is merely a newly coined term for convenience of use. Literally meaning "one belt one road", however, the term does not "imply balance, harmony, wholeness", as the report claimed, when the report undertook to compare Yidai Yilu to such Chinese set phrases as Yifu Yiqi (one man one wife) and Yixin Yiyi (one heart one soul), which no wonder sounds bizarre to a Chinese ear, and is misleading to international audiences.

To be clear, the purpose of such comparison was to approve a Mr. Eyck Freymann's claim in the report that the Chinese term evokes an image of China "going forth to encompass the world on land and sea, at once opening to the world and binding the world more closely to China", surely echoing ancient China's tributary system. I would say regretfully, that interpretation is overstretched at its best, and lunatic at its worst.

Second, regarding the English name change from the initial "One Belt One Road" to the current "Belt and Road Initiative", the report said, such change was only to conceal "a sense of China's return to historical greatness" from foreign audiences. Derived from Freymann's bizarre interpretation above, that claimed sense of concealed superiority is illogical and purely self-made-up. After all, does any English native speaker believe that the four English words— "One Belt One Road"—convey anything threatening to the West, as the report warned, and thus, that the official English name "Belt and Road Initiative" is warranted?

Instead, a real reason for such change is that BRI is more accurate than OBOR in characterizing the program. The official English name respects the fact of multiple belts and roads under the umbrella of the program. For example, under the cap of the Belt alone, there are at least six grand economic corridors; and under the cap of

Road, at least two routes reach across the Indian Ocean towards the Mediterranean and Africa, respectively, and a third towards South Pacific islands. And the number of belts and roads may grow as time goes by—the debut of the Polar Silk Road in 2017 and the Digital Silk Road in 2019 being the latest examples. Since the outbreak of COVID-19 pandemic, the Health Silk Road has become a new hit.

Third, the argument in *The Economist*'s special report about the BRI's name in both Chinese and English as above, was consistent with the general theme of that report, i.e., the China-led BRI aimed to revive the ancient tributary system, where all other countries centered around China in an orderly hierarchy and one's obligation depended on its relationship with China. It reflects a typical ignorance in the West about China's approach towards the world order.

The nation's true meaning and intention about the program may be reflected in the choice of "initiative" in the name of the BRI. The word "initiative" infers that the BRI is not pre-destined or self-contained. It conveys a sense of direction, but avoids dictating specifics. Such flexibility and openness as connoted in the name expresses a preferred approach of discussion and collaboration among participating nations on an equal footing. It surely contrasts the ancient tributary system, which featured inequality among states.

No doubt China is at the center of the BRI, sitting in the driver's seat. But it acts as no hegemon to impose its will on others, which is not its cultural gene. *Chinese* multilateralism as reflected therein contrasts *American* multilateralism, whereby the US as a missionary society is ready to convert others.

Technically, the usual discourse "hub-and-spoke arrangements" to describe the BRI is misleading. The "hub-and-spoke" is simply bilateral, but the BRI is a complex and more than bilateral: it has a multilateral Belt and Road Forum, a trilateral agreement on the China-Mongolia-Russia Economic Corridor, an MOU signed with six international organizations under the BRI, and various multi-stakeholder green BRI initiatives, to name a few.

President Xi depicts the world as "a community of shared future for mankind", which as a direction for mankind proves even more true during the global response to COVID-19. The BRI has been serving as a beacon shining for mankind still at this difficult moment. In contrast, Trump's banner "America First", at the expense of even the allies, has been degraded to "America Supremacy" (and domestically to "White Supremacy", against the labeling of "the Chinese Virus" and the killing of George Floyd), having brought chaos home and abroad. To some extent, Trump's world is even worse than the obsolete tributary system, where people and nations might still be able to expect their due positions in a set hierarchy.

(This article appeared in *China Daily*, June 17, 2020).

Americans are Wrong to Paint China as an Intellectual Property Thief

It has become politically correct in the US to call China a thief, bent on stealing American intellectual property. In 2018, this rhetoric was formalised in a "Sect. 301" investigation by the US trade representative. President Donald Trump used allegations of state-sponsored intellectual property (IP) theft as justification to trigger a prolonged trade war between the countries.

This week, the US and China are due to sign phase one of a trade deal to lessen tensions, under which China will boost imports from the US in return for a reduction in American tariffs. But the allegations of IP theft continue to sow mistrust between the two sides, bringing a long, co-operative relationship to the verge of collapse.

What the US calls theft began as technical co-operation 40 years ago, when the two countries committed to a closer relationship in the form of, for example, joint ventures or equity ownership, subject to governmental licences. Such agreements are reinterpreted today as evidence of the coerced transfer of technology—an act of American duplicity.

In a World Trade Organization case heard last summer, the US made the claim that China's IP theft violated "public morals" prevailing in US society, while noting that such behaviour "may not offend China's sense of public morals". That allegation is both wrong and offensive. IP violations bring about civil, administrative and even criminal penalties in China, as well as in the US. China cherishes a culture of fair competition and respect for innovation. "To steal a book is an elegant offence," has long been misread as a permissive aphorism peculiar to Chinese culture. But the short story by Lu Xun, if read carefully, has the opposite moral: the scholar is punished for his theft, and cut off by his neighbours.

IP protection is a necessary part of development. When an under-developed country tries to catch up with a developed one, it learns by imitation, by way of reverse engineering. It accumulates professionals and technology, and then starts to invest in research and innovation. When it wants to climb further up the ladder and expand, it may have to step into a technological no man's land, as the telecoms firm Huawei has in its 5G tech development.

The rise of the US at the turn of the nineteenth century was essentially a process of rampant IP theft from the UK, including of textile manufacturing tech. Some would argue that the laws governing IP protection then were light, and that the US's behaviour was thus tolerable.

That is simply not true. Before the American Revolution, England had passed laws to ban the export of textile machinery and tools that might assist in the manufacture of cotton, linen, wool, and silk. Skilled mechanics were forbidden to emigrate upon pain of imprisonment. The US government defied that law, raiding British industrial secrets and wooing knowledgeable British textile managers, as Ron Chernow has described in his biography, *Alexander Hamilton*. This amounted to state-sanctioned industrial espionage—more evidence of duplicity, given that the US constitution explicitly protected IP.

The story shows how the US has climbed the ladder to tech supremacy only to kick it away now that it has reached the top, just as Britain jealously blocked America's rise. China's IP model started from scratch 40 years ago, but its success is no less extraordinary. Former US Treasury secretary Lawrence Summers, once a stern critic of the policy, has said that China's technological progress comes from its own "terrific entrepreneurs" and "an educational system that's privileging excellence", but not from theft.

By prioritising fair competition and innovation, China will only keep enhancing IP protection, including that originally from the US, as its governmental and social governance capabilities improve.

(This article appeared in *The Financial Times*, January 16, 2020).

US, a Manipulator of Law, Will Be Disappointed

On August 5, the US Department of the Treasury designated China as a currency manipulator. The decision amounted to an escalation of the trade war into a currency war, in the name of responding to China's yuan depreciation, which had broken the milestone point of 7 to the US dollar earlier that day.

US President Donald Trump would not tolerate the yuan depreciation, because the depreciation has an economic effect of offsetting US tariff increases. Trump had earlier threatened to levy tariffs of 10% on the remaining $300 billion of Chinese goods, starting September.

The People's Bank of China (PBC), the country's central bank, said that the currency move reflects shifts in market dynamics and volatilities in global foreign exchange markets amid global economic developments and escalating trade frictions. It was, therefore, a market move in anticipation of the additional tariffs.

It is Trump that brought down the yuan value, by fighting his tariff war and making the world economy look gloomy. But he chose to blame China for "currency manipulation."

In fact, since March 2018 when Trump first initiated the tariff war, the yuan has depreciated from less than 6.3 to 7 to the US dollar. Each time the China-US negotiations appeared favorable to the market, the yuan went up, but when the negotiations halted and Trump weaponized the tariffs, the market felt the pinch and the yuan would go down.

It is evident that the yuan to US dollar exchange rate volatility reflects more of a typical "defensive depreciation" driven by market forces, rather than the alleged "competitive devaluation" advanced by China in order to gain an export edge.

Factoring in the trade frictions and global economic prospects, many currencies have depreciated against the US dollar since the start of August. It is not a phenomenon unique to the yuan, as PBC Governor Yi Gang explained in a press release. The PBC emphasized that the yuan remains the strongest among the G20 economies, appreciating 47% in real terms during the past 15 years.

Yi explicitly defended China's loyalty to the G20 consensus against "competitive devaluations," amid US Treasury accusations that the PBC "has extensive experience of manipulating its currency and remains prepared to do so on an ongoing basis."

The IMF basically requires two elements for proving currency manipulation: Objectively, a fundamental exchange rate misalignment must exist; and subjectively, such a misalignment must serve the purpose of gaining trade advantages. The US bluntly labeled China as a currency manipulator, without even bothering to refer to the established standards.

For the US, this is another outright violation of international rules, let alone its repetitive violations of WTO tariff commitments.

History shows that the US has never hesitated to pursue "America First" at the expense of international law. The US Congress used to propose various bills, including using antidumping or countervailing measures, to counter Chinese exports based on alleged currency manipulation. But it is clear that such bills, if passed into law, would be in violation of international rules.

The US Treasury's designation is even inconsistent with its domestic law. There are three criteria for establishing currency manipulation: a significant bilateral trade surplus (at least $20 billion); a material current account surplus (at least 2% of GDP); and persistent one-sided intervention in the forex market (net purchase of foreign currency of no less than 2% of an economy's GDP over a period of 12 months).

The Treasury's designation was arbitrary, given the sound evidence contrary to its claims, according to an IMF report released on August 9, shortly after the designation. It also contradicted the Treasury's own conclusion in a May 2019 report. For example, China's current account surplus was just 0.4% of GDP last year and will be 0.5% in 2019, far below the designated threshold; and on forex intervention, China did not meet the threshold either.

What comes next after the designation? US law directs its executive director in the IMF to call for "additional rigorous surveillance of the macroeconomic and exchange rate policies" of China and perhaps "formal consultations on findings of currency manipulation," among other things. The Treasury vowed to urge the IMF "to eliminate the unfair competitive advantage created by China's latest actions."

The US will effectively try to push the IMF to endorse its decision, which would be difficult as the IMF has just concluded in its Article IV consultation that the yuan is broadly in line with fundamentals, and is "not significantly overvalued or undervalued."

Nowadays, the IMF is not a puppet of the US Treasury any more. It is almost certain that Trump will be disappointed, and he may then threaten to withdraw from the organization. Nothing is impossible for Trump.

(This article appeared in *The Global Times*, August 18, 2019).

Five Myths About China Must Be Debunked Before the Trade War with the US Can End

The relationship between China and the United States has hit dangerous turbulence since trade talks ended without agreement last month. Ahead of the upcoming G20 Osaka summit, where both countries' leaders are expected to meet, it is now critical to clear up misconceptions about China that are so popular in the US that they threaten to undermine this precious opportunity for both sides to get back to the negotiating table.

The first misconception is that China steals intellectual property (IP) from the US, obsessed with a peculiar culture—to steal a book is an elegant offence. History has taught that almost no country can escape 'stealing' IP of others during its development. The rise of the US at the turn of twentieth century was inseparable from its rampant stealing of IP from the UK, including textile manufacturing technology and Dickson's novel copies. Now the US advocates the highest IP standard worldwide.

China followed a similar IP protection path as the US, but at a much quicker pace, during the past 40 years. Its IP system started from scratch and has climbed to a very high level today. The success is even more extraordinary than that of its economy, in terms of law stipulation and enforcement, as well as promotion of people's awareness through education. This developing country, prioritizing science and technology leadership, will only keep enhancing IP protection, as its governmental and social governance capabilities increase.

The second misconception is that Chinese government forces US companies to transfer technology when they plan to invest in China. The key is to assess whether the investment contract involving technology transfer is done out of willingness or coercion. If both sides are reasonable persons, well informed, desire to maximize respective benefits, and negotiate without duress, then the transaction is done out of willingness, not by force.

Chinese law requires that, for the sake of government approval, some contracts must take the form of joint venture, where Chinese counterparts sometimes must hold majority shares. The US cited such requirements to speculate 'forced technology transfer', but lacked concrete evidence of Chinese government imposing technology transfer requirements either during contract negotiation or approval procedures. Indeed, a recent landmark Chinese foreign investment law explicitly prohibits its government doing so.

The third misconception is about China's developing country status. No doubt, China is a superpower measured by economy and trade volume in aggregate; but by per capita GDP, China falls way behind 90 economies: Russia, Kazakhstan, Brazil, and Malaysia all perform better than it. China indeed has top metropolises such as Beijing and Shanghai; but aside them, you will surely see backward countryside everywhere.

China's developing country status is additionally decided by its limited governmental and social governance capabilities, as mentioned. There has been stark, widespread shortage of professionalism and institutional thinking both in government and society. On social governance, for example, garbage classification has yet become citizens' habits even in some first-tier cities, let alone in smaller ones and rural areas. China's impotence in soft power, alongside hard economy, contributes to its developing country status.

The fourth misconception is about the Party's role in Chinese economy. Some people imagine that China's state capitalism enables it to operate as China Inc., and that Party members occupy every important position in China. Such allegations are simply not true. Rather, private firms today occupy the lion's share of Chinese economy, contributing over 50% for tax revenue, over 60% for GDP growth, over 70% for tech innovation, over 80% for employment, and over 90% for enterprise quantity.

What does the Party committee, established as required by law, do in a company? Here is an illustrative analogy. The Party in China is like God among Christians, while its Party committee is like a church. The church calls upon congregation to be helpful to neighbors, while the Party committee asks members to be role model for corporate codes compliance. In daily operations, Chinese companies perform commercially and autonomously, uncontrolled by the Party; just like a Christian CEO doing business on his own, free from God's intervention.

The fifth misconception is that Chinese citizens must cooperate and spy, if requested by the Party. Such allegation only misinterprets China's 2017 intelligence law, but probably affirms American intelligence practices, as evidenced by Snowden.

China's intelligence apparatus must respect its citizens' lawful rights and interests. Thus, if the government asks Huawei, China's 5G equipment company, to spy on its European clients, Huawei has right to refuse; if it is forced to do so, it would violate Huawei's lawful rights under Article 8 of the intelligence law. After all, the law aims at deterring the activities meant to harm China's national security, not to authorize a preemptive act as to spy or steal information.

From a policy analysis perspective, the government would only avoid using Huawei to spy, because it simply cannot afford to put this hard-won world brand over the barrel and risk its future, in a world already full of venomous rumor and prejudice against both the country and the company.

(This article, in an edited version, appeared in *South China Morning Post*, June 15, 2019).

Two Public Goods that Are Truly Inclusive

The Belt and Road Initiative and the Asian Infrastructure Investment Bank are both manifestations of Chinese multilateralism.

The nexus between the Belt and Road Initiative and the Asian Infrastructure Investment Bank, both of which are ambitious global public goods initiated by China, has been a frequent topic of debate for the international community, with some people questioning the bank's purpose and querying whether it is just a vehicle for promoting China's Belt and Road Initiative.

But it should be noted that the AIIB is an international organization and not a specialized agency under China's Belt and Road Initiative program. The AIIB Articles of Agreement have no mention of it working for the Belt and Road Initiative in particular. Indeed, India, which has not joined the initiative, has so far received 1 in 3 US dollars of the AIIB's approved financing totaling $8 billion.

However, it is equally clear that the AIIB does not shy away from the Belt and Road Initiative, as it shares the same objectives and purposes: sustainable infrastructure and cross-border connectivity.

So why has the issue become so delicate and sensitive? There are both technical and ideological reasons for this.

The technical reason relates to the quality of the Belt and Road Initiative projects. Opponents claim that Belt and Road projects have poor records of transparency, fiscal sustainability, environmental protection, or community engagement, and thus fail to meet the standards of the AIIB.

The rule of thumb in infrastructure investment is that money talks. It is the privilege of the bank funding a project to apply its standards to the project. The Export–Import Bank of China applies its own policies and standards, rather than someone else's, in a project it funds. Similarly, a Belt and Road Initiative project using AIIB money is governed by the standards of the AIIB.

Thus, multilateral and bilateral financiers interested in the Belt and Road Initiative should cooperate and coordinate their efforts to ensure the standards are high and feasible, particularly in projects they are co-financing.

The deeper, ideological reason for attempts to keep the AIIB away from the Belt and Road Initiative is the prejudice of some developed countries toward China, which has long been framed as a significant threat to Western democracy and US supremacy. The United States is particularly unhappy about China changing the world it has long dominated. Neither is it happy about the way China is doing so: China's multilateralism.

Chinese multilateralism is a combination of well-established development theories, including the best practices of Western development, with developing countries' needs, in particular their limited capabilities.

Chinese multilateralism is essentially based on the multilateralism of the US, which contributed to long-term peace and prosperity under the framework of global governance rules, embroidered by international best practices, after the end of World War II.

However, the voice of developing countries was little heard, and because of this, the design and implementation of international rules and standards have failed to take their local conditions and needs into consideration, and thus failed to produce the hoped-for results. This in turn has harmed the reputation of US multilateralism.

Chinese multilateralism corrects this defect by being responsive to the needs of developing countries, while maintaining a rules-based, high-standard system. In this line, the voice of those often forgotten in other international organizations must be heard in the AIIB.

Chinese multilateralism is well positioned to improve US multilateralism, because of the successful development experiences of China and other Asian countries. China promotes "the principle of achieving shared growth through discussion and collaboration", enabling the needs and concerns of all stakeholders to be heard, including those of borrowers.

A typical question related to Chinese multilateralism is: Won't China be a hegemon once it becomes No 1 economy, as the US and the United Kingdom were? My reply is no. A hegemon has two composite elements: it must be powerful, that is a prerequisite, and then based on its power, impose its will on others. A powerful China will not interfere in the internal affairs of other countries.

China is prone to reflect inwardly on how it can improve and reform itself, it does not seek external solutions to handle challenges and solve problems. A good example is the overall approach China has chosen in handling the current trade frictions with the US. China has chosen to open up and better its business climate to mitigate conflict with the US, rather than conduct a tit-for-tat trade war, which would be chaotic for the two countries as well as for the world.

(This article appeared in *China Daily*, May 9, 2019).

Western Fears of Party Influence on Chinese Companies Are Overblown

Huawei, the Chinese telecoms equipment company, has aroused fresh concerns in the west about the role played by the Communist party in Chinese companies—whether these are either state- owned or private.

Western critics claim that companies in China are obliged to spy on foreign governments and companies, at the request of the party. Yet there is no provision in Chinese law requiring citizens to assist the party in spying on foreigners.

China's national intelligence law, in particular article 7 on the obligation of Chinese citizens to support national intelligence work, is often misunderstood. First, it does not authorise pre-emptive spying; national intelligence work must be defensive in nature. Second, the law requires that intelligence agencies respect the rights and interests of individuals and entities. That includes Huawei. Moreover, it is not clear that there is any incentive for China to risk the future of Huawei, a Chinese brand recognised around the world, by asking it to engage in spying.

My experience as a party member for about 10 years might help to throw some light on the subject. I studied in the US and then worked for an intergovernmental organisation in Geneva. During those years it never occurred to me that the party might ask me to do something on its behalf. I received precisely one request that mentioned my party membership, and that came from a Harvard law professor who invited me to talk to his class about China.

I also remember joining a heated debate with members of a Bible study group in Boston. We discussed the question of who or what should govern in China—Christianity, Confucianism, or Communism. I felt an obligation to help my American friends understand China and the Chinese Communist party.

There has been a widespread misperception in the west about what is sometimes called "China Inc". Yes, China is a market economy led by the party, but that does not mean that the political leadership intervenes to allocate resources on a daily basis. Instead, the market plays a decisive role.

Chinese company law requires that there be a party committee in a company with three or more party members. The question is what such committees actually do.

An analogy may be not perfectly proper, but illustrative nevertheless. The Party in China is like God among Christians, and the Party committee in a company is like a church community. The church calls upon its attendees to be role model citizens in the community, while the Party committee asks its members to be role model staff in the company, i.e., working hard and abiding by law and corporate code of ethics. The Party committee offers its members a sense of community, while not dictating the company in business operation. Similarly, God through Church never tells a CEO how much to invest in a particular transaction; a believer is on his own on it.

In Xi's New Era, the Party has been attaching great importance on building and strengthening such Party committees at all grassroots levels in China. Besides commercial companies discussed above, local communities have been called upon to rejuvenate their Party committees. I personally joined some interesting pro bono activities organized by the Party committee in my community, such as campaign for promoting garbage recycling, and tidying up the Ofo shared bikes scattered around.

However, some choose to be blind to what the Party does in China. In the US, the Trump administration has shown signs of adopting a closed-door policy towards Chinese businesses and people, under the cover of national security.

President Donald Trump often conjures up the image of the invisible hand of the Communist party operating through Huawei's global 5G networks. And this is having an effect. Statistics show that Chinese investment in the US dropped by more than 80% in 2018. And concerns are growing among overseas Chinese, increasing numbers of whom are choosing to leave the US and return to China each year.

(This article, in an edited version, appeared in *The Financial Times*, February 18, 2019).

AIIB Should Broaden Horizons to Gain Global Impact

The Asian Infrastructure Investment bank (AIIB) has had global ambitions ever since its establishment in December 2015. The bank has "three global goals"—global recruitment, global procurement and global investment prioritizing Asia.

However, the bank this year set a ceiling on non-regional investment, limiting it to 15% of total financing. This decision by the board of directors has the effect of curtailing the bank's ambitions, and it should be revoked in the best interest of the bank.

First, the bank's authorized capital—$100 billion—is subscribed by regional members (75%) and non-regional members (25%). The term "region" as defined by AIIB law refers to Asia and Oceania, consisting of Asian countries, as well as Russia, Australia, New Zealand, and the Pacific Islands.

There are various motives for a country to join the AIIB.

First, a country may want to have a say in the bank by subscribing its due capital share and placing its own nationals in bank management.

Second, a country may want to help its domestic enterprises obtain business opportunities—for example, by engaging in AIIB corporate or project procurement contracts.

Third, a country may want to receive AIIB loans and investment itself.

If non-regional members are only eligible to receive 15% of the AIIB's investment, while contributing 25% of the bank's capital, that will dim non-regional countries' enthusiasm for the bank as a member, or a potential member.

These disincentives could be mitigated by non-regional recruitment or by non-regional procurement. But these possibilities are uncertain, compared the clearly designated 15% ceiling for non-regional investment, so such moves are hardly convincing for non-regional members.

Even within the 15% portion, the eligibility requirements are demanding. In principle, a non-regional investment must benefit Asia significantly. But in practice, only regions that are geographically proximate to and closely economically integrated with Asia are most likely to be considered. For example, Egypt has been the only non-regional recipient of AIIB financing, because it has the territory of the Sinai Peninsula in the Asian continent.

This type of requirement must be changed. The bank must be eligible to invest globally, including in Africa, the Americas and Europe. With close cooperation with peer institutions of pertinent non-regions—African Development Bank, Inter-American Development bank, European Bank for Reconstruction and Development, and Eurasian Development Bank—the AIIB could expand its investment in those regions.

No doubt the bank has its DNA in Asia, since 22 Asian countries and regions signed the memorandum of understanding to establish the AIIB in 2014. What's more, regional members are privileged to subscribe 75% of bank capital, effectively preserving the lender's Asian character.

But now bank membership has already burgeoned to 87, with 37 non-regionals covering every continent except Antarctica. The letter "A" in the "AIIB" should thus represent Africa, the Americas and others, on top of Asia and Oceania. The momentum of openness should be maintained, not contained.

First, the 15% non-regional investment limit must be lifted, at least to a larger proportion, say 25%.

Second, the bank's decisions on potential non-regional investment should be flexible, rather than rigidly limited to geographically proximate areas.

Starting in January 2019, the bank will delegate its power to approve projects from the board to the president. This new development in bank governance has enormous exceptions, however; the president may still have to ask the board for project approval as before. A decision on non-regional investment is one such exception.

The reservation of non-regional financing approval to the board must be revoked. The reservation tends to increase bank bureaucracy, decrease operational efficiency, and obscure responsibility between the board and management, particularly when a project goes sour.

All those factors go against the intent of the bank's negotiators when they decided to establish a non-resident board for the bank, a major lesson the AIIB learned from traditional banks. With a resident board, those banks are often highly bureaucratic, politicized and unduly likely to delay project processing.

If the president has power to approve non-regional financing, the bank will be able to operate in a more efficient, professional and fiscally sustainable manner, with a pipeline of bankable projects selected globally, rather than locally.

So far, of the AIIB's approved financing of $6.4 billion in total, nearly one in three dollars has gone to India, the biggest recipient of AIIB financing. There may be various reasons for such a peculiar concentration of AIIB investment; for example, ideally India's proposed projects should be top quality.

But regional concentration can be financially risky for the bank, and a more diversified investment portfolio is conducive to all members, including non-regional economies.

Among non-regional members, developed countries typically need to rebuild their infrastructure after decades of use, but their local governments lack money to do the job. Since their deteriorating roads and facilities are potentially good projects, why can't the AIIB jump in? This would be a milestone in the 70-plus-year history of multilateral development financing, bringing welfare to local people in a developed member for the first time.

This will be attractive for the US and Japan, the only two powers still lingering outside the bank.

(This article appeared in *The Global Times*, December 16, 2018).

Annex B
My Review of an AIIB Book

Natalie Lichtenstein is in a most suitable position to write a book explaining the constituent legal document of the Asian Infrastructure Investment Bank (AIIB). Ms. Lichtenstein was technically the drafter of the AIIB Articles of Agreement (AOA, or the Charter), the treaty based on which the Bank was founded, in the position of Chief Counsel during the Bank's establishment process. She was also the Inaugural General Counsel after the Bank went into operation in January 2016.

Ms. Lichtenstein's book, entitled *A Comparative Guide of the Asian Infrastructure Investment Bank*, published by Oxford University Press in 2018, offers an authoritative introduction to the AIIB's Charter. She accurately explains each and every clause or term by comparing their counterparts in the charters of other multilateral development banks (MDBs). She clearly demonstrates in the book that the visions, principles, and rules pertaining to the Bank not only resemble those of peer institutions, but also innovate by echoing the needs of the twenty-first century, by drawing upon those peer MDBs, or by streamlining some piecemeal arrangements commonly seen in other MDBs.

In this review, I discuss five select matters Ms. Lichtenstein touched upon in her book, noting their significance to the AIIB. Such matters include: innovation in AIIB governance; relationship between AIIB Board of Directors (BoD) and its President; non-regional investment limit; nexus between AIIB and the Belt and Road Initiative; and investment in information and communications technology (ICT). I elaborate my own thoughts on those matters, some of which have been inspired by Ms. Lichtenstein but might be different from her viewpoints. I hope the following will encourage and facilitate further discussions among scholars and practitioners.

B. Gu, *Chinese Multilateralism in the Asian Infrastructure Investment Bank (AIIB)*, Modern China and International Economic Law,
https://doi.org/10.1007/978-981-97-1219-9

Governance Innovation

Lichtenstein's book devotes a section on "Heritage and Innovation" (paras 2.76–2.80 in Chap. 2). The non-resident Board of Directors embedded in the AIIB structure has been a prominent topic for discussion on AIIB governance. Although the non-resident nature of the Board is not unique to the AIIB, it is not seen among the leading traditional MDBs such as the World Bank and the Asian Development Bank.

In my mind, what is truly innovative about AIIB's governance is the "three circles" centered around the non-resident Board. Learning the lesson of other MDBs, the Chief Negotiators of the AIIB Charter decided to build a non-resident Board for the Bank, while placing a Complaints-resolution, Effectiveness and Integrity Unit (CEIU) in the Bank, checking/advising the President and his team in Bank operations. In that context, the Board decided to delegate project approval power to the President starting January 2019, nevertheless reserving a few exceptions whereby the Board retains the power. At this point, a commendable innovation by synergizing the "three circles" in bank governance—the non-resident Board, the President and the CEIU—is finally in shape. The "three-circle" arrangement is unique to the AIIB, not seen elsewhere.

Relationship Between BoD and President

Lichtenstein rightly points out that the AIIB should highlight "the centrality of productive governance relationships", reflecting on the tensions between the President and the Board in some leading MDBs, including the World Bank and the African Development Bank, in their early years of operations (paras 10.27–10.28 in Chap. 10). Those traditional MDBs all have a resident Board, whereas the AIIB has a non-resident one, but the tension between the Board and President can similarly arise at some point in AIIB, though predictably boasting some different features.

The key for AIIB is to appropriately demarcate the relationship between the President and the CEIU, two of the "three circles" as discussed. The CEIU resides within the Bank and reports directly to the Board, which is non-resident and absent from Bank headquarters in daily operations. But to carry out its function, does the CEIU have to check and balance the power of the President, or can it be cooperative while looking over the shoulder of the President and his team? An optimal way is to advise or consult the President when (and even before) issues of concern arise. Alternatively, since the President delegates essential elements of operational power to his Vice President, the CEIU may be restrained to monitor up to the level of Vice President in carrying out its function, leaving room for the President to (re)act. It seems that the latter option is preferred, as evidenced in the newly approved Project-affected People's Mechanism.[1]

[1] The Project-affected People's Mechanism (PPM) was approved by the Board of the AIIB in December 2018. In the PPM, the term "Management" is defined to be Vice President and Chief

Non-regional Investment Limit

Lichtenstein discussed the AIIB's investment scope in para 3.13 in Chap. 3, para 4.08 in Chap. 4, and paras 5.23–5.27 and 5.33 in Chap. 5. The Charter permits the AIIB to invest beyond Asia if such investment aims to "foster sustainable economic development, create wealth and improve infrastructure connectivity *in Asia*".[2] In implementing this Charter provision, the Board approved the *Strategy on Financing Operations in Non-regional Members* in February 2018. The *Strategy* decides that the ceiling on non-regional investment as a share of total approved Bank financing is 15%. Non-regional investment must have "significant benefits" to Asia; a global spillover or general equilibrium argument alone is insufficient to justify it, pursuant to the *Strategy*.

Lichtenstein interpreted the Charter requirement on non-regional investment as to "contribute to economic development in Asia" in para 5.33 in Chap. 5. But since the book was written before the date of the *Strategy*, it made no comment on the *Strategy*.

I personally agree on Lichtenstein's flexible interpretation, rather than a rigid one as demonstrated in the *Strategy*. The interpretation of "significant benefits" in the *Strategy* probably has an effect of curtailing the Bank's ambition to operate globally.[3] The 15% non-regional investment limit should be lifted; at least it may be lifted to a bigger percentage, say 25%, the same percentage non-regional members are entitled to subscribe to the AIIB's capital stock.

Even within the 15% non-regional financing, the eligibility requirement sounds rigid, and thus is subject to change. The Bank must be eligible to invest globally, including in Africa, America, and Europe. In that same column, I suggested that the approval authority on non-regional investment should be delegated to the President, one exceptional situation where the Board reserves its approval power, next time when the Board considers revising its *Accountability Framework*.

Nexus Between the AIIB and the Belt and Road Initiative

Lichtenstein touched upon the nexus between the AIIB and the Belt and Road Initiative (BRI), two impressive initiatives made by China for the international community against a backdrop of turbulence for globalization. She mentioned in particular an

---

Investment Officer; and Vice President, Policy and Strategy. Only when Management fails to satisfy CEIU in a situation involving a complaint made by project-affected people, the head of CEIU may notice the President; and if the President fails to act appropriately (within 30 working days upon notice), then the CEIU head shall report to the Board on a confidential basis. *AIIB Policy on the Project-affected People's Mechanism* Dec.7, 2018, paras. 1.3, and 7.2–7.3.

[2] AIIB AOA Arts. 1.1 and 11.1 (a).

[3] See my argument in a recent newspaper column. Gu Bin, 'AIIB should broaden horizons to gain global impact', *The Global Times*, December 16, 2018, http://www.globaltimes.cn/content/1132140.shtml (visited February 1, 2019).

MOU signed between the Chinese Ministry of Finance and six leading international financial institutions including AIIB in connection with the BRI, and appropriately commented that while the BRI "is not part of AIIB's Charter or other basic documents, the overlap of AIIB membership with Belt and Road geography makes it likely that many AIIB investment operations may fall within the Initiative's scope." (para 3.15 in Chap. 3).

Since AIIB and the Chinese government indeed have matters of common interest under the BRI, they may collaborate by signing agreements encompassing "commitments, cost-sharing or cost recovery" under certain BRI activities or projects.[4] I argued in my AIIB law book that the AIIB should consider two conditions in deciding upon a BRI project proposal:[5] first, the proposed project must be bankable for the purposes of the Bank's fiscal sustainability; second, the project must live up to the Bank's high standards, such as social and environmental standards, and corporate and project procurement standards. An example of collaboration between AIIB and BRI is Oman Broadband Infrastructure Project,[6] an important ICT project co-financed by the AIIB and the Silk Road Fund,[7] a fund established by the Chinese government under the BRI.

Investment in ICT

AIIB's investment sectoral focus is laid out broadly in its purpose under AIIB AOA Article 1, as Lichtenstein commented in para 3.12 in Chap. 3, and para 4.07 in Chap. 4. AIIB investment breaks down into two sectors in legal text: "infrastructure"

[4] The MOU mentioned in Lichtenstein's book identifies five focused areas for collaboration: (i) Enhanced support to infrastructure and connectivity projects; (ii) Building stable, diversified, and sustainable development financing mechanisms; (iii) Improving the business climate; (iv) Strengthening coordination and capacity building; and (v) Supporting the implementation of the UN 2030 agenda for Sustainable Development, the achievement of the Sustainable Development Goals, and the Paris Agreement on Climate Change. *Memorandum of Understanding on Collaboration on Matters of Common Interest under the Belt and Road Initiative* between Ministry of Finance of the People's Republic of China and the Asian Development Bank, the Asian Infrastructure Investment Bank, the European Bank for Reconstruction and Development, the European Investment Bank, the New Development Bank, the World Bank Group, dated May 14, 2017, Art. I.

[5] Gu Bin, *The Law and Governance of the Asian Infrastructure Investment Bank*, Wolters Kluwer, 2019, pp 14–17.

[6] The AIIB approved the project proposal in 2017. https://www.aiib.org/en/projects/approved/2017/broadband-infrastructure-project.html (visited February 2, 2019).

[7] It is a B Loan program, whereby the AIIB is the only lender of record in signing contracts with the Oman borrower, i.e., Oman Broadband Company SAOC. The Silk Road Fund participates as a B loan lender but does not appear in lending contracts with the borrower.

http://www.silkroadfund.com.cn/cnweb/19930/19938/37552/index.html (visited February 2, 2019)

and "other productive sectors". "Infrastructure" itself is a broad sector, encompassing both physical and electronic content. "Other productive sectors" can be even broader, echoing the term "productive" first used in the International Bank for Reconstruction and Development (IBRD) Charter in 1944, whereby the word choice meant to exclude "such non-productive lending as financing of war and budget deficits and refinancing of old debts".

As an MDB committed to embracing the twenty-first century, the AIIB must answer the call of the new industrial era featuring digitalization and artificial intelligence (AI). So far the AIIB has focused on traditional hard infrastructure in three identified sectors: energy, transport, and urban development.[8] The AIIB must pioneer in updating the concept of infrastructure by spending more resources on infrastructure relating to ICT, such as 5G networks and quantum information science, thereby digitalizing the traditional infrastructure and developing the digital infrastructure itself.[9] I recall that AIIB President Jin Liqun, then AIIB President-designate, articulated the importance of investment in ICT for the Bank even back in early 2016.[10] Enterprises of Korea as the host country made impressive ICT presentations at the second annual meeting of the AIIB in June 2017.[11] The AIIB now plans to develop an ICT strategy that will focus on "investment in broadband and other connectivity-focused projects".[12] The AIIB must be ready and contribute to the era of digital economy.

(This book review originally appeared in *Manchester Journal of International Economic Law*, Volume16, Issue 1, April 2019).

[8] AIIB Annual Report and Accounts 2016, p. 13.

[9] AIIB Report on Asian Infrastructure Finance 2019, pp. 2 and 106–8.

[10] Jin Liqun, "AIIB improves collaboration in international economy and finance" (AIIB, the "promoter of international economic and financial cooperation and development") January 5, 2016, http://opinion.people.com.cn/n1/2016/0105/c1003-28011508.html (visited February 2, 2019).

[11] Gu Bin, "AIIB boosts sustainable infrastructure" (AIIB: a "propeller" for sustainable infrastructure) *FT Chinese*, June 28, 2017 , http://www.ftchinese.com/story/001073176?archive (visited February 2, 2019).

[12] AIIB News Release, "Infrastructure Investment Needs to Scale Up to Ensure Long-Term Growth in Asia: AIIB Report" January 29, 2019, https://www.aiib.org/en/news-events/news/2019/20190129_001.html (visited February 2, 2019).

Annex C
AIIB Articles of Agreement

Asian Infrastructure Investment Bank

Articles of Agreement

The countries on whose behalf the present Agreement is signed agree as follows:

Considering the importance of regional cooperation to sustain growth and promote economic and social development of the economies in Asia and thereby contribute to regional resilience against potential financial crises and other external shocks in the context of globalization;

Acknowledging the significance of infrastructure development in expanding regional connectivity and improving regional integration, thereby promoting economic growth and sustaining social development for the people in Asia, and contributing to global economic dynamism;

Realizing that the considerable long-term need for financing infrastructure development in Asia will be met more adequately by a partnership among existing multilateral development banks and the Asian Infrastructure Investment Bank (hereinafter referred to as the "Bank");

Convinced that the establishment of the Bank as a multilateral financial institution focused on infrastructure development will help to mobilize much needed additional resources from inside and outside Asia and to remove the financing bottlenecks faced by the individual economies in Asia, and will complement the existing multilateral development banks, to promote sustained and stable growth in Asia;

Have Agreed to establish the Bank, which shall operate in accordance with the following:

B. Gu, *Chinese Multilateralism in the Asian Infrastructure Investment Bank (AIIB)*, Modern China and International Economic Law,
https://doi.org/10.1007/978-981-97-1219-9

CHAPTER I

Purpose, Functions and Membership

Article 1 Purpose

1. The purpose of the Bank shall be to: (i) foster sustainable economic development, create wealth and improve infrastructure connectivity in Asia by investing in infrastructure and other productive sectors; and (ii) promote regional cooperation and partnership in addressing development challenges by working in close collaboration with other multilateral and bilateral development institutions.
2. Wherever used in this Agreement, references to "Asia" and "region" shall include the geographical regions and composition classified as Asia and Oceania by the United Nations, except as otherwise decided by the Board of Governors.

Article 2 Functions

To implement its purpose, the Bank shall have the following functions:

(i) to promote investment in the region of public and private capital for development purposes, in particular for development of infrastructure and other productive sectors;
(ii) to utilize the resources at its disposal for financing such development in the region, including those projects and programs which will contribute most effectively to the harmonious economic growth of the region as a whole and having special regard to the needs of less developed members in the region;
(iii) to encourage private investment in projects, enterprises and activities contributing to economic development in the region, in particular in infrastructure and other productive sectors, and to supplement private investment when private capital is not available on reasonable terms and conditions; and
(iv) to undertake such other activities and provide such other services as may further these functions.

Article 3 Membership

1. Membership in the Bank shall be open to members of the International Bank for Reconstruction and Development or the Asian Development Bank.

    (a) Regional members shall be those members listed in Part A of Schedule A and other members included in the Asia region in accordance with paragraph 2 of Article 1. All other members shall be non-regional members.
    (b) Founding Members shall be those members listed in Schedule A which, on or before the date specified in Article 57, shall have signed this Agreement and shall have fulfilled all other conditions of membership before the final date specified under paragraph 1 of Article 58.

2. Members of the International Bank for Reconstruction and Development or the Asian Development Bank which do not become members in accordance with Article 58 may be admitted, under such terms and conditions as the Bank shall

determine, to membership in the Bank by a Special Majority vote of the Board of Governors as provided in Article 28.

3. In the case of an applicant which is not sovereign or not responsible for the conduct of its international relations, application for membership in the Bank shall be presented or agreed by the member of the Bank responsible for its international relations.

CHAPTER II

Capital

Article 4 Authorized Capital

1. The authorized capital stock of the Bank shall be one hundred billion United States dollars ($100,000,000,000), divided into one million (1,000,000) shares having a par value of 100,000 dollars ($100,000) each, which shall be available for subscription only by members in accordance with the provisions of Article 5.
2. The original authorized capital stock shall be divided into paid-in shares and callable shares. Shares having an aggregate par value of twenty billion dollars ($20,000,000,000) shall be paid-in shares, and shares having an aggregate par value of eighty billion dollars ($80,000,000,000) shall be callable.
3. The authorized capital stock of the Bank may be increased by the Board of Governors by a Super Majority vote as provided in Article 28, at such time and under such terms and conditions as it may deem advisable, including the proportion between paid-in and callable shares.
4. The term "dollar" and the symbol "$" wherever used in this Agreement shall be understood as being the official currency of payment of the United States of America.

Article 5 Subscription of Shares

1. Each member shall subscribe to shares of the capital stock of the Bank. Each subscription to the original authorized capital stock shall be for paid-in shares and callable shares in the proportion two (2) to eight (8). The initial number of shares available to be subscribed by countries which become members in accordance with Article 58 shall be that set forth in Schedule A.
2. The initial number of shares to be subscribed by countries which are admitted to membership in accordance with paragraph 2 of Article 3 shall be determined by the Board of Governors; provided, however, that no such subscription shall be authorized which would have the effect of reducing the percentage of capital stock held by regional members below seventy-five (75) percent of the total subscribed capital stock, unless otherwise agreed by the Board of Governors by a Super Majority vote as provided in Article 28.
3. The Board of Governors may, at the request of a member, increase the subscription of such member on such terms and conditions as the Board may determine by a Super Majority vote as provided in Article 28; provided, however, that

no such increase in the subscription of any member shall be authorized which would have the effect of reducing the percentage of capital stock held by regional members below seventy-five (75) percent of the total subscribed capital stock, unless otherwise agreed by the Board of Governors by a Super Majority vote as provided in Article 28.

4. The Board of Governors shall at intervals of not more than five (5) years review the capital stock of the Bank. In case of an increase in the authorized capital stock, each member shall have a reasonable opportunity to subscribe, under such terms and conditions as the Board of Governors shall determine, to a proportion of the increase of stock equivalent to the proportion which its stock theretofore subscribed bears to the total subscribed capital stock immediately prior to such increase. No member shall be obligated to subscribe to any part of an increase of capital stock.

Article 6 Payment of Subscriptions

1. Payment of the amount initially subscribed by each Signatory to this Agreement which becomes a member in accordance with Article 58 to the paid-in capital stock of the Bank shall be made in five (5) installments, of twenty (20) percent each of such amount, except as provided in paragraph 5 of this Article. The first installment shall be paid by each member within thirty (30) days after entry into force of this Agreement, or on or before the date of deposit on its behalf of its instrument of ratification, acceptance or approval in accordance with paragraph 1 of Article 58, whichever is later. The second installment shall become due one (1) year from the entry into force of this Agreement. The remaining three (3) installments shall become due successively one (1) year from the date on which the preceding installment becomes due.
2. Each installment of the payment of initial subscriptions to the original paid-in capital stock shall be paid in dollars or other convertible currency, except as provided in paragraph 5 of this Article. The Bank may at any time convert such payments into dollars. All rights, including voting rights, acquired in respect of paid-in and associated callable shares for which such payments are due but have not been received shall be suspended until full payment is received by the Bank.
3. Payment of the amount subscribed to the callable capital stock of the Bank shall be subject to call only as and when required by the Bank to meet its liabilities. In the event of such a call, payment may be made at the option of the member in dollars or in the currency required to discharge the obligations of the Bank for the purpose of which the call is made. Calls on unpaid subscriptions shall be uniform in percentage on all callable shares.
4. The Bank shall determine the place for any payment under this Article, provided that, until the inaugural meeting of the Board of Governors, the payment of the first installment referred to in paragraph 1 of this Article shall be made to the Government of the People's Republic of China, as Trustee for the Bank.
5. A member considered as a less developed country for purposes of this paragraph may pay its subscription under paragraphs 1 and 2 of this Article, as an alternative, either:

(a) entirely in dollars or other convertible currency in up to ten (10) installments, with each such installment equal to ten (10) percent of the total amount, the first and second installments due as provided in paragraph 1, and the third through tenth installments due on the second and subsequent anniversary dates of the entry into force of this Agreement; or

(b) with a portion in dollars or other convertible currency and a portion of up to fifty (50) percent of each installment in the currency of the member, following the schedule of installments provided in paragraph 1 of this Article. The following provisions shall apply to payments under this sub-paragraph (b):

   (i) The member shall advise the Bank at the time of subscription under paragraph 1 of this Article of the proportion of payments to be made in its own currency.

   (ii) Each payment of a member in its own currency under this paragraph 5 shall be in such amount as the Bank determines to be equivalent to the full value in terms of dollars of the portion of the subscription being paid. The initial payment shall be in such amount as the member considers appropriate hereunder but shall be subject to such adjustment, to be effected within ninety (90) days of the date on which such payment was due, as the Bank shall determine to be necessary to constitute the full dollar equivalent of such payment.

   (iii) Whenever in the opinion of the Bank, the foreign exchange value of a member's currency has depreciated to a significant extent, that member shall pay to the Bank within a reasonable time an additional amount of its currency required to maintain 6 the value of all such currency held by the Bank on account of its subscription.

   (iv) Whenever in the opinion of the Bank, the foreign exchange value of a member's currency has appreciated to a significant extent, the Bank shall pay to that member within a reasonable time an amount of that currency required to adjust the value of all such currency held by the Bank on account of its subscription.

   (v) The Bank may waive its rights to payment under sub-paragraph (iii) and the member may waive its rights to payment under sub-paragraph (iv).

6. The Bank shall accept from any member paying its subscription under sub-paragraph 5 (b) of this Article promissory notes or other obligations issued by the Government of the member, or by the depository designated by such member, in lieu of the amount to be paid in the currency of the member, provided such amount is not required by the Bank for the conduct of its operations. Such notes or obligations shall be non-negotiable, non-interest-bearing, and payable to the Bank at par value upon demand.

Article 7 Terms of Shares

1. Shares of stock initially subscribed by members shall be issued at par. Other shares shall be issued at par unless the Board of Governors by a Special Majority

vote as provided in Article 28 decides in special circumstances to issue them on other terms.

2. Shares of stock shall not be pledged or encumbered in any manner whatsoever, and they shall be transferable only to the Bank.
3. The liability of the members on shares shall be limited to the unpaid portion of their issue price.
4. No member shall be liable, by reason of its membership, for obligations of the Bank.

Article 8 Ordinary Resources

As used in this Agreement, the term "ordinary resources" of the Bank shall include the following:

(i) authorized capital stock of the Bank, including both paid-in and callable shares, subscribed pursuant to Article 5;
(ii) funds raised by the Bank by virtue of powers conferred by paragraph 1 of Article 16, to which the commitment to calls provided for in paragraph 3 of Article 6 is applicable;
(iii) funds received in repayment of loans or guarantees made with the resources indicated in sub-paragraphs (i) and (ii) of this Article or as returns on equity investments and other types of financing approved under sub-paragraph 2 (vi) of Article 11 made with such resources;
(iv) income derived from loans made from the aforementioned funds or from guarantees to which the commitment to calls set forth in paragraph 3 of Article 6 is applicable; and
(v) any other funds or income received by the Bank which do not form part of its Special Funds resources referred to in Article 17 of this Agreement.

CHAPTER III

Operations of the Bank

Article 9 Use of Resources

The resources and facilities of the Bank shall be used exclusively to implement the purpose and functions set forth, respectively, in Articles 1 and 2, and in accordance with sound banking principles.

Article 10 Ordinary and Special Operations

1. The operations of the Bank shall consist of:

   (i) ordinary operations financed from the ordinary resources of the Bank, referred to in Article 8; and
   (ii) special operations financed from the Special Funds resources referred to in Article 17.

The two types of operations may separately finance elements of the same project or program.

2. The ordinary resources and the Special Funds resources of the Bank shall at all times and in all respects be held, used, committed, invested or otherwise disposed of entirely separately from each other. The financial statements of the Bank shall show the ordinary operations and special operations separately.
3. The ordinary resources of the Bank shall, under no circumstances, be charged with, or used to discharge, losses or liabilities arising out of special operations or other activities for which Special Funds resources were originally used or committed.
4. Expenses appertaining directly to ordinary operations shall be charged to the ordinary resources of the Bank. Expenses appertaining directly to special operations shall be charged to the Special Funds resources. Any other expenses shall be charged as the Bank shall determine.

Article 11 Recipients and Methods of Operation

1. (a) The Bank may provide or facilitate financing to any member, or any agency, instrumentality or political subdivision thereof, or any entity or enterprise operating in the territory of a member, as well as to international or regional agencies or entities concerned with economic development of the region.
   (b) The Bank may, in special circumstances, provide assistance to a recipient not listed in sub-paragraph (a) above only if the Board of Governors, by a Super Majority vote as provided in Article 28: (i) shall have determined that such assistance is designed to serve the purpose and come within the functions of the Bank and is in the interest of the Bank's membership; and (ii) shall have specified the types of assistance under paragraph 2 of this Article that may be provided to such recipient.
2. The Bank may carry out its operations in any of the following ways:
   (i) by making, co-financing or participating in direct loans;
   (ii) by investment of funds in the equity capital of an institution or enterprise;
   (iii) by guaranteeing, whether as primary or secondary obligor, in whole or in part, loans for economic development;
   (iv) by deploying Special Funds resources in accordance with the agreements determining their use;
   (v) by providing technical assistance in accordance with Article 15; or
   (vi) through other types of financing as may be determined by the Board of Governors, by a Special Majority vote as provided in Article 28.

Article 12 Limitations on Ordinary Operations

1. The total amount outstanding of loans, equity investments, guarantees and other types of financing provided by the Bank in its ordinary operations under sub-paragraphs 2 (i), (ii), (iii) and (vi) of Article 11 shall not at any time be increased, if by such increase the total amount of its unimpaired subscribed capital, reserves and retained earnings included in its ordinary resources would be exceeded.

Notwithstanding the provisions of the preceding sentence, the Board of Governors may, by a Super Majority vote as provided in Article 28, determine at any time that, based on the Bank's financial position and financial standing, the limitation under this paragraph may be increased, up to 250% of the Bank's unimpaired subscribed capital, reserves and retained earnings included in its ordinary resources.

2. The amount of the Bank's disbursed equity investments shall not at any time exceed an amount corresponding to its total unimpaired paid-in subscribed capital and general reserves.

Article 13 Operating Principles

The operations of the Bank shall be conducted in accordance with the principles set out below.

1. The Bank shall be guided by sound banking principles in its operations.
2. The operations of the Bank shall provide principally for the financing of specific projects or specific investment programs, for equity investment, and for technical assistance in accordance with Article 15.
3. The Bank shall not finance any undertaking in the territory of a member if that member objects to such financing.
4. The Bank shall ensure that each of its operations complies with the Bank's operational and financial policies, including without limitation, policies addressing environmental and social impacts.
5. In considering an application for financing, the Bank shall pay due regard to the ability of the recipient to obtain financing or facilities elsewhere on terms and conditions that the Bank considers reasonable for the recipient, taking into account all pertinent factors.
6. In providing or guaranteeing financing, the Bank shall pay due regard to the prospects that the recipient and guarantor, if any, will be in a position to meet their obligations under the financing contract.
7. In providing or guaranteeing financing, the financial terms, such as rate of interest and other charges and the schedule for repayment of principal shall be such as are, in the opinion of the Bank, appropriate for the financing concerned and the risk to the Bank.
8. The Bank shall place no restriction upon the procurement of goods and services from any country from the proceeds of any financing undertaken in the ordinary or special operations of the Bank.
9. The Bank shall take the necessary measures to ensure that the proceeds of any financing provided, guaranteed or participated in by the Bank are used only for the purposes for which the financing was granted and with due attention to considerations of economy and efficiency.
10. The Bank shall pay due regard to the desirability of avoiding a disproportionate amount of its resources being used for the benefit of any member.
11. The Bank shall seek to maintain reasonable diversification in its investments in equity capital. In its equity investments, the Bank shall not assume responsibility

for managing any entity or enterprise in which it has an investment and shall not seek a controlling interest in the entity or enterprise concerned, except where necessary to safeguard the investment of the Bank.

Article 14 Terms and Conditions for Financing

1. In the case of loans made or participated in or loans guaranteed by the Bank, the contract shall establish, in conformity with the operating principles set forth in Article 13 and subject to the other provisions of this Agreement, the terms and conditions for the loan or the guarantee concerned. In setting such terms and conditions, the Bank shall take fully into account the need to safeguard its income and financial position.
2. Where the recipient of loans or guarantees of loans is not itself a member, the Bank may, when it deems it advisable, require that the member in whose territory the project concerned is to be carried out, or a public agency or any instrumentality of that member acceptable to the Bank, guarantee the repayment of the principal and the payment of interest and other charges on the loan in accordance with the terms thereof.
3. The amount of any equity investment shall not exceed such percentage of the equity capital of the entity or enterprise concerned as permitted under policies approved by the Board of Directors.
4. The Bank may provide financing in its operations in the currency of the country concerned, in accordance with policies that minimize currency risk.

Article 15 Technical Assistance

1. The Bank may provide technical advice and assistance and other similar forms of assistance which serve its purpose and come within its functions.
2. Where expenditures incurred in furnishing such services are not reimbursable, the Bank shall charge such expenditures to the income of the Bank.

CHAPTER IV

Finances of the Bank

Article 16 General Powers

In addition to the powers specified elsewhere in this Agreement, the Bank shall have the powers set out below.

1. The Bank may raise funds, through borrowing or other means, in member countries or elsewhere, in accordance with the relevant legal provisions.
2. The Bank may buy and sell securities the Bank has issued or guaranteed or in which it has invested.
3. The Bank may guarantee securities in which it has invested in order to facilitate their sale.
4. The Bank may underwrite, or participate in the underwriting of, securities issued by any entity or enterprise for purposes consistent with the purpose of the Bank.

5. The Bank may invest or deposit funds not needed in its operations.
6. The Bank shall ensure that every security issued or guaranteed by the Bank shall bear on its face a conspicuous statement to the effect that it is not an obligation of any Government, unless it is in fact the obligation of a particular Government, in which case it shall so state.
7. The Bank may establish and administer funds held in trust for other parties, provided such trust funds are designed to serve the purpose and come within the functions of the Bank, under a trust fund framework which shall have been approved by the Board of Governors.
8. The Bank may establish subsidiary entities which are designed to serve the purpose and come within the functions of the Bank, only with the approval of the Board of Governors by a Special Majority vote as provided in Article 28.
9. The Bank may exercise such other powers and establish such rules and regulations as may be necessary or appropriate in furtherance of its purpose and functions, consistent with the provisions of this Agreement.

Article 17 Special Funds

1. The Bank may accept Special Funds which are designed to serve the purpose and come within the functions of the Bank; such Special Funds shall be resources of the Bank. The full cost of administering any Special Fund shall be charged to that Special Fund.
2. Special Funds accepted by the Bank may be used on terms and conditions consistent with the purpose and functions of the Bank and with the agreement relating to such Funds.
3. The Bank shall adopt such special rules and regulations as may be required for the establishment, administration and use of each Special Fund. Such rules and regulations shall be consistent with the provisions of this Agreement, except for those provisions expressly applicable only to ordinary operations of the Bank.
4. The term "Special Funds resources" shall refer to the resources of any Special Fund and shall include:

   (i) funds accepted by the Bank for inclusion in any Special Fund;
   (ii) funds received in respect of loans or guarantees, and the proceeds of any equity investments, financed from the resources of any Special Fund which, under the rules and regulations of the Bank governing that Special Fund, are received by such Special Fund;
   (iii) income derived from investment of Special Funds resources; and
   (iv) any other resources placed at the disposal of any Special Fund.

Article 18 Allocation and Distribution of Net Income

1. The Board of Governors shall determine at least annually what part of the net income of the Bank shall be allocated, after making provision for reserves, to retained earnings or other purposes and what part, if any, shall be distributed to the members. Any such decision on the allocation of the Bank's net income to other purposes shall be taken by a Super Majority vote as provided in Article 28.

2. The distribution referred to in the preceding paragraph shall be made in proportion to the number of shares held by each member, and payments shall be made in such manner and in such currency as the Board of Governors shall determine.

Article 19 Currencies

1. Members shall not impose any restrictions on currencies, including the receipt, holding, use or transfer by the Bank or by any recipient from the Bank, for payments in any country.
2. Whenever it shall become necessary under this Agreement to value any currency in terms of another or determine whether any currency is convertible, such valuation or determination shall be made by the Bank.

Article 20 Methods of Meeting Liabilities of the Bank

1. In the Bank's ordinary operations, in cases of arrears or default on loans made, participated in, or guaranteed by the Bank, and in cases of losses on equity investment or other types of financing under sub-paragraph 2 (vi) of Article 11, the Bank shall take such action as it deems appropriate. The Bank shall maintain appropriate provisions against possible losses.
2. Losses arising in the Bank's ordinary operations shall be charged:

   (i) first, to the provisions referred to in paragraph 1 above;
   (ii) second, to net income;
   (iii) third, against reserves and retained earnings;
   (iv) fourth, against unimpaired paid-in capital; and
   (v) last, against an appropriate amount of the uncalled subscribed callable capital which shall be called in accordance with the provisions of paragraph 3 of Article 6.

CHAPTER V

Governance

Article 21 Structure

The Bank shall have a Board of Governors, a Board of Directors, a President, one or more Vice-Presidents, and such other officers and staff as may be considered necessary.

Article 22 Board of Governors: Composition

1. Each member shall be represented on the Board of Governors and shall appoint one Governor and one Alternate Governor. Each Governor and Alternate Governor shall serve at the pleasure of the appointing member. No Alternate Governor may vote except in the absence of his principal.
2. At each of its annual meetings, the Board shall elect one of the Governors as Chairman who shall hold office until the election of the next Chairman.

3. Governors and Alternate Governors shall serve as such without remuneration from the Bank, but the Bank may pay them reasonable expenses incurred in attending meetings.

Article 23 Board of Governors: Powers

1. All the powers of the Bank shall be vested in the Board of Governors.
2. The Board of Governors may delegate to the Board of Directors any or all its powers, except the power to:

   (i) admit new members and determine the conditions of their admission;
   (ii) increase or decrease the authorized capital stock of the Bank;
   (iii) suspend a member;
   (iv) decide appeals from interpretations or applications of this Agreement given by the Board of Directors;
   (v) elect the Directors of the Bank and determine the expenses to be paid for Directors and Alternate Directors and remuneration, if any, pursuant to paragraph 6 of Article 25;
   (vi) elect the President, suspend or remove him from office, and determine his remuneration and other conditions of service;
   (vii) approve, after reviewing the auditors' report, the general balance sheet and the statement of profit and loss of the Bank;
   (viii) determine the reserves and the allocation and distribution of the net profits of the Bank;
   (ix) amend this Agreement;
   (x) decide to terminate the operations of the Bank and to distribute its assets; and
   (xi) exercise such other powers as are expressly assigned to the Board of Governors in this Agreement.

3. The Board of Governors shall retain full power to exercise authority over any matter delegated to the Board of Directors under paragraph 2 of this Article.

Article 24 Board of Governors: Procedure

1. The Board of Governors shall hold an annual meeting and such other meetings as may be provided for by the Board of Governors or called by the Board of Directors. Meetings of the Board of Governors shall be called by the Board of Directors whenever requested by five (5) members of the Bank.
2. A majority of the Governors shall constitute a quorum for any meeting of the Board of Governors, provided such majority represents not less than two-thirds of the total voting power of the members.
3. The Board of Governors shall by regulation establish procedures whereby the Board of Directors may obtain a vote of the Governors on a specific question without a meeting and provide for electronic meetings of the Board of Governors in special circumstances.

4. The Board of Governors, and the Board of Directors to the extent authorized, may establish such subsidiary entities, and adopt such rules and regulations, as may be necessary or appropriate to conduct the business of the Bank.

Article 25 Board of Directors: Composition

1. The Board of Directors shall be composed of twelve (12) members who shall not be members of the Board of Governors, and of whom:

   (i) nine (9) shall be elected by the Governors representing regional members; and
   (ii) three (3) shall be elected by the Governors representing non-regional members.

   Directors shall be persons of high competence in economic and financial matters and shall be elected in accordance with Schedule B. Directors shall represent members whose Governors have elected them as well as members whose Governors assign their votes to them.

2. The Board of Governors shall, from time to time, review the size and composition of the Board of Directors, and may increase or decrease the size or revise the composition as appropriate, by a Super Majority vote as provided in Article 28.
3. Each Director shall appoint an Alternate Director with full power to act for him when he is not present. The Board of Governors shall adopt rules enabling a Director elected by more than a specified number of members to appoint an additional Alternate Director.
4. Directors and Alternate Directors shall be nationals of member countries. No two or more Directors may be of the same nationality nor may any two or more Alternate Directors be of the same nationality. Alternate Directors may participate in meetings of the Board but may vote only when the Alternate Director is acting in place of the Director.
5. Directors shall hold office for a term of two (2) years and may be re-elected.

   (a) Directors shall continue in office until their successors shall have been chosen and assumed office.
   (b) If the office of a Director becomes vacant more than one hundred and eighty (180) days before the end of his term, a successor shall be chosen in accordance with Schedule B, for the remainder of the term, by the Governors who elected the former Director. A majority of the votes cast by such Governors shall be required for such election. The Governors who elected a Director may similarly choose a successor if the office of a Director becomes vacant one hundred and eighty (180) days or less before the end of his term.
   (c) While the office of a Director remains vacant, an Alternate Director of the former Director shall exercise the powers of the latter, except that of appointing an Alternate Director.

6. Directors and Alternate Directors shall serve without remuneration from the Bank, unless the Board of Governors shall decide otherwise, but the Bank may pay them reasonable expenses incurred in attending meetings.

Article 26 Board of Directors: Powers

The Board of Directors shall be responsible for the direction of the general operations of the Bank and, for this purpose, shall, in addition to the powers assigned to it expressly by this Agreement, exercise all the powers delegated to it by the Board of Governors, and in particular:

(i) prepare the work of the Board of Governors;
(ii) establish the policies of the Bank, and, by a majority representing not less than three-fourths of the total voting power of the members, take decisions on major operational and financial policies and on delegation of authority to the President under Bank policies;
(iii) take decisions concerning operations of the Bank under paragraph 2 of Article 11, and, by a majority representing not less than three-fourths of 16 the total voting power of the members, decide on the delegation of such authority to the President;
(iv) supervise the management and the operation of the Bank on a regular basis, and establish an oversight mechanism for that purpose, in line with principles of transparency, openness, independence and accountability;
(v) approve the strategy, annual plan and budget of the Bank;
(vi) appoint such committees as deemed advisable; and
(vii) submit the audited accounts for each financial year for approval of the Board of Governors.

Article 27 Board of Directors: Procedure

1. The Board of Directors shall meet as often as the business of the Bank may require, periodically throughout the year. The Board of Directors shall function on a non-resident basis except as otherwise decided by the Board of Governors by a Super Majority vote as provided in Article 28. Meetings may be called by the Chairman or whenever requested by three (3) Directors.
2. A majority of the Directors shall constitute a quorum for any meeting of the Board of Directors, provided such majority represents not less than two-thirds of the total voting power of the members.
3. The Board of Governors shall adopt regulations under which, if there is no Director of its nationality, a member may send a representative to attend, without right to vote, any meeting of the Board of Directors when a matter particularly affecting that member is under consideration.
4. The Board of Directors shall establish procedures whereby the Board can hold an electronic meeting or vote on a matter without holding a meeting.

Article 28 Voting

1. The total voting power of each member shall consist of the sum of its basic votes, share votes and, in the case of a Founding Member, its Founding Member votes.

    (i) The basic votes of each member shall be the number of votes that results from the equal distribution among all the members of twelve (12) percent of the aggregate sum of the basic votes, share votes and Founding Member votes of all the members.

(ii) The number of the share votes of each member shall be equal to the number of shares of the capital stock of the Bank held by that member.

(iii) Each Founding Member shall be allocated six hundred (600) Founding Member votes.

In the event a member fails to pay any part of the amount due in respect of its obligations in relation to paid-in shares under Article 6, the number of share votes to be exercised by the member shall, as long as such failure continues, be reduced proportionately, by the percentage which the amount due and unpaid represents of the total par value of paid-in shares subscribed to by that member.

2. In voting in the Board of Governors, each Governor shall be entitled to cast the votes of the member he represents.

   (i) Except as otherwise expressly provided in this Agreement, all matters before the Board of Governors shall be decided by a majority of the votes cast.
   (ii) A Super Majority vote of the Board of Governors shall require an affirmative vote of two-thirds of the total number of Governors, representing not less than three-fourths of the total voting power of the members.
   (iii) A Special Majority vote of the Board of Governors shall require an affirmative vote of a majority of the total number of Governors, representing not less than a majority of the total voting power of the members.

3. In voting in the Board of Directors, each Director shall be entitled to cast the number of votes to which the Governors who elected him are entitled and those to which any Governors who have assigned their votes to him, pursuant to Schedule B, are entitled.

   (i) A Director entitled to cast the votes of more than one member may cast the votes for those members separately.
   (ii) Except as otherwise expressly provided in this Agreement, all matters before the Board of Directors shall be decided by a majority of the votes cast.

Article 29 The President

1. The Board of Governors, through an open, transparent and merit-based process, shall elect a president of the Bank by a Super Majority vote as provided in Article 28. He shall be a national of a regional member country. The President, while holding office, shall not be a Governor or a Director or an Alternate for either.
2. The term of office of the President shall be five (5) years. He may be re-elected once. The President may be suspended or removed from office when the Board of Governors so decides by a Super Majority vote as provided in Article 28.

   (a) If the office of the President for any reason becomes vacant during his term, the Board of Governors shall appoint an Acting President 18 for a temporary period or elect a new President, in accordance with paragraph 1 of this Article.

3. The President shall be Chairman of the Board of Directors but shall have no vote, except a deciding vote in case of an equal division. He may participate in meetings of the Board of Governors but shall not vote.
4. The President shall be the legal representative of the Bank. He shall be chief of the staff of the Bank and shall conduct, under the direction of the Board of Directors, the current business of the Bank.

Article 30 Officers and Staff of the Bank

1. One or more Vice-Presidents shall be appointed by the Board of Directors on the recommendation of the President, on the basis of an open, transparent and merit-based process. A Vice-President shall hold office for such term, exercise such authority and perform such functions in the administration of the Bank, as may be determined by the Board of Directors. In the absence or incapacity of the President, a Vice-President shall exercise the authority and perform the functions of the President.
2. The President shall be responsible for the organization, appointment and dismissal of the officers and staff in accordance with regulations adopted by the Board of Directors, with the exception of Vice-Presidents to the extent provided in paragraph 1 above.
3. In appointing officers and staff and recommending Vice-Presidents, the President shall, subject to the paramount importance of securing the highest standards of efficiency and technical competence, pay due regard to the recruitment of personnel on as wide a regional geographical basis as possible.

Article 31 The International Character of the Bank

1. The Bank shall not accept Special Funds, loans or assistance that may in any way prejudice, limit, deflect or otherwise alter its purpose or functions.
2. The Bank, its President, officers and staff shall not interfere in the political affairs of any member, nor shall they be influenced in their decisions by the political character of the member concerned. Only economic considerations shall be relevant to their decisions. Such considerations shall be weighed impartially in order to achieve and carry out the purpose and functions of the Bank.
3. The President, officers and staff of the Bank, in the discharge of their offices, owe their duty entirely to the Bank and to no other authority. Each member of the Bank shall respect the international character of this duty and shall refrain from all attempts to influence any of them in the discharge of their duties.

CHAPTER VI

General Provisions

Article 32 Offices of the Bank

1. The principal office of the Bank shall be located in Beijing, People's Republic of China.
2. The Bank may establish agencies or offices elsewhere.

Article 33 Channel of Communication; Depositories

1. Each member shall designate an appropriate official entity with which the Bank may communicate in connection with any matter arising under this Agreement.
2. Each member shall designate its central bank, or such other institution as may be agreed upon with the Bank, as a depository with which the Bank may keep its holdings of currency of that member as well as other assets of the Bank.
3. The Bank may hold its assets with such depositories as the Board of Directors shall determine.

Article 34 Reports and Information

1. The working language of the Bank shall be English, and the Bank shall rely on the English text of this Agreement for all decisions and for interpretations under Article 54.
2. Members shall furnish the Bank with such information it may reasonably request of them in order to facilitate the performance of its functions.
3. The Bank shall transmit to its members an annual report containing an audited statement of its accounts and shall publish such report. It shall also transmit quarterly to its members a summary statement of its financial position and a profit and loss statement showing the results of its operations.
4. The Bank shall establish a policy on the disclosure of information in order to promote transparency in its operations. The Bank may publish such reports as it deems desirable in the carrying out of its purpose and functions.

Article 35 Cooperation with Members and International Organizations

1. The Bank shall work in close cooperation with all its members, and, in such manner as it may deem appropriate within the terms of this Agreement, with other international financial institutions, and international organizations concerned with the economic development of the region or the Bank's operational areas.
2. The Bank may enter into arrangements with such organizations for purposes consistent with this Agreement, with the approval of the Board of Directors.

Article 36 References

1. References in this Agreement to Article or Schedule refer to Articles and Schedules of this Agreement, unless otherwise specified.
2. References in this Agreement to a specific gender shall be equally applicable to any gender.

CHAPTER VII

Withdrawal and Suspension of Members

Article 37 Withdrawal of Membership

1. Any member may withdraw from the Bank at any time by delivering a notice in writing to the Bank at its principal office.
2. Withdrawal by a member shall become effective, and its membership shall cease, on the date specified in its notice but in no event less than six (6) months after the date that notice has been received by the Bank. However, at any time before the withdrawal becomes finally effective, the member may notify the Bank in writing of the cancellation of its notice of intention to withdraw.
3. A withdrawing member shall remain liable for all direct and contingent obligations to the Bank to which it was subject at the date of delivery of the withdrawal notice. If the withdrawal becomes finally effective, the member shall not incur any liability for obligations resulting from operations of the Bank effected after the date on which the withdrawal notice was received by the Bank.

Article 38 Suspension of Membership

1. If a member fails to fulfill any of its obligations to the Bank, the Board of Governors may suspend such member by a Super Majority vote as provided in Article 28.
2. The member so suspended shall automatically cease to be a member one (1) year from the date of its suspension, unless the Board of Governors decides by a Super Majority vote as provided in Article 28 to restore the member to good standing.
3. While under suspension, a member shall not be entitled to exercise any rights under this Agreement, except the right of withdrawal, but shall remain subject to all its obligations.

Article 39 Settlement of Accounts

1. After the date on which a country ceases to be a member, it shall remain liable for its direct obligations to the Bank and for its contingent liabilities to the Bank so long as any part of the loans, guarantees, equity investments or other forms of financing under paragraph 2 (vi) of Article 11 (hereinafter, other financing) contracted before it ceased to be a member is outstanding, but it shall not incur liabilities with respect to loans, guarantees, equity investments or other financing entered into thereafter by the Bank nor share either in the income or the expenses of the Bank.
2. At the time a country ceases to be a member, the Bank shall arrange for the repurchase of such country's shares by the Bank as a part of the settlement of accounts with such country in accordance with the provisions of paragraphs 3 and 4 of this Article. For this purpose, the repurchase price of the shares shall be the value shown by the books of the Bank on the date the country ceases to be a member.

3. The payment for shares repurchased by the Bank under this Article shall be governed by the following conditions:

    (i) Any amount due to the country concerned for its shares shall be withheld so long as that country, its central bank or any of its agencies, instrumentalities or political subdivisions remains liable, as borrower, guarantor or other contracting party with respect to equity investment or other financing, to the Bank and such amount may, at the option of the Bank, be applied on any such liability as it matures. No amount shall be withheld on account of the contingent liability of the country for future calls on its subscription for shares in accordance with paragraph 3 of Article 6. In any event, no amount due to a member for its shares shall be paid until six (6) months after the date on which the country ceases to be a member.
    (ii) Payments for shares may be made from time to time, upon surrender of the corresponding stock certificates by the country concerned, to the extent by which the amount due as the repurchase price in accordance with paragraph 2 of this Article exceeds the aggregate amount of liabilities, on loans, guarantees, equity investments and other financing referred to in sub-paragraph (i) of this paragraph, until the former member has received the full repurchase price.
    (iii) Payments shall be made in such available currencies as the Bank determines, taking into account its financial position.
    (iv) If losses are sustained by the Bank on any loans, guarantees, equity investments or other financing which were outstanding on the date when a country ceased to be a member and the amount of such losses exceeds the amount of the reserve provided against losses on that date, the country concerned shall repay, upon demand, the amount by which the repurchase price of its shares would have been reduced if the losses had been taken into account when the repurchase price was determined. In addition, the former member shall remain liable on any call for unpaid subscriptions in accordance with paragraph 3 of Article 6, to the same extent that it would have been required to respond if the impairment of capital had occurred and the call had been made at the time the repurchase price of its shares was determined.

4. If the Bank terminates its operations pursuant to Article 41 within six (6) months of the date upon which any country ceases to be a member, all rights of the country concerned shall be determined in accordance with the provisions of Articles 41 to 43. Such country shall be considered as still a member for purposes of such Articles but shall have no voting rights.

CHAPTER VIII

Suspension and Termination of Operations of the Bank

Article 40 Temporary Suspension of Operations

In an emergency, the Board of Directors may temporarily suspend operations in respect of new loans, guarantees, equity investment and other forms of financing under sub-paragraph 2 (vi) of Article 11, pending an opportunity for further consideration and action by the Board of Governors.

Article 41 Termination of Operations

1. The Bank may terminate its operations by a resolution of the Board of Governors approved by a Super Majority vote as provided in Article 28.
2. After such termination, the Bank shall forthwith cease all activities, except those incident to the orderly realization, conservation and preservation of its assets and settlement of its obligations.

Article 42 Liability of Members and Payments of Claims

1. In the event of termination of the operation of the Bank, the liability of all members for uncalled subscriptions to the capital stock of the Bank and in respect of the depreciation of their currencies shall continue until all claims of creditors, including all contingent claims, shall have been discharged.
2. All creditors holding direct claims shall first be paid out of the assets of the Bank and then out of payments to the Bank or unpaid or callable subscriptions. Before making any payments to creditors holding direct claims, the Board of Directors shall make such arrangements as are necessary, in its judgment, to ensure a pro rata distribution among holders of direct and contingent claims.

Article 43 Distribution of Assets

1. No distribution of assets shall be made to members on account of their subscriptions to the capital stock of the Bank until:

    (i) all liabilities to creditors have been discharged or provided for; and
    (ii) the Board of Governors has decided, by a Super Majority vote as provided in Article 28, to make such distribution.

2. Any distribution of the assets of the Bank to the members shall be in proportion to the capital stock held by each member and shall be effected at such times and under such conditions as the Bank shall deem fair and equitable. The shares of assets distributed need not be uniform as to type of asset. No member shall be entitled to receive its share in such a distribution of assets until it has settled all of its obligations to the Bank.
3. Any member receiving assets distributed pursuant to this Article shall enjoy the same rights with respect to such assets as the Bank enjoyed prior to their distribution.

CHAPTER IX

Status, Immunities, Privileges and Exemptions

Article 44 Purposes of Chapter

1. To enable the Bank to fulfill its purpose and carry out the functions entrusted to it, the status, immunities, privileges and exemptions set forth in this Chapter shall be accorded to the Bank in the territory of each member.
2. Each member shall promptly take such action as is necessary to make effective in its own territory the provisions set forth in this Chapter and shall inform the Bank of the action which it has taken.

Article 45 Status of the Bank

The Bank shall possess full juridical personality and, in particular, the full legal capacity:

(i) to contract;
(ii) to acquire, and dispose of, immovable and movable property;
(iii) to institute and respond to legal proceedings; and
(iv) to take such other action as may be necessary or useful for its purpose and activities.

Article 46 Immunity from Judicial Proceedings

1. The Bank shall enjoy immunity from every form of legal process, except in cases arising out of or in connection with the exercise of its powers to raise funds, through borrowings or other means, to guarantee obligations, or to buy and sell or underwrite the sale of securities, in which cases actions may be brought against the Bank only in a court of competent jurisdiction in the territory of a country in which the Bank has an office, or has appointed an agent for the purpose of accepting service or notice of process, or has issued or guaranteed securities.
2. Notwithstanding the provisions of paragraph 1 of this Article, no action shall be brought against the Bank by any member, or by any agency or instrumentality of a member, or by any entity or person directly or indirectly acting for or deriving claims from a member or from any agency or instrumentality of a member. Members shall have recourse to such special procedures for the settlement of controversies between the Bank and its members as may be prescribed in this Agreement, in the by-laws and regulations of the Bank, or in the contracts entered into with the Bank.
3. Property and assets of the Bank shall, wheresoever located and by whomsoever held, be immune from all forms of seizure, attachment or execution before the delivery of final judgment against the Bank.

Article 47 Immunity of Assets and Archives

1. Property and assets of the Bank, wheresoever located and by whomsoever held, shall be immune from search, requisition, confiscation, expropriation or any other form of taking or foreclosure by executive or legislative action.

2. The archives of the Bank, and, in general, all documents belonging to it, or held by it, shall be inviolable, wheresoever located and by whomsoever held.

Article 48 Freedom of Assets from Restrictions

To the extent necessary to carry out the purpose and functions of the Bank effectively, and subject to the provisions of this Agreement, all property and assets of the Bank shall be free from restrictions, regulations, controls and moratoria of any nature.

Article 49 Privilege for Communications

Official communications of the Bank shall be accorded by each member the same treatment that it accords to the official communications of any other member.

Article 50 Immunities and Privileges of Officers and Employees

All Governors, Directors, Alternates, the President, Vice-Presidents and other officers and employees of the Bank, including experts and consultants performing missions or services for the Bank:

(i) shall be immune from legal process with respect to acts performed by them in their official capacity, except when the Bank waives the immunity and shall enjoy inviolability of all their official papers, documents and records;
(ii) where they are not local citizens or nationals, shall be accorded the same immunities from immigration restrictions, alien registration requirements and national service obligations, and the same facilities as regards exchange regulations, as are accorded by members to the representatives, officials and employees of comparable rank of other members; and
(iii) shall be granted the same treatment in respect of travelling facilities as is accorded by members to representatives, officials and employees of comparable rank of other members.

Article 51 Exemption from Taxation

1. The Bank, its assets, property, income and its operations and transactions pursuant to this Agreement, shall be exempt from all taxation and from all customs duties. The Bank shall also be exempt from any obligation for the payment, withholding or collection of any tax or duty.
2. No tax of any kind shall be levied on or in respect of salaries, emoluments and expenses, as the case may be, paid by the Bank to Directors, Alternate Directors, the President, Vice-Presidents and other officers or employees of the Bank, including experts and consultants performing missions or services for the Bank, except where a member deposits with its instrument of ratification, acceptance, or approval a declaration that such member retains for itself and its political subdivisions the right to tax salaries, and emoluments , as the case may be, paid by the Bank to citizens or nationals of such member.
3. No tax of any kind shall be levied on any obligation or security issued by the Bank, including any dividend or interest thereon, by whomsoever held:

(i) which discriminates against such obligation or security solely because it is issued by the Bank; or
(ii) if the sole jurisdictional basis for such taxation is the place or currency in which it is issued, made payable or paid, or the location of any office or place of business maintained by the Bank.

4. No tax of any kind shall be levied on any obligation or security guaranteed by the Bank, including any dividend or interest thereon, by whomsoever held:

   (i) which discriminates against such obligation or security solely because it is guaranteed by the Bank; or
   (ii) if the sole jurisdictional basis for such taxation is the location of any office or place of business maintained by the Bank.

Article 52 Waivers

1. The Bank at its discretion may waive any of the privileges, immunities and exemptions conferred under this Chapter in any case or instance, in such manner and upon such conditions as it may determine to be appropriate in the best interests of the Bank.

CHAPTER X

Amendment, Interpretation and Arbitration

Article 53 Amendments

1. This Agreement may be amended only by a resolution of the Board of Governors approved by a Super Majority vote as provided in Article 28.
2. Notwithstanding the provisions of paragraph 1 of this Article, the unanimous agreement of the Board of Governors shall be required for the approval of any amendment modifying:

   (i) the right to withdraw from the Bank;
   (ii) the limitations on liability provided in paragraphs 3 and 4 of Article 7; and
   (iii) the rights pertaining to purchase of capital stock provided in paragraph 4 of Article 5.

3. Any proposal to amend this Agreement, whether emanating from a member or the Board of Directors, shall be communicated to the Chairman of the Board of Governors, who shall bring the proposal before the Board of Governors. When an amendment has been adopted, the Bank shall so certify in an official communication addressed to all members. Amendments shall enter into force for all members three (3) months after the date of the official communication unless the Board of Governors specifies therein a different period.

Article 54 Interpretation

1. Any question of interpretation or application of the provisions of this Agreement arising between any member and the Bank, or between two or more members

of the Bank, shall be submitted to the Board of Directors for decision. If there is no Director of its nationality on that Board, a member particularly affected by the question under consideration shall be entitled to direct representation in the Board of Directors during such consideration; the representative of such member shall, however, have no vote. Such right of representation shall be regulated by the Board of Governors.

2. In any case where the Board of Directors has given a decision under paragraph 1 of this Article, any member may require that the question be referred to the Board of Governors, whose decision shall be final. Pending the decision of the Board of Governors, the Bank may, so far as it deems necessary, act on the basis of the decision of the Board of Directors.

Article 55 Arbitration

If a disagreement should arise between the Bank and a country which has ceased to be a member, or between the Bank and any member after adoption of a resolution to terminate the operations of the Bank, such disagreement shall be submitted to arbitration by a tribunal of three arbitrators. One of the arbitrators shall be appointed by the Bank, another by the country concerned, and the third, unless the parties otherwise agree, by the President of the International Court of Justice or such other authority as may have been prescribed by regulations adopted by the Board of Governors. A majority vote of the arbitrators shall be sufficient to reach a decision which shall be final and binding upon the parties. The third arbitrator shall be empowered to settle all questions of procedure in any case where the parties are in disagreement with respect thereto.

Article 56 Approval Deemed Given

Whenever the approval of any member is required before any act may be done by the Bank except under paragraph 2 of Article 53, approval shall be deemed to have been given unless the member presents an objection within such reasonable period as the Bank may fix in notifying the member of the proposed act.

CHAPTER XI

Final Provisions

Article 57 Signature and Deposit

1. This Agreement, deposited with the Government of the People's Republic of China (hereinafter called the "Depository"), shall remain open until December 31, 2015 for signature by the Governments of countries whose names are set forth in Schedule A.
2. The Depository shall send certified copies of this Agreement to all the Signatories and other countries which become members of the Bank.

Article 58 Ratification, Acceptance or Approval

1. This Agreement shall be subject to ratification, acceptance or approval by the Signatories. Instruments of ratification, acceptance or approval shall be deposited with the Depository not later than December 31, 2016, or if necessary, until such later date as may be decided by the Board of Governors by a Special Majority vote as provided in Article 28. The Depository shall duly notify the other Signatories of each deposit and the date thereof.
2. A Signatory whose instrument of ratification, acceptance or approval is deposited before the date on which this Agreement enters into force, shall become a member of the Bank, on that date. Any other Signatory which complies with the provisions of the preceding paragraph, shall become a member of the Bank on the date on which its instrument of ratification, acceptance or approval is deposited.

Article 59 Entry into Force

This Agreement shall enter into force when instruments of ratification, acceptance or approval have been deposited by at least ten (10) Signatories whose initial subscriptions, as set forth in Schedule A to this Agreement, in the aggregate comprise not less than fifty (50) percent of total of such subscriptions.

Article 60 Inaugural Meeting and Commencement of Operations

1. As soon as this Agreement enters into force, each member shall appoint a Governor, and the Depository shall call the inaugural meeting of the Board of Governors.
2. At its inaugural meeting, the Board of Governors:

   (i) shall elect the President;
   (ii) shall elect the Directors of the Bank in accordance with paragraph 1 of Article 25, provided that the Board of Governors may decide to elect fewer Directors for an initial period shorter than two years in consideration of the number of members and Signatories which have not yet become members;
   (iii) shall make arrangements for the determination of the date on which the Bank shall commence its operations; and
   (iv) shall make such other arrangements as necessary to prepare for the commencement of the Bank's operations.

3. The Bank shall notify its members of the date of the commencement of its operations.

DONE at Beijing, People's Republic of China on June 29, 2015, in a single original deposited in the archives of the Depository, whose English, Chinese and French texts are equally authentic.

Schedule A

Initial Subscriptions to the Authorized Capital Stock for Countries Which May Become Members in accordance with Article 58

	Number of Shares	Capital Subscription (in million $)
Part A Regional members		
Australia	36,912	3,691.2
Azerbaijan	2541	254.1
Bangladesh	6605	660.5
Brunei Darussalam	524	52.4
Cambodia	623	62.3
China	297,804	29,780.4
Georgia	539	53.9
India	83,673	8,367.3
Indonesia	33,607	3,360.7
Iran	15,808	1,580.8
Israel	7499	749.9
Jordan	1192	119.2
Kazakhstan	7293	729.3
Korea	37,388	3,738.8
Kuwait	5360	536.0
Kyrgyz Republic	268	26.8
Lao People’s Democratic Republic	430	43.0
Malaysia	1095	109.5
Maldives	72	7.2
Mongolia	411	41.1
Myanmar	2645	264.5
Nepal	809	80.9
New Zealand	4615	461.5
Oman	2592	259.2
Pakistan	10,341	1,034.1
Philippines	9791	979.1
Qatar	6,044	604.4
Russia	65,362	6,536.2
Saudi Arabia	25,446	2,544.6
Singapore	2500	250.0
Sri Lanka	2690	269.0
Tajikistan	309	30.9
Thailand	14,275	1,427.5

(continued)

(continued)

	Number of Shares	Capital Subscription (in million $)
Part A Regional members		
Turkey	26,099	2,609.9
United Arab Emirates	11,857	1,185.7
Uzbekistan	2198	219.8
Vietnam	6633	663.3
Unallocated	16,150	1,615.0
Total	750,000	75,000.0
Part B Non-regional members		
Austria	5008	500.8
Brazil	31,810	3,181.0
Denmark	3695	369.5
Egypt	6505	650.5
Finland	3103	310.3
France	33,756	3,375.6
Germany	44,842	4,484.2
Iceland	176	17.6
Italy	25,718	2,571.8
Luxembourg	697	69.7
Malta	136	13.6
Netherlands	10,313	1,031.3
Norway	5506	550.6
Poland	8318	831.8
Portugal	650	65.0
South Africa	5905	590.5
Spain	17,615	1,761.5
Sweden	6300	630.0
Switzerland	7064	706.4
United Kingdom	30,547	3,054.7
Unallocated	2336	233.6
Total	**250,000**	**25,000.0**
Grand Total	**1,000,000**	**100,000.0**

Schedule B

Election of Directors

The Board of Governors shall prescribe rules for the conduct of each election of Directors, in accordance with the following provisions.

1. ***Constituencies***. Each Director shall represent one or more members in a constituency. The total aggregate voting power of each constituency shall consist of the votes which the Director is entitled to cast under paragraph 3 of Article 28.
2. ***Constituency Voting Power***. For each election, the Board of Governors shall establish a Minimum Percentage for constituency voting power for Directors to be elected by Governors representing regional members (Regional Directors) and a Minimum Percentage for constituency voting power for Directors to be elected by Governors representing non-regional members (Non-Regional Directors).

   (a) The Minimum Percentage for Regional Directors shall be set as a percentage of the total votes eligible to be cast in the election by the Governors representing regional members (Regional Governors). The initial Minimum Percentage for Regional Directors shall be 6%.
   (b) The Minimum Percentage for Non-Regional Directors shall be set as a percentage of the total votes eligible to be cast in the election by the Governors representing non-regional members (Non-Regional Governors). The initial Minimum Percentage for Non-Regional Directors shall be 15%.

3. ***Adjustment Percentage***. In order to adjust voting power across constituencies when subsequent rounds of balloting are required under paragraph 7 below, the Board of Governors shall establish, for each election, an Adjustment Percentage for Regional Directors and an Adjustment Percentage for Non-Regional Directors. Each Adjustment Percentage shall be higher than the corresponding Minimum Percentage.

   (a) The Adjustment Percentage for Regional Directors shall be set as a percentage of the total votes eligible to be cast in the election by the Regional Governors. The initial Adjustment Percentage for Regional Directors shall be 15%.
   (b) The Adjustment Percentage for Non-Regional Directors shall be set as a percentage of the total votes eligible to be cast in the election by the Non-Regional Governors. The initial Adjustment Percentage for Non-Regional Directors shall be 60%.

4. ***Number of Candidates***. For each election, the Board of Governors shall establish the number of Regional Directors and Non-Regional Directors to be elected, in light of its decisions on the size and composition of the Board of Directors pursuant to paragraph 2 of Article 25.

   (a) The initial number of Regional Directors shall be nine.
   (b) The initial number of Non-Regional Directors shall be three.

5. ***Nominations***. Each Governor may only nominate one person. Candidates for the office of Regional Director shall be nominated by Regional Governors. Candidates for the office of Non-Regional Director shall be nominated by Non-Regional Governors.

6. ***Voting***. Each Governor may vote for one candidate, casting all of the votes to which the member appointing him is entitled under paragraph 1 of Article 28. The election of Regional Directors shall be by ballot of Regional Governors. The election of Non-Regional Directors shall be by ballot of Non-Regional Governors.
7. ***First Ballot***. On the first ballot, candidates receiving the highest number of votes, up to the number of Directors to be elected, shall be elected as Directors, provided that, to be elected, a candidate shall have received a sufficient number of votes to reach the applicable Minimum Percentage.

    (a) If the required number of Directors is not elected on the first ballot, and the number of candidates was the same as the number of Directors to be elected, the Board of Governors shall determine the subsequent actions to complete the election of Regional Directors or the election of Non-Regional Directors, as the case may be.

8. ***Subsequent Ballots***. If the required number of Directors is not elected on the first ballot, and there were more candidates than the number of Directors to be elected on the ballot, there shall be subsequent ballots, as necessary. For subsequent ballots:

    (a) The candidate receiving the lowest number of votes in the preceding ballot shall not be a candidate in the next ballot.
    (b) Votes shall be cast only by: (i) Governors who voted in the preceding ballot for a candidate who was not elected; and (ii) Governors whose votes for a candidate who was elected are deemed to have raised the votes for that candidate above the applicable Adjustment Percentage under (c) below.
    (c) The votes of all the Governors who cast votes for each candidate shall be added in descending order of number, until the number of votes representing the applicable Adjustment Percentage has been exceeded. Governors whose votes were counted in that calculation shall be deemed to have cast all their votes for that Director, including the Governor whose votes brought the total over the Adjustment Percentage. The remaining Governors whose votes were not counted in that calculation shall be deemed to have raised the candidate's total votes above the Adjustment Percentage, and the votes of those Governors shall not count towards the election of that candidate. These remaining Governors may vote in the next ballot.
    (d) If in any subsequent ballot, only one Director remains to be elected, the Director may be elected by a simple majority of the remaining votes. All such remaining votes shall be deemed to have counted towards the election of the last Director.

9. ***Assignment of Votes***. Any Governor who does not participate in voting for the election or whose votes do not contribute to the election of a Director may assign the votes to which he is entitled to an elected Director, provided that such Governor shall first have obtained the agreement of all those Governors who have elected that Director to such assignment.

10. ***Founding Member Privileges***. The nomination and voting by Governors for Directors and the appointment of Alternate Directors by Directors shall respect the principle that each Founding Member shall have the privilege to designate the Director or an Alternate Director in its constituency permanently or on a rotating basis.

Report on the Articles of Agreement of the Asian Infrastructure Investment Bank

The Asian Infrastructure Investment Bank (AIIB) stems from an initiative by China, joined by the parties to the Memorandum of Understanding of October 24, 2014 (MOU), recognizing the importance of infrastructure to the development of Asia and the need for considerable additional long-term financing for infrastructure in the region.

A Special Ministerial Meeting of the signatories to the MOU set up a forum to prepare the establishment of the AIIB, the Chief Negotiators' Meetings, joined by representatives of the parties to the MOU. These parties, having signed or later endorsed the MOU, are the Prospective Founding Members of the AIIB, to become Founding Members following their signature and ratification of the AIIB Articles of Agreement (the AIIB Articles).

The first Chief Negotiators' Meeting took place in Kunming, China in November 2014.[13] The second Chief Negotiators' Meeting took place in Mumbai, India in January 2015, co-chaired by India.[14] The third Chief Negotiators' Meeting took place in Almaty, Kazakhstan in March 2015, co-chaired by Kazakhstan.[15] The fourth Chief Negotiators' Meeting took place in Beijing, China in April 2015.[16] The fifth Chief Negotiators' Meeting took place in Singapore in May 2015, co-chaired by Singapore.[17] The final text of the Articles of Agreement of the Asian Infrastructure Investment Bank was adopted on May 22, 2015 at the Singapore meeting.

During the discussions on the draft AIIB Articles, the representatives came to the view that certain formulations in the text represented general understandings which needed to be recorded. It was therefore agreed that a report summarizing these understandings would form part of the AIIB's basic documents, for future reference in interpreting the AIIB Articles. The explanatory paragraphs attached to this introduction should be viewed against that background.

---

[13] Prospective Founding Members: Bangladesh, Brunei Darussalam, Cambodia, China, India, Indonesia, Kazakhstan, Kuwait, Lao PDR, Malaysia, Mongolia, Myanmar, Nepal, Oman, Pakistan, Philippines, Qatar, Singapore, Sri Lanka, Thailand, Uzbekistan and Vietnam.

[14] Maldives, New Zealand, Saudi Arabia and Tajikistan joined as Prospective Founding Members.

[15] Jordan, Luxembourg, Switzerland and the United Kingdom joined as Prospective Founding Members.

[16] Australia, Austria, Azerbaijan, Brazil, Denmark, Egypt, Finland, France, Georgia, Germany, Iceland, Iran, Israel, Italy, Korea, Kyrgyz Republic, Malta, Netherlands, Norway, Poland, Portugal, Russia, Spain, South Africa, Sweden, Turkey, and United Arab Emirates joined as Prospective Founding Members.

[17] Representatives from all Prospective Founding Members participated.

Chief Negotiators for Establishing the Asian Infrastructure Investment Bank

Singapore May 22, 2015

Explanatory Notes

Preamble. Representatives highlighted that the Bank would be established as a multilateral financial institution to promote sustained and stable growth in Asia.

Article 1, paragraph 2. Representatives noted that the current geographical region and composition listing for Asia and Oceania by the United Nations for statistical purposes formed the basis for their consideration of "Asia" and "region". The listing can be found at http://unstats.un.org/unsd/methods/m49/m49regin.htm.

Representatives further noted that future decisions on regional classification, if needed, would be made by the Board of Governors under paragraph 2 of Article 1, and that decisions on new members would be made by the Board of Governors under paragraph 2 of Article 3.

Article 5, paragraphs 2 and 3. While representatives recognized that the Board of Governors might need to exercise some flexibility in the future that would reduce the regional shareholding percentage in paragraphs 2 and 3 below 75%, representatives agreed that a minimum of 70% regional shareholding would be important in preserving the regional character of the Bank. Representatives noted that, in Schedule A, unallocated shares had been shown for regional members (Part A) and non-regional members (Part B), respectively, in anticipation of additional members joining in each category.

Article 5, paragraph 4. Representatives noted that the basic parameter for allocation of capital stock to members would be the relative share of the global economy of members within the regional and non-regional groupings, respectively. Members' shares of the global economy would be measured by reference to Gross Domestic Product (GDP), with the understanding that GDP share would be indicative only for non-regional members.

Representatives further noted that reviews of capital stock by the Board of Governors need not result in a capital increase, and any such increase would require Board of Governors' approval in accordance with paragraph 3 of Article 4.

Article 6, paragraph 5. Representatives agreed that a member that is eligible to borrow from the International Development Association (but not from the International Bank for Reconstruction and Development) would be considered a less developed country for purposes of this paragraph.

Article 11, paragraph 1. Representatives noted that the Preamble and the functions and purposes of the Bank in Articles 1 and 2 focus on the economic development of the Asia region. To the extent permitted under its operational policies, the Bank could provide financing to recipients located outside the region under Article 11, paragraph 1, consistent with its purpose and functions.

Article 13, paragraph 4. Representatives emphasized that the operational and financial policies of the Bank, referred to in paragraph 4, would be subject to approval by the Board of Directors in accordance with Article 26 and should be based on international best practices. These policies would include, among others, environmental and social frameworks, disclosure, procurement, and debt sustainability. A policy on operations in disputed areas would provide that, for financing in a disputed area, member consent is obtained in accordance with paragraph 3, and the Bank does not take a position on territorial claims.

Article 15, paragraph 1. Representatives noted that the inclusion of "other similar forms of assistance" was intended to permit the possibility of investment grants and similar instruments commonly used in infrastructure financing by multilateral development banks and others. Project preparation support could also be provided under this paragraph.

Article 16, paragraph 1. Representatives noted that the reference to "relevant legal provisions" was not intended to restrict the Bank from the benefits of treatment commonly extended to multilateral development banks by member countries in their markets.

Article 16, paragraph 8. Representatives noted that this paragraph, together with paragraph 4 of Article 24, provided the framework for the establishment of subsidiary entities with the approval of the Board of Governors. The establishment of offices of the Bank under paragraph 2 of Article 32 would be regulated under the By-Laws of the Bank.

Article 25. Representatives noted that the Board of Governors would consider rules at its inaugural meeting to enable each Director in a constituency of more than a specified number of members to appoint an additional Alternate Director. Such rules would require a Director appointing an additional Alternate Director to designate which Alternate Director shall act for the Director: (i) in his absence; and (ii) when the office of the Director is vacant under sub-paragraph 5 (c).

Article 26. Representatives noted that major policies established by the Board of Directors under Article 26 (ii) would include such policies as environmental and social impact and procurement (Article 13) and disclosure (Article 34).

A higher three-quarters majority of total voting power would be required for decisions by the Board of Directors to approve major operational and financial policies, delegate authority to the President under Bank policies, and for decisions on delegation of the Board's authority to take decisions on operations.

Representatives agreed that the oversight mechanism to be established by the Board of Directors under Article 26 (iv) would be designed in line with the principles of transparency, openness, independence and accountability, and would address such areas as audit, evaluation, fraud and corruption, project complaints and staff grievances, and reflect the Bank's character as a multilateral financial institution focused on infrastructure development.

Article 60. Representatives agreed that, until the Articles of Agreement had entered into force, the Prospective Founding Members would continue to convene Chief Negotiators' Meetings to provide a broader consultation mechanism for the establishment of the AIIB. Once the Articles of Agreement had entered into force, and until the final date under Article 58, paragraph 1, Interim Arrangements would provide an opportunity for Prospective Founding Members to continue to participate in AIIB governance, pending their completion of the steps for membership. In that period, the Boards would accommodate non-voting representatives as follows, in order to ensure that major decisions will be supported by adequate consultation of all Signatories and reached by consensus to the maximum extent possible.

a. ***Board of Governors***. Each Signatory that has not yet become a member could send a representative to attend meetings of the Board of Governors as an observer.
b. ***Board of Directors***. Signatories could agree on notional constituency groupings, recognizing that actual constituencies would be formed when members' Governors cast their votes for or assign their votes to a Director. Based on these notional constituency groupings, each constituency would either be represented by a Director if one has been elected by a member or members in the constituency, or, if there is no Director yet for the constituency, by a special Constituency Representative selected by the constituency members through consultations. Constituency Representatives could participate in Board of Directors' meetings without voting. A Director would informally represent the Signatories in the constituency that had not yet become members, as well as formally representing the Governors who had cast their votes for or assigned their votes to the Director. Each constituency group would be represented by a Director or by a Constituency Representative, but not both.

Once the deadline has passed for Signatories to complete the steps for membership and become members under Article 58, the period to become Founding Members would end. At that point, all Founding Members would participate in AIIB governance under normal AIIB governance arrangements, and these Interim Arrangements would terminate.

The manufacturer's authorised representative in the EU is Springer Nature Customer Service Centre GmbH, Europaplatz 3, 69115 Heidelberg, Germany. If you have any concerns regarding our products, please contact ProductSafety@springernature.com

Printed and bound by CPI Group (UK) Ltd, Croydon, CR0 4YY
01/10/2026
02225864-0003